SHAPE-UP AND HIRING HALL

SHAPE-UP
AND
HIRING HALL

A COMPARISON OF
HIRING METHODS AND
LABOR RELATIONS ON THE
NEW YORK AND SEATTLE WATERFRONTS

CHARLES P. LARROWE

UNIVERSITY OF CALIFORNIA PRESS
BERKELEY AND LOS ANGELES : 1955

UNIVERSITY OF CALIFORNIA PRESS
BERKELEY AND LOS ANGELES, CALIFORNIA

CAMBRIDGE UNIVERSITY PRESS
LONDON, ENGLAND

DESIGNED BY JOHN B. GOETZ

To Fritz

Preface

Longshoring in the United States has provided some of the most colorful chapters in American labor history. In several respects, the industry is unique. No other industry has offered a more extreme form of casual employment, nor such diversity in hiring methods. In most industries, especially after they have been unionized, the trend has been toward the development of uniform working conditions and industrial practices. But in longshoring, despite the fact that operational problems in East and West Coast ports are virtually the same, and that many of the same stevedoring companies operate on both coasts, vastly different hiring systems have evolved. These divergent systems — the shape-up and the hiring hall — have profoundly influenced the collective-bargaining relationship and the character of the unions representing longshoremen on the two coasts. The East Coast union — the International Longshoremen's Association — has been expelled from the AFL on charges of "racketeering and accepting bribes from employers," while the West Coast union — the International Longshoremen's and Warehousemen's Union — has been expelled from the CIO on charges of "following the Communist Party line." Here, then, is an industry which invites investigation.

The New York waterfront was an obvious choice for studying the shape-up. Although intolerable conditions on the New York docks have, of late, received nation-wide publicity and the ILA has long been recognized as a classic example of "labor racketeering," the role played by employers and public officials in creating these conditions has never been adequately described. Nor has the relationship of the shape-up to racketeering been fully treated. As to the hiring-hall system, any major West Coast port could have been used as an example, because hiring practices are much the same in all ILWU ports. Seattle was chosen because it has the distinction of having been the first American port to establish a central hiring hall for longshoremen, in 1921. The system was put into operation by the employers themselves.

To provide a common basis for comparing the shape-up and the hiring hall, it was convenient to set up tests for judging how well a hiring system operates. The first part of this book describes the evolution of the shape-up in New York and judges it in terms of these tests. The second part treats the Seattle hiring hall in the same manner. The last chapter analyzes the reforms instituted in New York in 1953.

It was difficult to decide on an appropriate breaking-off point for the book. At the time of writing, conditions on the New York waterfront were still highly fluid, with dramatic new developments occurring almost every week, while West Coast labor-management relations and the status of the hiring hall had been stable since 1948. The late summer of 1953 was a logical termination point since, by that time, the New York and New Jersey legislatures had outlawed the shape-up on the piers, and the ILA had been expelled from the AFL. These two events are of lasting importance, but it was too soon to evaluate the permanent effect of any subsequent developments. Happily, it has been possible to include an epilogue, written in January, 1955, in which the first year's experience with the government-operated hiring halls set up as part of the New York reform program could be reviewed.

The author acknowledges with pleasure the assistance of many persons in the longshore industry, in government agencies, and in the academic profession, who aided in the preparation of this study. Special thanks go to Darrell W. Cornell, Washington area manager of the Pacific Maritime Association; Charles Appel, president of Local 19, ILWU; and Lincoln Fairley, research director of the ILWU, for their thoughtful criticisms of the Seattle chapters. Anne Rand, ILWU librarian, and Corinne Lightburn, Pacific Maritime Association librarian, were unstinting in their assistance and in making available original documents. Bill Gettings, Northwest regional director of the ILWU, and the Seattle staff of the National Labor Relations Board were equally generous in helping trace the background of labor relations in Seattle.

For their help in uncovering New York hiring practices, I am particularly indebted to William Keating of the New York City Anti-Crime Committee; Robert P. Patterson, Jr., of the New York State Crime Commission; Walter P. Hedden of the Port of New York Authority; Anthony (Tony Mike) de Vincenzo of Hoboken; Rev. John M. Corridan, S.J., of the Xavier Institute of Industrial Relations; and the staff of the NLRB in New York.

More than to anyone else, I am indebted to my wife, Pat, who not only typed the manuscript but collaborated closely in every phase of the research and writing of this book—who is, in truth, its coauthor. I am also heavily in the debt of Vern and Vera Countryman, who permitted me to make exorbitant demands upon them for intellectual assistance and moral support. Not the least of these was for guidance through the labyrinthine passages of the Taft-Hartley Act. Invaluable assistance in suggesting lines of inquiry and putting the subject matter in perspective was given by Neil Chamberlain, E. Wight Bakke, and Charles E. Lindblom, all of Yale University. They, with Vern Countryman, gave most generously of their time when they served as members of the committee which directed the original study—a dissertation presented for the degree of Doctor of Philosophy in Yale University—on which this book has been based.

For their patience in reading the manuscript and their annoying suggestions for improvement, I want to express my gratitude to John Pagani of the University of Utah, Frances Herring of Oberlin College, William S. Hopkins of the University of Washington, John P. Hardt of the Research Studies Institute, Air University, Marilyn and Walter Webb of Redwood City, California, Ruth Wright of Salt Lake City, and Maxwell E. Knight of the Editorial Department, University of California Press.

Contents

1

The New York Waterfront

"A Pirate's Nest"

The Port of New York is preëminent among United States harbors, both for its physical size and for the amount of crime, graft, and political corruption which have infested its piers. Unsavory conditions on New York docks were exposed as early as 1914, and widely decried for almost forty years. Yet in 1953, the words of the governor of New York as he opened public hearings on waterfront labor conditions showed that the need for reform was more urgent than ever:

> Unless there is a better method of conducting business than by murder, none of us are fit to govern, to hold public office, and if intimidation is inherent in conducting a business there is a tragic gap in our society.[1]

The sheer size of the port has been an important factor in shaping its history and in complicating attempts at reform. The waterfront has more than 700 miles of shoreline, and its 350 principal piers are scattered over two states and six different municipalities. Longshoring became concentrated in several distinct areas, almost as though it were a series of separate ports rather than one big harbor, but this compartmentalization of the industry did not bring the problem of reform down to more manageable size because the interchangeable nature of the shipping industry precluded piecemeal improvements. If steamship companies became dissatisfied with conditions in one area of the port, they could easily shift their operations to another because few companies owned the pier facilities. To be effective, any reform had to encompass the entire port.

For America's largest and busiest port, New York's cargo-handling facilities are surprisingly inadequate—another factor which has shaped the history of the industry. All but one of the railroads serving the harbor come in on the New Jersey side while most piers where steamships are loaded are on the New York side, in Manhattan and South Brooklyn. An extensive system of freight-car barges and lighters must be used to move freight back and forth across the harbor. In addition, many piers are so narrow that warehouse space is at a premium. Since cargo cannot be stored on the piers, the marginal streets are obstructed by long lines of trucks which sometimes wait for hours to pick up cargo just arrived in port or to deliver freight to out-bound ships. The New York waterfront is chronically the scene of chaos and congestion far exceeding the normal hubbub of a busy port, and speed in completing the job assumes even greater importance than is customary in longshoring.

The irregularity of employment traditionally associated with longshoring is especially marked in New York. In any port, the number of longshoremen needed to work at any particular time fluctuates widely and rapidly depending on the type of ships being worked. Intercoastal, coastwise, and interport trade requires a relatively stable labor force, while deep-sea traffic is highly irregular. In the Port of New York, foreign trade has accounted for as much as 30 per cent of the total volume of waterborne commerce—a larger percentage than in most ports. Since coastwise and intercoastal shipments also show some irregularity, the number of men needed to work cargo in New York would have fluctuated more widely than in most ports even in the absence of poor storage facilities on its piers.

Irregularity of employment was further intensified by the hiring system used on the New York waterfront until 1953, when it was abolished—not by collective bargaining, but by special sessions of the New York and New Jersey legislatures called for the specific purpose of remedying waterfront evils. Under the traditional hiring system, longshoremen seeking jobs "shaped up" each morning at the docks where they usually worked. They waited in the street until a hiring foreman came out of the door of the pier warehouse and blew his whistle, then formed a sort of horseshoe around him. From this group—which typically outnumbered the available jobs—he picked the men for the day's work. Men who were picked in the "shape-up" were guaranteed only four hours work.

Taken together, these conditions—the size and complexity of the port, and the traditional hiring system—contributed to the development of a most unusual collective-bargaining relationship and a waterfront aptly described as a "pirate's nest." Racketeers and thugs represented the longshoremen and negotiated contracts with the employers, many of whom were equally corrupt but whose practices were more subtle.

The employers are, for the most part, contracting stevedores although

2

some steamship companies operate their own stevedoring subsidiaries. The employers have been represented by the New York Shipping Association[2], which includes 175 members.[3] Only one large employer of longshoremen—the United Fruit Company—is outside the association. The NYSA negotiated collective-bargaining agreements with the Atlantic Coast District of the International Longshoremen's Association—an unusual arrangement, because the employers' association represented only the Port of New York, while the union represented the entire Atlantic Coast.[4] In practice, the master agreement between these parties became the standard contract for all ports from Portland, Maine, to Norfolk, Virginia, by action of the employers' associations and ILA locals in those ports.[5]

Two other aspects of the port which added to its uniqueness were the almost complete absence of information about the size of the labor force and the air of mystery surrounding the union. Until recent years, every study of the New York waterfront contained a statement which said, in effect, "Nobody knows how many longshoremen work in the port, nor how many belong to the ILA." It was not until 1951 that information on employment in the port became available when a state board of inquiry, created to investigate the causes of a wildcat strike which tied up the port for 22 days, secured employment figures from the employers. The NYSA reported to the board of inquiry that members of the association—who employed well over 90 per cent of all waterfront workers—had hired more than 36,500 longshoremen in 1950.[6]

Since the International Longshoremen's Association had been the sole bargaining representative of New York waterfront workers since 1916, the board was interested in ascertaining how many of these 36,500 longshoremen were members of the union. After hearing extensive testimony from both union officials and employers, the board was able to report only:

> Present membership in the International Longshoremen's Association is estimated at 55,000 to 60,000. . . . At the present time, about forty per cent [i.e., 22,000–24,000] of its members belong to locals in this port.[7]

Even if the figure of 24,000 were accepted as the total ILA membership in the port (other evidence indicates that this estimate is too liberal), not all these men would have been longshoremen, since the union included other waterfront crafts such as dock foremen. Even using the ILA's own figures, this meant that well over 12,000 men who did not belong to the ILA were competing for jobs in the shape-up against union members.

A peculiar feature of the ILA's internal structure was the way the union

3

was gerrymandered. A total of 31 separate longshore locals were distributed throughout the port as shown on the map in figure 1. (The probable reasons for such a large number of locals, in view of the size of the ILA's membership in the port, are discussed in chapter 3. The other locals shown in the map were the locals of checkers, cargo repairmen, etc.) The 31 longshore locals were:

Hoboken	6 locals, (Nos. 306, 867, 881, 890, 1064, 1198)
Newark	2 locals (Nos. 1233, 1235)
Jersey City	1 local (No. 1247)
Bayonne	2 locals (Nos. 1588, 1589)
Brooklyn	10 locals (Nos. 327, 327-1, 338, 338-1, 808, 975, 968, 1199, 1199-1, 1195)
Staten Island . . .	1 local (No. 920)
Manhattan	9 locals (Nos. 791, 824, 824-1, 856, 866, 895, 964, 1124, 1258)

These locals were all affiliated with the New York District Council of the ILA, which encompassed the same area as the New York Shipping Association. While the district council presumably existed to administer the collective-bargaining agreement, the history of collective bargaining indicates that relations with the employers were largely carried on through the union president. This arrangement was amicable and highly informal. Agreements were often verbal rather than written, a practice most frustrating to the rank-and-file longshoremen—not to mention the student of the industry.

Here in America's largest port, where working conditions had been determined by collective bargaining for almost forty years, was a system of hiring which has been variously described as "inefficient," "archaic," "brutal and degrading," "a spawning place for crime," "a system which promotes chronic unemployment among longshoremen." From 1914 to 1953, every official study of the New York waterfront had condemned the shape-up. Why did the shape-up—abandoned decades ago in other ports—stubbornly persist in New York, in a country which takes pride in the ability of its social and economic institutions to adapt to changing conditions?

Union organization on the New York waterfront passed through several distinct phases from its inception in the 1830's to its domination by rack-

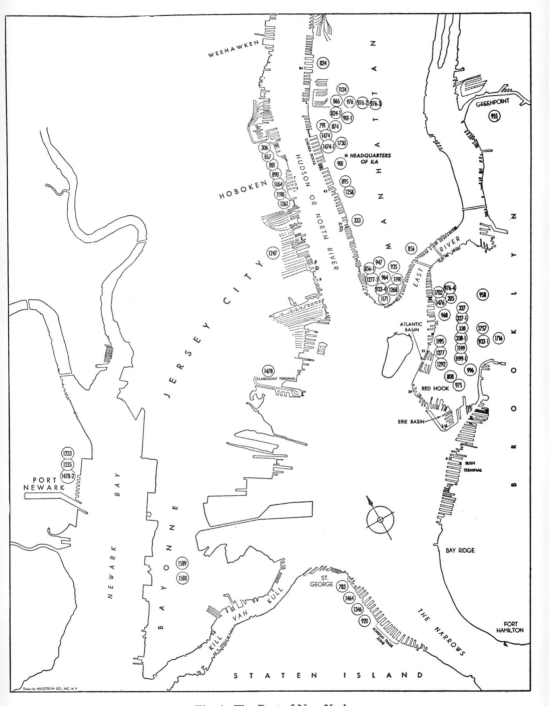

Fig. 1. The Port of New York

5

eteers in the 1930's. While it is now apparent that the failure to eliminate the shape-up earlier was largely responsible for the ultimate degradation of the union, in each phase compelling reasons prevented the union from focusing its primary attention on abolishing the shape-up. The long and tragic history can be summarized as follows:

Before the ILA was established in the port, the sporadic attempts at organizing longshoremen that enjoyed even limited success resulted in small, weak local unions, each independent of the others. The shape-up, which had evolved as the hiring system of the longshoring industry, worked great hardship on the men—as it always had—but union officials turned their attention to what seemed to them the first order of business—getting some sort of security for their unions. When the ILA finally integrated the locals and emerged as a relatively permanent organization, union leaders wanted to improve hiring practices, as well as wages, but they had little knowledge of alternatives to the shape-up and evidently lacked the imagination necessary to improvise any substitute. Consequently, the shape-up remained basically unchanged even after a strong, centralized union had been established and had obtained what amounted to a closed shop.

This combination of circumstances—the power now vested in union officials to pass judgment on who could be hired, coupled with the ever-present surplus of job-seekers in the shape-up—encouraged the corruption of union officials by offering them opportunities to use their positions in a variety of petty rackets. Many of these officials gradually came to regard their jobs solely as valuable sources of personal income and prestige, and ultimately they lost any feeling of common interest with the union members. The movement toward dictatorial control of the union was accelerated in the 1930's when racketeers, attracted to the waterfront by the opportunities for graft and extortion, entered longshoring—and the union—in substantial numbers. By the time knowledge of workable alternatives to the shape-up became fairly widespread among the men, it was too late for a peaceful transition. By then, too many union officials saw the preservation of the shape-up as the means for perpetuating their positions. No continuing attempts to force reforms were made by union members, partly because they feared retaliation from union officials, but also because, by that time, the rank and file had so little confidence in their officials that they viewed the shape-up with all its abuses as a lesser evil than a system of centralized hiring which would concentrate even more power in the hands of these officials. The comment of a New York longshoreman pointed up the dilemma of the rank and file: "You've got to have a clean union before you can have a hiring hall."

Early History

Before the ILA was organized on the New York waterfront, the long-shoremen's attempts to unionize were hampered by the conflict between their need to achieve port-wide solidarity and their fear of centralizing the power of the union. Some attention was given to hiring practices in this period but the main emphasis of union activity was on wage rates.

The earliest recorded strike of New York longshoremen occurred in 1836. The men demanded a wage increase and shorter hours, but the strike was broken when the mayor "ordered the military under arms . . . and threatened them with ball cartridges."[8] After this setback, organizational efforts of longshoremen took the form of "benevolent societies," similar to the early Friendly Societies in Britain. They complained of irregularity of employment which kept their earnings down when they formed the Alongshoremen's United Benefit Society in 1853, but the first organization to propose regulating "the time and manner of employment" was the Long-shoremen's Union Protective Association, No. 2, of the City of New York, incorporated in 1866.[9]

The first sizable strike occurred in 1874 as a protest against a reduction in wages, and involved between 8,000 and 10,000 members of the five LUPA locals in Manhattan and Brooklyn. The locals failed to form any central body to coördinate their actions and, after five weeks during which strikebreakers were used widely, the strike collapsed and the men returned to work on the employers' terms. Available records do not indicate that hiring practices were an issue.

During the next two decades, there were sporadic attempts to organize but even where these were successful the locals covered only limited geographic areas and functioned independently of each other. When the Knights of Labor were organizing successfully in the late 1880's, New York longshoremen joined the Knights in such large numbers that port-wide solidarity seemed within reach. The new union's first test came in the "big strike" of 1887. The tie-up was begun by the coastwise longshoremen who were soon supported by 50,000 waterfront workers in the Knights.* The strikers agreed to make the dispute of another craft—the coal handlers—the main issue, on the grounds that if it could be won the coastwise employers would also settle. When the demands of the coal handlers were subsequently met, the Knights immediately proclaimed a victory and

---

* Ironically enough, the coastwise men were protesting an employer proposal that they be hired by the week at $12 for 60 hours instead of at the prevailing rate of $.25 an hour—presumably because a reduction in earnings was involved. The history of the waterfront might have been a much happier one had weekly employment been established in the 1880's.

declared the strike ended, leaving the coastwise longshoremen's dispute unsettled. Realizing their isolated position, the coastwise men began shaping at the piers without even waiting for the action of their own locals. The longshoremen's disgust with the Knights was so great that within a year there were no longshore locals in the port.

The men remained unorganized until 1896, when the British Dockers' Union sent Edward McHugh to the United States to organize longshoremen in this country.[10] McHugh was highly successful in New York and Philadelphia, and formed the American Longshoremen's Union. He was a single-taxer, and Henry George and some of his associates were interested in the organization. The new union demanded a wage increase and that saloonkeepers be prevented from paying off the men but, historically, the most significant of their demands were that the shape-up be restricted to three fixed times a day (men were being "shaped" whenever a ship came in or a job was to be done) and that men who were hired be guaranteed four hours' pay. None of these demands was met and the union was dissolved within two years after its founding when the general secretary absconded with the funds.

With the disastrous experience of two centralized organizations behind them, the men reëstablished the Longshoremen's Union Protective Association in 1898. This time, the locals retained their own funds and possessed greater autonomy than in the old organizations. The only concession to the need for a port-wide unit was the creation of a port council, delegates to which—as well as local officers—were elected twice a year. Over the next nine years, a few improvements in conditions were negotiated by the union, including preference of employment for its members at certain piers.

By 1907 the membership of the LUPA locals was about 3,100. Unrest was widespread in the port and a May Day demonstration among longshoremen in Brooklyn touched off a spontaneous, unplanned strike throughout the port. The walk-out was not recognized by union officials until the port council met five days later and decided to call an official strike for a wage increase. As in the 1874 strike, the shape-up was not an issue. A temporary feeling of solidarity developed among the men, over 9,000 of whom joined the LUPA during the strike. More than 30 employers formed a committee to coördinate their resistance, and strikebreakers were used extensively. The union persuaded some of the latter to quit and paid their fares "back to where they came from." The longshoremen received no support from other unions and returned to work after six weeks on the terms which had existed when the strike began.

A pattern can be seen evolving in the 1907 strike which was to be repeated on numerous later occasions. Unplanned and unauthorized, the

8

walk-out was well under way when the union officials declared it to be an official strike. The delay in this strike, unlike that in more recent strikes, was apparently caused by the decentralized nature of the union and by inadequate communication between the separate areas of the port, rather than by a disinclination to disrupt harmonious relations with the employers.

The International Longshoremen's Association

The ineffectiveness of the LUPA resulted in disaffiliation of many of its locals, which then affiliated with a new waterfront union—the International Longshoremen's Association, then in the AFL.[11] Rivalry between the two unions continued until 1914, when the LUPA locals were all brought under the ILA banner.

Two years later, the ILA secured its first port-wide collective agreement with New York employers. It provided for a wage increase and preference of employment for union members, but was silent with respect to other aspects of hiring.[12] While this was the first signed agreement, it merely formalized a condition which had been developing in the port. Charles Barnes, the author of the first study of the industry, had commented in 1915:

> Curiously enough, throughout the history of unionism in this port, there has never been a signed wage scale, just as there has never been official recognition of any union. The lack of any uniform and official wage scale in New York is all the more noteworthy in that the differing rate in different parts of the port was in the early days a prime cause of perpetuating the animosity of the men and in preventing any coming together of the unions . . . [while not recognizing the unions] the companies discern in them a certain intangible power of making trouble and accordingly do not allow their foremen to reject union men. Union men are, generally speaking, the best, and if it were discovered that any company discriminated against them, they would all quietly quit work.[13]

In retrospect, it seems strange that the ILA did not attempt, after achieving preference for union members, to devise some system for regularizing employment. Evidently, at this time, officials could not think of any way in which this could be done. This was reflected in their testimony given before the United States Commission on Industrial Relations in 1914. The first witness was John F. Riley, an ILA international organizer. After offering page after page of testimony on kickbacks, long hours, abuse of power by foremen, and other undesirable aspects of the shape-up, the only reform he proposed was that three regular times a day for shaping be

9

established.[14] Walter B. Holt, another ILA organizer, gave testimony much like Riley's but offered the opinion "the shape is the best for the men, due to the fact that the stevedore employs practical longshoremen, which will prevent accidents."[15] Dennis Delaney, a longshoreman for 24 years and a foreman for part of that time, took the same position in his testimony. Asked by Commissioner John R. Commons, "Have you any way of equalizing the work around amongst your members?" Holt answered, "No . . . all we try to see is that he (the stevedore) hires all union men."[16]

Looking back on the history of the ILA in the port, it is apparent that when the union obtained preference of employment for union members but failed to limit the labor supply and to regularize hiring, it laid the groundwork for its ultimate corruption.

Labor Statesmanship

The signing of the 1916 agreement ushered in a new era in union–employer relations. The forerunner of the present employers' association was established in the Standing Committee of Steamship Agents and Contracting Stevedores. The activities of all ILA locals in the port were coördinated through the New York District Council. The 1916 agreement was the first of a 30-year series negotiated by officials of the union and the employers without a threat of a strike or lockout. There were to be strikes—some of them port-wide and prolonged—during the next 30 years, but none of them was to receive the official blessing of the leadership.

The newly elected officials spent most of their time during these early years quarreling among themselves, rather than confronting the employers with demands for contract improvements. When the ILA absorbed the rival LUPA locals, it inherited a legacy of minority opposition and personal rivalries. The presidential election in the 1917 convention was a hotly contested affair between President T. V. O'Connor (who, like the first ILA president, Dan Keefe, was a Great Lakes tugboat captain) and Richard J. Butler (a former official of the LUPA). The ILA faction won the election but the contest left smoldering resentments.[17]

The union had also inherited a pattern of differential wage rates throughout the port, and these were the cause of serious animosities among ILA members. Resentments came to the surface in 1918 when other ILA members in the port refused to participate in a strike of the coastwise longshoremen who were protesting an award of the National Adjustment Commission. [18] Despite the lack of support, the coastwise men were successful in forcing the commission to amend its award, and their success had important implications for the wildcat strike which developed one year later.[19]

10

The 1919 Strike

It is possible to discern, even in this early phase of the union's development, a gradual separation of the leadership from the members, seriously weakening the ability of the officials to represent the desires of the membership. This was demonstrated in the 1919 strike.

The port was troubled, early in 1919, by a series of minor strikes. In March, the men employed on harbor craft (lighters and tugs) walked out in protest of a War Labor Board decision. President O'Connor held the strike to be in violation of a commitment by the ILA to accept board decisions and refused to support the men. Without official support, the strikers were forced to settle for terms less favorable than those which had prevailed before the walk-out. Ill-feeling among this craft toward the union leadership was exacerbated when the executive council removed Paul Vaccarelli, an official of one of the striking locals, from his position as fifth vice-president of the international because of his participation in the strike.

At the convention in July, President O'Connor was empowered to open negotiations with the employers on the basis of demands formulated by representatives of all the North Atlantic locals.* The demands included a wage increase of 35 cents an hour for straight time and 90 cents for overtime. Hiring practices were not mentioned. Negotiations with the employers soon broke down, and it was agreed to refer the matter directly to the National Adjustment Commission, of which O'Connor and Joseph P. Ryan (then an ILA vice-president) were members. The commission began hearings in September on the demands of one of the crafts but, before an award could be made, longshoremen in Brooklyn lost patience and walked off their jobs. They were persuaded to return to work, however, and on October 6 the commission voted three to two—O'Connor and Ryan dissenting —to award an increase of 5 cents for straight time and 10 cents for overtime, with a provision for reopening the wage issue on December 1. Although they dissented from the award, O'Connor and Ryan undertook to accept it on behalf of the ILA. The membership disagreed and 4,000 to 5,000 dissatisfied members in the Chelsea area struck in protest on October 7. On the same day, a riot in which two men were killed occurred in Brooklyn between men who wanted to continue the strike and others who supported O'Connor's appeal to accept the award.

Confusion existed as to whether O'Connor and Ryan had exceeded their

---

*The convention initially refused to seat either the ousted Vaccarelli or R. J. Butler (the former LUPA official) as delegates. Ultimately Vaccarelli was seated to permit him to contest the executive council's action, and he ran unsuccessfully for his former post. Butler was excluded "for the reason that he is connected with a detective agency . . . which agency is detrimental to the best interest of our international association." *Proceedings of the International Longshoremen's Convention* (1919), p. 22, as quoted in the *Monthly Labor Review*, IX (Dec., 1919), 109.

authority in accepting the award. The 1919 convention had voted to reconstitute the commission, which was interpreted by the officials to commit the ILA to accept decisions of the commission as binding.[20] The longshoremen, on the other hand, felt that their officials were bound by demands formulated by the North Atlantic locals. Also, they remembered the precedent which had been set when the coastwise men's strike had forced the commission to amend its award a year earlier.

O'Connor denounced the walkout, which by October 9 was port-wide, asserting, "the strike was engineered by the IWW working with the radical elements in . . . the Union. The men are dominated by Bolsheviki and the IWW."* On the third day of the strike, a meeting in Tammany Hall was addressed by John Riley (president of the New York District Council) and Joseph Ryan, both of whom urged the men "to place their case for guidance in the hands of their officials." At the meeting, Riley was elected chairman of a three-man committee to place the strikers' case before their international president and the employers for reconsideration.

Posters began appearing on the waterfront, some of which caricatured O'Connor and read: "You Can't Make a Five and Ten Cent Store out of the ILA." The board's decision became popularly known among the men as the "Woolworth award."

A volley of appeals to return to work was then directed at the strikers from several quarters. Ben Tillett, secretary of the British Dock Workers' Union, stated in New York that British dockers would not support the strike because it was unauthorized.† At a meeting of the strikers, President O'Connor reiterated his opposition, and Riley, chairman of the strike committee, urged the men to return to work with the words, "You men are not licked, if you go back. You don't go back losing anything." Professor William Z. Ripley of Harvard, chairman of the commission, addressed the same meeting, promising to reopen the wage matter on December 1, but stating that the commission would not change its present decision. He fur-

---

* The Industrial Workers of the World, a group not usually bashful about accepting credit for a strike, disclaimed having instigated this one. The *New York Times* reported: "Agents of the Department of Justice, it was learned, are paying particular attention at this time to persons known, or believed to be, members, or in sympathy with the IWW." At a meeting the next day, the strikers passed a resolution denouncing the IWW.

† Tillett was quoted a few days later as saying to a strike meeting: "I've never feared capitalists in my life, the only thing I fear is my own class when it takes the bit in its teeth and does some very radical things." Secretary of War Newton D. Baker announced that troops would be sent to work Army cargo, and Samuel Gompers added his voice to criticism of the strikers. On the other hand, Thomas A. Edison spoke to Local 791, telling the men they were entitled to more pay and suggesting a 50–50 profit-sharing arrangement if they were unable to get a wage increase.

ther advised the men that if the wage rate were too high, "floaters will enter the work force and make a surplus of labor attracted by the high rate of pay."

Local 968 in Brooklyn voted to return to work on October 14, and strike-leader Riley announced he was sure the entire port would be working by the end of the week. By the end of the week Local 791—the largest local in the port—had heard O'Connor and Riley urge them to return to work, then had voted overwhelmingly to stay on strike. O'Connor's comment on this action was: "If every one of the 40,000 longshoremen in the Port of New York vote to remain out on strike I will still refuse to endorse or support their action in any manner." The leader of the strike committee commented, "Well, they did it. Some of them will be peddling shoelaces if they don't look out."

The federal government took a hand in trying to settle the strike on October 19, when the secretary of labor appointed a special conciliation commission. The chairman was John F. Hylan, mayor of New York, and the two other members were James L. Hughes, immigration commissioner in Philadelphia, and Paul Vaccarelli. The employers—who had been discreetly keeping out of the dispute—expressed approval, both of the commission's appointment and its personnel. O'Connor was highly critical of both, asserting, "There is nothing to mediate and nothing to conciliate." He also protested the appointment of Vaccarelli.* The conciliation commission was unsuccessful in its efforts to induce O'Connor to demand a rehearing before the National Adjustment Commission, and when Mayor Hylan issued a statement criticizing the ILA officers, O'Connor replied, "The Mayor is preventing a solution to the strike."

A dramatic incident occurred on October 21, when a group of international officers, including O'Connor and Ryan, went to Hoboken to try to persuade the men there to go back to work. When the party arrived at the Hoboken hall, they were booed by the strikers, and after one of the visitors jumped off the stage and knocked down a longshoreman who was coming toward it, a riot ensued. The men "went at O'Connor [and his group] and were handling them in a rough manner when Captain Garrick of the First Precinct and Captain Sullivan of the Second Precinct arrived with police reserves." Ryan and two others in the party (one of whom was carrying a gun) were arrested for inciting the riot, the court commenting:

> It is a serious matter if Hoboken working men, whether on
> strike or not, could not hold a meeting without having New York

---

* The choice of Vaccarelli as a conciliator was indeed intriguing. He was a precursor of the modern labor racketeer and had set up a dual union—the International Union of Riverfront, Harbor and Interior Workers—after his defeat at the ILA convention. The AFL had refused Vaccarelli's petition for a charter.

13

"gunmen" and "roughnecks" come over and try to break up the meeting.

On October 25, O'Connor suspended three locals—866 (in which Butler was influential), 783, and 908. On the following day, the insurgents
—who claimed to have 22,000 in their camp—launched a newspaper
known as *The Loyal Labor Legion Review*. Riley countered with an assertion which was to become familiar in subsequent rank-and-file revolts:

> The entire organization at the port still recognizes T. V.
> O'Connor as their leader . . . I talked to them today. The men
> now see the folly of listening to golden promises made to them
> by Vaccarelli and Butler, and feel that Vaccarelli and Butler
> have done nothing but injure them. I found that it was the con-
> sensus of opinion among the men that they will return to work
> in a body at 7 o'clock tomorrow morning and stand up for their
> organization hereafter.

The men did not return, and on October 28 the employers openly
entered the dispute by announcing that they would employ "men willing
to work, whether union or non-union." When some strikebreakers were
discovered working in Jersey City two days later, Mayor Frank Hague
(the "union mayor" as he was then known) caused police to remove them
from the docks declaring, "There will be no strikebreakers used in Jersey
City." The mayor's determination was short-lived. When the same men
returned the following day, they were not molested.

Finally, on November 6, after having shut down the port for 30 days
in the face of vigorous opposition from their union spokesmen, the rank
and file gave in. On the previous day, Butler had for the first time urged
them to go back, and Vaccarelli had told them to return to work "not in
a surly or vindictive spirit, but with the determination to give the employers a full dollar's worth of work for every dollar they pay." The men
went back at the rate set originally by the conciliation commission. On
November 21, the commission held its scheduled rehearing and raised the
wage rate another 10 cents as of December 1.

Later developments indicate that ILA officials drew two conclusions
from the 1919 strike. First, the successful revolt of the membership—in
many cases by official action of their locals—seems to have convinced
top union officials that the existing degree of local autonomy weakened
the union as a port-wide entity. Second, the actions of Mayors Hylan and
Hague, and the authorities in Hoboken, evidently suggested the notion
that effective control of the waterfront required the establishment of cordial relations with city officials. Mayor Hylan's statements during the strike

had been strongly critical of the international officers. Speaking as head of the conciliation commission, he had declared:

> The Longshoremen say they are not making a living wage because of the high cost of necessities and owing to the fact that they are obliged to go from one dock to another to seek employment, often wait many hours, sometimes days, to secure work, and that they average only about $28 a week.
> The crux of the matter seems to be that the men feel that their national officers and members of the National Adjustment Commission have not dealt fairly with them and they resent the 5-and-10 cent award.
> The men informed me last night that they prefer to deal directly with their employers rather than through the National Adjustment Commission, because of lack of confidence in some of its personnel.*

The Long Sleep

In the 26 years from 1919 to 1945, there were no major strikes or lock-outs and the New York waterfront received little public attention. This was the period when the corruption of the union was accomplished, although information about the industry and the union is so meager that it is impossible to state precisely when the process began.[21]

During these 26 years, only one significant change in the hiring system occurred. This was in 1921, when an agreement was signed setting three fixed times for shaping; men ordered for any other hours were to be notified at the regular shape; and those picked for work were guaranteed two hours' pay.† Having gained preference of employment (in 1916) and regular shaping times, the ILA made no further efforts to modify hiring practices in the port. Whether it can be concluded from this that the majority of the rank and file were satisfied with the shape-up in the 1920's and 1930's is uncertain. In other ports, ILA locals established alternative

---

* B. M. Squires, "The Strike of Longshoremen in the Port of New York," *Monthly Labor Review*, IX (Dec., 1919), 95–115. The author of this article, who was commissioner of conciliation in New York and secretary of the National Adjustment Commission, drew different conclusions than Mayor Hylan. In his analysis of the strike Squires attributed the work stoppage to factionalism and personal rivalry within the union.

† *Monthly Labor Review*, XIV (Jan., 1922), 152–153. This agreement also reduced wages from $.80 and $1.20 to $.65 and $1.00. By 1921, T. V. O'Connor had become director of the Marine and Dock Industrial Relations Division of the U.S. Shipping Board. In the board's 1922 report, O'Connor made an extraordinary statement for a former union president. Commenting on the success of the board's policy in handling labor relations, he said: "That we have been able within the past few months to inaugurate so great a saving in longshore and marine labor wages without serious interruption tends to justify that policy" (p. 3).

hiring devices. In Tacoma, Washington, Local 38-30 had required since 1919 that longshoremen be hired from the union hall; in Buffalo, ILA grain handlers had set up a system to equalize their earnings.[22] And in 1934, hiring halls operated jointly by the ILA locals and the employers were established in all Pacific Coast ports.

A clue that some New York longshoremen were dissatisfied with the shape-up in this period is found in the 1938 testimony of the representative of the "Rank-and-File Members of the ILA, Local 791" before the Senate Committee on Commerce. Stating that the shape-up created insecurity and low earnings, sometimes forcing men to work long hours when they were able to obtain employment, he testified:

> Our west coast brothers enjoy something that we are all striving for—job security. Under their system there is no partiality or favoritism. . . .
> The great majority of the east coast longshoremen are aware of the gains made by their west coast brethren, and realize that to a great extent the conditions under which we suffer here on the east coast have been eliminated on the west coast. This can be proved by the fact that numerous ILA locals on the east coast have already endorsed the west-coast program, among them being locals 808, 968, 800, 1195, 306, 890, and even Mr. Ryan's own Local 791.[23]

While the ILA did not engage in aggressive collective bargaining, the union was active on the political front. On the national level, it secured passage in 1927 of the Longshoremen's and Harbor Workers' Compensation Act, which covered longshoremen injured while working on board ships. Before that year, only men working on the docks were covered by state accident-compensation laws.

The importance of political action at the local level was not ignored, however. Quietly, but with consummate skill, ILA officials established an extraordinary degree of political influence, beginning in the late 1920's. This seems to have been accomplished through the medium of the Joseph P. Ryan Association.* The association originated as a social club but its annual banquets at which testimonials of gratitude and loyalty were tendered to "our great leader, Joseph P. Ryan" came to perform a money-raising as well as a political function. In 1931, the net proceeds of a Bon

---

* Ryan was elected international president in 1927. He had first worked as a longshoreman on the Chelsea docks in 1912. After about a year, he was injured in a dock accident and was elected to office in Local 791. In 1915 he became the local's delegate to the New York District Council and by 1919 he was an international vice-president. In 1928 he became president of the New York City Central Trades and Labor Council, a position he held for a decade. During most of the thirties, he was also chairman of the New York State Parole Board.

Voyage dinner were $8,000 which provided Ryan with a trip to Europe with his wife, two daughters, and a niece.[24]

As an indication of the prominent role the ILA attained in New York politics, the association was able to list as honorary chairmen at the 1931 dinner such persons as Governor Franklin D. Roosevelt, former Governor Alfred E. Smith, and Mayor James J. Walker.* Not only did the association effect a close political liaison with Tammany Hall, but it served as a medium for political influence on lower levels. The testimony of one of Ryan's critics showed how far this had been carried by 1938:

> It is a well-known fact that the Joseph P. Ryan Association has many policemen in its membership. We can testify here that Mr. Ryan still has sufficient influence in certain police precincts to pack his local meetings with plain-clothes policemen who participate in the union meetings, even to the extent of voting.[25]

One appeal of membership in the association to relatively low paid policemen was the opportunity it afforded them to make contacts which were helpful in getting work on the waterfront during their off-duty hours.

It is not possible to fix precisely the point when the ILA changed from a legitimate, if weak, union (not unlike many other unions in the 1920's), into an organization which existed largely for the benefit of a few officials and their cronies, but the transition appears to have coincided roughly with the election of Joseph P. Ryan as international president. Indications of a major change in the character of the union began to appear as early as 1931 when Ryan, whose salary had just been raised from $6,000 to $8,000, recommended that local union funds should henceforth not be used to pay death benefits (a traditional practice in most AFL unions) because "the men made good wages and the locals needed the money for other purposes."[26] The significance of Ryan's recommendation can be appreciated in the light of conclusions drawn by Barnes in 1916:

> The benefit feature has been an important factor in attracting members in so hazardous a trade. . . . Some longshoremen at the present time keep up their dues after they have ceased to work at their trade so that their families may receive the death benefit.[27]

Although it did not receive publicity at the time, an incident which

---

* *Longshoremen's Journal* (Buffalo: International Longshoremen's Association, 1931). Among the guests at the 1951 dinner were William J. McCormack, an important New York businessman with extensive waterfront interests; Harry Durning, Port of New York customs collector; Mayor Vincent Impelliteri of New York; John A. Coleman, former chairman of the board of governors, New York Stock Exchange; Thomas J. Curran, secretary of state of New York; and Police Inspector William McQuade. *Compass* (New York), Dec. 2, 1951.

occurred as early as 1930 suggests that the turning point had been reached then. A committee of 50 citizens had been appointed to investigate waterfront rackets. Frank Hogan, district attorney of New York County, has summarized the committee's findings:

> . . . the waterfront was described as one of the most lucrative fields for racketeers. The shape-up, the loading racket and other economic antiquities which have been regularly exposed since the days of (Mayor John Purroy) Mitchel were adjudged to be responsible for the evil conditions.
> One member of the committee of fifty protested strongly—in "fairness" as he put it, to the shippers of our great city. His name was Joseph P. Ryan—then and now the chief stumbling block to any and all remedial action in that area.[28]

In another area of the union's jurisdiction, the conduct of the international president demonstrated his lack of identification with the membership. In 1934, ILA locals on the West Coast were engaged in a coast-wide strike to obtain control of hiring and a coast-wide agreement. Ryan flew to San Francisco in the middle of the strike and shortly after his arrival announced a settlement. Not only did his plan fail to include the primary objectives of the longshoremen, but he signed it without referring it to the membership. The men flatly rejected his efforts and Ryan left for the East, commenting, "I've done all I can. If they want to carry on this strike forever I can't do anything about it."*

In 1935, Ryan began collecting contributions from New York employers "for a confidential fund to be used to fight Communism on the waterfront." The total amount of these contributions is not known but the Daniels & Kennedy Stevedoring Company made secret payments of at least $1,500 a year to Ryan from 1935 to 1952. The existence of this arrangement was not disclosed to the union membership, and Ryan kept the money in his own personal bank account.[29]

The true nature of the "anti-Communist fund" is a matter for conjecture. After the fund's existence was exposed by the Crime Commission in 1953, the ILA Executive Council offered the following explanation:

> These annual sums were contributions initiated some eighteen years ago by Arthur Kennedy, then president of Daniels & Kennedy, to a confidential anti-Communist fund set up by our international for use by our international president in combating Communist activity.
> These contributions were started by Mr. Kennedy at the time

---

* *Seattle Times,* June 29, 1934. The West Coast longshoremen remained on strike and ultimately secured most of their demands. Three years later, most West Coast ILA members withdrew and joined the newly formed CIO.

18

when Harry Bridges and his Communist allies were in the midst of their vicious . . . drive to capture . . . the maritime industry generally.[30]

This may have been a reference to an attempt in 1935 to unify West Coast maritime unions in the Maritime Federation of the Pacific—an effort in which Harry Bridges, then president of the San Francisco ILA local, was an important figure.* An alternative explanation would be that the employers were simply including the international president in the group of ILA officials to whom, it was later discovered, they were giving sizable cash amounts to "preserve good will."[31] Support for this view is found in the testimony secured from employers by the Crime Commission in 1953. The president of Daniels & Kennedy, for example, first denied attempting to influence union policies, but later conceded:

> Q. Didn't you pay that money for the purpose of influencing these union officials?   A. You might call it that.
> Q. Your motive was to pay the money, and hope that it would keep you out of trouble?   A. Yes, sir.[32]

The middle 1930's were also marked by the appearance on the waterfront of thugs and gangsters in substantial numbers. Having gained experience in strong-arm methods during the bootlegging era, they were left high and dry by the repeal of Prohibition—if the metaphor is permitted—and they moved onto the docks. How did such individuals become a part of the industry? Some were brought in by stevedoring companies as hiring foremen. One company official explained his rationale for this policy:

> Yes, our labor policy is tough. It has to be . . . because it is a rough, tough business. Now about criminals working on the docks: this may sound terrible to you, but I don't care whether they are criminals or not, just so long as they don't hurt me. In fact, to be perfectly frank, if I had a choice of hiring a tough ex-convict or a man without a criminal record I am more inclined to take the ex-con. Know why? Because if he is in a boss job he'll keep the men in line and get the maximum work out of them. They'll be afraid of him.[33]

In another case, when probation officers asked an official of the Standard Fruit and Steamship Company why the firm had hired Albert Ackalitis, a former convict and waterfront tough, as a foreman, he answered, "We would like to have 20 Ackalitises. He gets more work out of the men than

---

* The federation was originally composed of ten unions, nine of which were AFL affiliates. In 1935, the president of the federation was Harry Lundeberg, secretary-treasurer of the Sailors' Union of the Pacific, and president of the Seafarers' International Union, AFL.

anybody else. We're not interested in his personal affairs."[34] The extent to which the employment of hoodlums was carried by some firms is suggested by the following report:

> At least one stevedore is known to have assured himself of a sufficient number of muscle men by pleading with state parole officials to release 200 men from prison so that they could go to work for him. Through collusion with union officials such men were provided with union books as soon as they were released.[35]

Another means of entering the industry was through the union. Over the years, many men whose chief qualifications seemed to be previous convictions for crimes of violence or their general reputation for toughness, were appointed to important union positions, despite the fact that few of them had ever worked as longshoremen. President Ryan explained the use of his position on the parole board in recruiting these officials:

> They talk about us giving jobs to men who've gone wrong and have served time. Where are these poor devils to go? Because a man's done wrong once, it don't show he's a criminal. Why, a man can't get paroled unless somebody'll give him a job, and those are the very men who stop other men from stealing. Many times, we've heard of a fellow who's got a record stopping men who are broaching cargo. Lay off, boys, he'll say. That'll go against me.[36]

One example of such appointees was Edward McGrath, who shortly after completing a prison term for robbery, felonious assault, and parole violation, was appointed international organizer although he had never previously worked on the waterfront. This position gave McGrath control over the important piers along Manhattan's lower West Side.[37] Another example was Alex Di Brizzi, an ex-convict who was appointed international organizer for Staten Island. In addition, Di Brizzi became president of local 920 and a vice-president of the ILA Atlantic District. Some years later, when he was asked about the local's funds, he testified that the local had no bank account but that he had received $56,175 from the union in the previous five-year period. He had also received substantial cash gifts from stevedoring companies during the same period. [38] Still another Ryan appointee was Ed Florio, a convicted bootlegger, who was made international organizer for New Jersey and who dominated Hoboken piers until 1952 when he was convicted of perjury. While holding union office, Florio made $25,000 between 1948 and 1952 operating a loading concession and employing members of his own union.[39]

The third avenue by which strong-arm men entered the industry was by

20

forcing their way in. Their first penetration came in the "public loading" area. Shortly after World War I, a practice peculiar to the Port of New York developed on the waterfront. Known as "public loading," it grew up as the pier areas became congested and trucks and wagons were forced to wait in line to pick up cargo from the docks. Since men were always available to help in the loading, trucking companies began sending drivers alone to the pier and having them hire casual laborers as they needed them. Some men began to specialize in this type of loading, and, in time, asserted monopoly rights to certain areas. They were not employees of the steamship companies or stevedores who had traditionally refused to accept responsibility for this necessary service. They were "public" loaders, that is, independent contractors performing a function similar to stevedores except that they confined themselves to loading trucks taking goods away from the piers. Having established monopolies, the loaders charged what the traffic would bear. Often, the service they rendered degenerated into a racket. For a bribe, loaders would service trucks ahead of their turn and, in the most flagrant cases, would extort loading charges even when stevedores or the truck driver himself had done the loading. These opportunities for extortion attracted men to the waterfront who were willing to use force to obtain "loading concessions" on the various piers. As early as the 1920's, several murders were committed in gaining control of these concessions.[40]

Frequently, men who seized control of pier areas to obtain loading concessions forced themselves into positions of power in the local union. This gave them a two-fold advantage. They then had control over the local's treasury, as well as the power to order a strike on the pier if the steamship company or stevedore raised objections to any of their practices as public loaders. This power was frequently exercised.*

An example of the tie-in between control of a public-loading concession and control of the local union is furnished in the history of the North River piers, which offered especially lucrative opportunities for the public-loading racket because they are used by major European passenger lines. In 1939, two murders were committed to obtain control of this area. The method by which the Bowers gang moved into the resultant vacuum has

---

* Some public loaders became employers of their fellow union members on a much larger scale than Florio in Hoboken. For example, George Sellenthin, Inc., which did all the public loading on Staten Island, had gross receipts of close to two million dollars for the years 1947 through 1951 and conducted a daily shape-up for jobs in its loading work. Its 31 stockholders were all ILA members. *Fourth Report of the New York State Crime Commission (Port of New York Waterfront) to the Governor, the Attorney General and the Legislature of the State of New York,* Leg. Doc. 70 (Albany: 1953), pp. 47–48, hereafter cited as *Fourth Report of Crime Commission.*

been described by Dominick (Joe) Genova, who was then a longshoreman in the area:

> "After the Bandit (Richard Gregory) was knocked off," said Joe, "there was a fight for power on the upper West Side. Suddenly a new mob walked in and took over. This was the Bowers mob, and I started paying dues to those boys. We got a membership book for $26, a cut rate. The official rate was $50. The mob never put stamps in our book. I guess 2,000 men paid off in this way. The collector was Harold Bowers, Mickey's cousin."[41]

After establishing control over the longshoremen, the gang organized Allied Stevedores, Inc., which collected at least $75,000 in the next two-and-one-half years by "renting" two Hi-Lo machines to the firm which actually did the loading. These machines could have been purchased new for about $10,000.[42]

The extent to which thugs and criminals became a part of the industry is indicated in a statement in the final report of a state board of inquiry, in 1951:

> The Board has evidence that a number of organizers, public loaders, hiring bosses, and others in the . . . [union] . . . have substantial criminal records. The Board can understand men working on the waterfront who have run afoul of the law and are in search of an opportunity to earn an honest living and to support their families. The Board is concerned, however, with the explanation it received that one of the reasons for the utilization in key positions of so many men with criminal records is to enforce a strong-arm system for domination of the waterfront. For the most part such key positions cannot be attained without the approval or support of the . . . [union]. . . . Furthermore, in many instances, the utilization of men with substantial criminal records in positions of authority cannot prevail unless condoned by the business interests involved.[43]

The rank and file might have been expected to revolt against this strong-arm system. What happened to one longshoreman who tried indicates why others did not. In 1937, six Brooklyn locals controlled by Albert Anastasia were amalgamated without an election. Pete Panto, a young longshoreman, led the opposition to Anastasia's seizure and by 1939 had rallied more than a thousand supporters of his demands for regular meetings and elections when he suddenly disappeared from the waterfront. A year later, his body was found in a lime pit. District Attorney William O'Dwyer, in the course of the murder investigation, arrested several ILA officials and interrogated hundreds of longshoremen. He reported that gunmen had taken over the six locals, looted their treasuries of hundreds of thousands of dollars, and destroyed the books. Panto's murder was never solved, nor were convictions obtained for the other crimes described by O'Dwyer.[44]

During the course of his investigation, O'Dwyer urged President Ryan to clean up these locals—known as the Camarda Locals—and Ryan gave his assurance that reforms would be carried out. His failure to effect any significant change in the clique which dominated them is shown below.

OFFICERS OF SIX BROOKLYN ILA LOCALS BEFORE AND AFTER THE 1940 INVESTIGATION BY
THE KINGS COUNTY DISTRICT ATTORNEY'S OFFICE

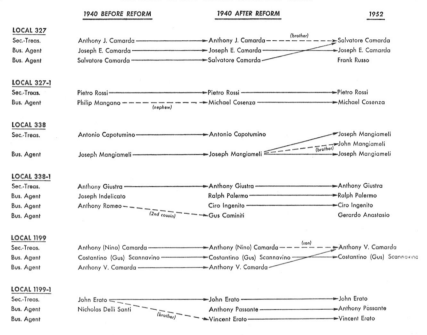

Ryan admitted that the same group in control of the locals under Albert Anastasia remained in control after the reform but defended his inaction by asserting that he found "Communist groups" in the locals that frustrated reorganization and made him fear for his life.[45]

District Attorney O'Dwyer's tolerance toward waterfront criminals was shared by other government officials. This was revealed in an extraordinary incident which occurred during World War II. Early in his 1948 waterfront series, Malcolm Johnson made the startling announcement: "It will be shown that the mobsters can exert powerful influence in high places, this influence even extending to Washington."[46] He referred to John Dunn, a public loader and reputed "boss of the waterfront." In September, 1941, Dunn and three accomplices assaulted Edward J. Kelly, a hiring boss at Pier 51, to force him to hire certain longshoremen in the shape-up. Kelly refused to be intimidated, and Dunn then forced a strike at the pier causing a British freighter to miss two convoys to England. Soon after, Dunn was sentenced for the Kelly beating to an indeterminate term up to three years in the penitentiary.

Early in 1942, New York City Councilman Powell urged Dunn's parole, stating that he was doing so at the request of some of Dunn's friends, and Congressman Tinkham of Massachusetts also interceded on his behalf. Dunn was paroled in 1942, but was recommitted on January 25, 1943, after he violated his parole. Four days later, an official of the War Department in Washington called the warden at Rikers Island Prison, urging Dunn's release, and on February 1 Lt. Col. Charles E. Martin, the chief of the U.S. Army Transportation Corps, Industrial Relations Division; Major John J. Lane of the Washington headquarters of the Transportation Corps; and John Bridge, a high civilian official of the Transportation Corps made a trip from Washington to New York to intercede for Dunn. Again, on February 3, Col. Frederick C. Horner, another Transportation Corps officer, wrote the New York State parole board urging Dunn's release on the grounds that he was "necessary to the war effort."[47] When Mayor La Guardia discovered what was going on, he scotched the efforts of the Army officials by explaining the true nature of the case to Secretary of War Stimson who ordered them to cease intervening on Dunn's behalf. Dunn was eventually released from Rikers Island and returned to the waterfront. In 1949, he was executed for murdering Anthony Hintz, a hiring foreman who, like Kelly, refused to pick Dunn's nominees in the shape-up.[48]

Public-loading concessions attracted numerous individuals of Dunn's type, and by 1942 public-loading charges had become so arbitrary that the New York trucking industry became concerned about the possibility of a serious loss of business, since importers and exporters—who ultimately pay the loading charges—were threatening to divert their freight to other ports. Now that their own interests had become directly involved, the trucking concerns appealed to Ryan for relief. After a series of meetings, a Truck Loading Authority was set up in February, 1943, and a schedule of rates established. The Authority's functions were to police the agreement, hear complaints of truckers or loaders, and negotiate changes in rates through a committee of five ILA members and five representatives of the truckers.[49] The agreement specifically excluded jurisdiction over the *unloading* of trucks, which was supposed to be a province of the Teamsters Union. This did not deter the public loaders from demanding to unload trucks, but merely left unloading operations unsupervised.[50]

Like other reforms in the port, the establishment of the Authority did not really solve the problem and, in 1947, the Motor Carriers' Association unilaterally began urging its members not to pay more than the loading rates specified in the schedule. In the following year, shippers began submitting complaints of unreasonable charges to the Port of New York Authority. After a considerable volume of such complaints had been filed, the city administration decided to take action. The shipping companies— that is, the lessees of the city-owned piers where public loaders operated— were asked to accept responsibility for loading, or to designate the public loaders for their piers. The shipping companies refused to do either, claiming that the loaders were independent contractors, and urged the city to license them. They were finally persuaded to designate the loaders on their piers when the city threatened not to renew their pier leases, but they merely named the loaders who, by a process of squatters' rights, had previously established concessions on the piers. Ryan then issued an ILA charter for Local 1757, known as the "loaders' local," which began negotiating contracts with the Motor Carriers' Association. None of these maneuvers resulted in any meaningful change, and the cost and inconvenience of public loading remained an important cause of the diversion of cargo from New York to other Atlantic ports.*

While the industry in the port was focusing its attention on the public-loading problem, the federal government during World War II was concerning itself with the over-all efficiency of the harbor as it related to the war effort. In 1943, the Senate Subcommittee on War Mobilization studied hiring practices in New York and other United States ports. Its report contained the following indictment of the shape-up:

> Labor is much more fully utilized on the west coast than on the east coast. There are three times as many longshoremen in New York than in San Francisco, while the tonnage handled in

---

* *Complaints Regarding Public Loaders on Piers in New York Harbor* (a mimeographed statement submitted by Walter Hedden, director of port development, Port of New York Authority, to the board of inquiry investigating the 1951 waterfront strike). Joseph M. Adelizzi, co-chairman with Ryan of the ineffectual Truck Loading Authority, differed with the Port Authority as to the seriousness of public loading when he testified before the Crime Commission in January, 1953. After Adelizzi stated that the union had brought about uniformity in services and fees among public loaders and unloaders, he was asked, "These public loaders exercise the power to make you hire them whether you need them or not?" Adelizzi responded, "Yes, but I don't think their charges are unduly high." He conceded, however, that loaders caused delays in pier trucking. *New York Times,* Jan. 21, 1953. When he testified again in June of that year, this time on behalf of the Empire State Highway Transportation Association, he urged that "public loaders as such should be eliminated, that the services provided by them should be taken over by the steamship companies." See *Record of the Public Hearings Held by Governor Thomas E. Dewey on the Recommendations of the New York State Crime Commission for Remedying Conditions on the Waterfront of the Port of New York* (New York: 1953), p. 193, hereafter cited as the *Dewey Hearings.*

New York is nowhere near triple the San Francisco tonnage.
. . . Men [in New York] are hired each day by the traditional
"shape-up" system, and their tenure is by the hour. There is no
mechanism by which men who "shape" at one pier, but are not
hired, are shifted to another pier. Thus there are "shortages"
of men at some piers, while at others men are turned away. The
shape-up system of hiring is wasteful and inefficient; it has been
condemned for over 30 years; it should be tolerated no longer.[51]

As they had all previous reform proposals, the parties disregarded the
subcommittee's recommendations.

The year 1943 was significant in another respect—the ILA decided
to dispense with the practice of reëlecting its president every four years
and elected Joseph P. Ryan to the office of international president "for
life." In 1943, the fate of the New York waterfront appeared to be sealed.
Despite occasional complaints from federal and local officials, some business men in the area, and a few private groups, the New York Shipping
Association and the ILA hierarchy seemed destined to prolong indefinitely
their pattern—already 24 years old—of mutual coöperation and cordiality,
coupled with complete disregard for the interests of the rank and file and
the public.

But two years later a different protest, and one which could not be
ignored, was registered when all longshoremen in the port walked off their
jobs in the first major strike since 1919. Like that earlier strike, this was
a spontaneous walkout and was vigorously opposed by the union hierarchy.
Although the two strikes were similar in a number of respects, there were
also significant differences. In 1919, ILA officials had what many believed
to be a completely legitimate issue on which to base their opposition to the
men's action—their belief that the union's participation in the National
Adjustment Commission obligated them to accept rulings of the commission. In 1945, the opposition of union officials could only be interpreted as
an effort to protect the intricate and mutually rewarding structure which
had grown up among union officials, hoodlums, and employers. In the
earlier walkout, the union was still reasonably democratic, and the men
could have waited for a rehearing of their grievances by the commission.
By 1945, denied meaningful participation in union affairs, the longshoremen could express their dissatisfaction only by direct action.

The 1945 Strike

The collective agreement between the ILA and NYSA expired on September 30, 1945. In his customary fashion, Ryan announced on October 1
that he had negotiated a "fine new contract," providing for an increase of

10 cents an hour, a 40-hour week, and a few minor changes in working conditions. That afternoon, 1,500 members of Local 791 voted with their feet, rejecting the contract by walking off their jobs. Within three days the entire port was shut down. At the outset, no one knew what the central issue was, although Ryan's failure to obtain a 2,240-pound limit on sling loads was mentioned by some strikers as the initial cause of the walkout. (It was reported that rope cargo slings were being sometimes loaded with as much as 7,000 pounds.) As the strike continued, demands were voiced that the number of men in a gang be increased and that the number of shape-ups be reduced to two per day by dropping the evening shape.

The walkout, which in the beginning had no central leadership, remained port-wide despite Ryan's almost daily statements—reminiscent of similar statements by O'Connor in 1919—that he was certain the strike would end the following morning. The New York District Council went through the motions of voting to return to work, but the rank and file ignored their actions. Meeting at first in vacant lots, later in public buildings rented for the occasion, the men elected a committee to carry on negotiations with the shipowners. For the first eleven days, the leaders of the revolt remained incognito because they were afraid of physical retaliation by ILA officials.

In accordance with the pattern developed many years earlier, the employers remained on the sidelines waiting for the ILA heirarchy to resume control. Calling attention to the many years of bargaining without interruption, J. V. Lyon, chairman of the NYSA, stated:

> At no time in the history of collective bargaining between the representatives of the employers and of the employees of this port, has there been a stoppage of work once their respective committees had agreed orally on the terms of renewal.

On the eighth day of the strike, again following the example of O'Connor who had blamed the 1919 strike on the "IWW and the Bolsheviki," Ryan began charging that "outside influences are fostering the strike."* Attempting to start a back-to-work movement, Ryan appeared at a meeting of the strikers in Brooklyn two days later but was booed, hissed, and shouted off the stage by 2,500 insurgent Brooklyn members—just as he and O'Connor had been booed and shouted off a Hoboken stage in 1919.

Not until the strike was in its tenth day did Ryan concede it was permanent and accept the assistance of the U.S. Conciliation Service. After John

---

* Gene Sampson, business agent of Local 791, who was regarded by the New York press as the champion of the rank and file and a rival of President Ryan, assured reporters that this was not a reference to a statement of support offered to the insurgents by the National Maritime Union (CIO).

27

A. Burke, federal conciliator assigned to the dispute, had toured the docks and talked with the strikers, the *New York Times* reported, "Mr. Burke said he got the impression that the membership had lost confidence in its leaders." On the same day, Ryan repeated his charge that outside influences were preventing a return to work but again failed to identify them. This time, however, Gene Sampson asserted that the influences were "Communists." Despite his earlier denial, this was interpreted by the press as a reference to the action of two CIO unions—the Marine Cooks and Stewards and the National Maritime Union—which had distributed leaflets on the waterfront urging the ILA rank and file to "Stay in the AFL and fight for your rights." On the other hand, the AFL Central Trades and Labor Council of Greater New York, the New York State Federation of Labor, and the eastern representative of the AFL, supported the ILA hierarchy.

After the strike had been under way for two weeks, Mayor La Guardia proposed an election "in which all longshoremen in the port of New York could have their choice of two factions, the insurgents or the present ILA officials." The insurgents—whose leaders were now out in the open—accepted this suggestion; the employers declined to comment; and Ryan, reacting as O'Connor had to Mayor Hylan's conciliation efforts in 1919, characterized it as "the silliest thing I ever heard of." Various AFL bodies in the area sharply criticized the mayor for interfering in the union's internal affairs.

A few longshoremen began straggling back to work on October 16, the number increased the following day, and on October 18 the walkout ended. When the leader of the insurgents—a young longshoreman named William Warren—shaped for work in Brooklyn the next morning, he was assaulted and beaten, as were some newspaper reporters who attempted to defend him. Later in the day, Ryan announced that Warren had been expelled from the ILA for "failure to pay dues," and another potential leader of rank-and-file revolt was eliminated from the waterfront.

ILA officials and employers resumed negotiations, but agreement was prevented by the employers' refusal to limit sling loads and to increase the number of men in longshore gangs. The parties decided to arbitrate the dispute and William H. Davis was appointed arbitrator. He handed down his decision on December 31, 1945. The award granted a wage increase of 25 cents an hour (15 cents more than Ryan's original settlement); reduction of the work week to 40 hours (Ryan's original settlement); a minimum of four hours' pay when men were picked for work (a new gain, not mentioned in the original settlement); two shape-ups per day instead of three (a new gain); paid vacations for men who had worked 1,350 hours in the previous year (a new gain). The men's request for a limitation on the size of sling loads—the initial cause of the strike—was denied, as was their demand for an increase in the size of gangs. The shape-up had not been in dispute, but Davis' award contained the following *obiter dictum:*

> The members of the New York Shipping Association and the Longshoremen are in basic agreement that the shape system of hiring should be maintained in the Port of New York, in preference to the system of rotation through hiring halls. They agree that the inconveniences of this system are more than offset by its advantages. They also agree in a mutual desire to minimize the inconvenience of the "shape-up" system wherever that desirable purpose can be reconciled with the fact that the longer you spread the time from the moment of actual hiring, to the time when the man returns to work, the greater the risk he takes of unexpected happenings and uncertain weather conditions.[52]

The 1945 strike was significant for several reasons. For the first time in 26 years, the rank and file had attempted a concerted revolt which, to be sure, was a rebellion against their working conditions and their employers, but perhaps more than either of these, an insurrection against their own officials and corrupt practices in their union. Opposed by other AFL bodies, and with negligible support from outside, the longshoremen found that direct action could be effective. The advances obtained through the strike were substantial—indeed, the men not only secured a much larger wage increase than their representatives had accepted, but also the first change in the shape-up since 1921.

Apparently alarmed by the implications of the revolt, Ryan attempted to redress some of the men's grievances by undertaking reforms within the union. He and the union attorney, Louis Waldman, sent a letter to all New York ILA locals directing them to hold regular meetings and regular elections of officers, and to maintain books which could be quickly audited. Later investigations revealed the extent to which union officials complied with these directives from their president and the union's legal counsel. Charles Spencer can serve as an example. Spencer was secretary-treasurer of the Atlantic Coast District, president of Local 901-1, secretary-treasurer and business agent of Local 866, and a salaried "adviser" of the port watchmen's local. He testified (in 1951) that Local 866 had held no elections since 1935, had held one meeting in 1945, one in 1948, and another in 1951 (each the year of a major strike).* He testified (in 1953) as follows:

---

* After Spencer had been interrogated by public officials in these hearings, the union attorney cross-examined his own client. The unusual line of questioning pur-

(Note continued on following page.)

29

Q. Did you keep any disbursements books?　A. No, sir.

Q. Did you keep any record of any expenditures that were made?　A. No, sir.

Q. Did you keep any daily record of receipts of dues from its members?　A. No, sir.

. . .

Q. As a matter of fact, Mr. Spencer, to be brutally frank about it, what you did with the money of that union that was left over after paying expenses was to put it in your own pocket, isn't that right?　A. That's right.[53]

Similar testimony was obtained from numerous other officials, and it was clear that Ryan's 1945 "clean up" attempt was as unsuccessful as had been his attempt to reform the Camarda locals in 1940.

The 1947 Strike

For the rest of the maritime industry—indeed, for the country as a whole —1946 was a year of hectic and prolonged strike activity as labor relations returned to a peacetime basis, but New York longshoremen stayed on the job. As the time for renewal of the agreement approached in 1947, however, the wage-scale committee of the union formulated a set of demands which were remarkably more ambitious than had been customary on the New York waterfront. The union demanded a wage increase of 25 cents an hour, a more liberal vacation allowance, an employer-supported welfare fund, and a guarantee of eight hours' work when picked in the shape-up. One other issue was involved in the negotiations. Earlier in the year, the Taft-Hartley Act had been passed. The new law prohibited collective-bargaining agreements which gave preference in employment to union members but it contained a proviso that such agreements, if signed before August 22, 1947, would be permitted for one year. When it was learned, two days before the August deadline, that Ryan was planning to accept the employers' offer of a 10-cent increase and to abandon all other de-

---

sued by Waldman apparently grew out of the attorney's annoyance that his directive of six years earlier had not been obeyed. For example:

Q.　Mr. Spencer, as an official for the District Council, an important official, don't you regard the absence of a meeting by your local as rather setting a bad example to other locals where representatives rise as high in the official family of the ILA?

A.　Yes, sir.

Q.　Do you feel that conduct by a local official, whatever the excuse may appear to be in not holding a meeting for a long period of time, casts a bad reflection on the ILA and its governing body?

A.　I know that now.

Transcript of Hearings before the [New York State] Board of Inquiry into the Longshoremen's Situation (New York: 1951), 10th Session.

mands in order to preserve the preference in employment language in the agreement, members of Local 791 walked off the job. Locals 895 and 1258 followed their lead the next day.[54]

The reaction of ILA officials and the press to the walkout was markedly different from what it had been in 1945. Ryan absented himself from his office and was not seen there or on the waterfront at any time during the six-day work stoppage which ensued. The press, which in 1945 had taken at face value his daily statements that the men would not persevere in their strike, treated this walkout with respect. The employers indicated a fear that the strike would spread over the entire port as it had in 1945, but they saw a basis for optimism:

> The principal hope for a return to work today [lies] in the fact that by working and signing today, the ILA workers would gain advantages not allowed after the labor law deadline.

The agreement negotiated by Ryan was signed just a few minutes before the deadline with the three locals, involving about 3,000 men, still striking in protest. Walter B. Holt, first vice-president, signed for the ILA since Ryan was still unavailable.

The strike appeared to be spreading to Brooklyn when six locals in that section walked out after a group of 150 men toured their area urging them to quit work. These locals were persuaded to return the same day by Joseph Moriarty, business agent and secretary of Local 1195, and an international vice-president. Moriarty offered the usual "official" explanation of the brief work stoppage:

> The men now know that they have been fooled. It was communistic all the way. I spoke to one of the stevedores and he told me there were not two longshoremen in the group of 150 men who called our men out.

From the beginning, the protest was destined to fail. Except for an expression of moral support from the National Maritime Union, the insurgents were faced with disapproval on all sides. On the third day, Gene Sampson joined the other ILA officials in urging the men to accept the contract. On August 26, Local 791 voted to return to work and the strike ended. Later that day, Ryan reappeared at his office where he commented to newsmen, "I am glad the men took the ballot vote. That certainly ought to settle it, because the majority rules."

After a quarter century of labor-management peace, the occurrence of two wildcat strikes within two years indicated that the system by which the ILA rank and file were kept under control was weakening. The union officials showed their awareness of this change by their behavior in the next strike, which came one year later and which provided an eloquent testimonial to the hierarchy's respect for the new-found power of an aroused membership. For the first time in the ILA's 32 years of collective bargaining in the port, a major strike was to be declared official.

The 1948 Strike

As the date for renewal of the contract approached in 1948, it appeared that the parties would not be able to agree on a new contract—a situation unique in their collective-bargaining history. President Truman invoked the national-emergency provisions of the Taft-Hartley Act and appointed a board of inquiry to ascertain whether a strike was impending and, if so, the causes of the dispute.[55] The board reported on August 18 that the union was demanding an increase of 50 cents an hour, but that the main obstacle to agreement was the union's insistence on the application of the recent Supreme Court decision concerning the payment of "overtime on over-time."[56] Since a work stoppage seemed probable, the U.S. attorney general secured an 80-day injunction which postponed any strike action until November.

The National Labor Relations Board then made preparations to conduct a vote among ILA members in the port on the employers' last offer.[57] The NLRB was faced with a difficult problem in deciding who would be eligible to vote, since no one—including the ILA officials—seemed to know who the regular longshoremen were. The board initially decided that the voting unit would include "All employees covered by the General Cargo Agreement . . . who were on the vacation list for the year ending September 30, 1947, and who remained on such vacation list for the quarter ending June 30, 1948." Upon announcing this criterion, the NLRB was immediately informed that a large number of union members had not worked the 900 hours necessary to place them on the vacation list in that period and would consequently be ineligible to vote. The voting unit was then changed to include "all those who have worked in the Shipping Industry in this area since June 1st, 1948, and are still available for such employment." Even on this basis, only 12,664 longshoremen in the port were eligible to vote.[58]

The National Labor Relations Board conducted the vote on the employers' last offer on November 4 and 5. This was a modest offer, indeed. In substance, the employers proposed to reduce the vacation eligibility requirement from 1,350 to 1,250 hours. The wage rate was to remain unchanged for one year, but they offered to reopen the wage issue for negotiation in August, 1949. The thorny overtime-on-overtime issue was no longer in dispute. It had been disposed of during the injunction period when ILA officials had coöperated with the employers in working out a special arrangement with the government exempting the industry from the Supreme Court's decision.[59] Voting on this offer gave ILA members what was probably their first experience with orderly balloting procedures since the 1920's. The NLRB required that men vote only in their own local union offices, and board officials supervised the secret balloting. To qualify for a ballot, longshoremen were required to present their union-dues book and social-security card. The employers' offer was rejected by a vote of 10,623 to 698.

Union officials immediately resumed negotiations with the employers and announced on December 8 (the date on which the 80-day injunction terminated) that a new agreement had been reached. Declaring, "we've got a very fine agreement and we are going to recommend strongly to the membership that it accept it," Ryan announced that it provided for a 10-cent wage increase (a 10-cent improvement over the employers' offer), a one-year agreement (an improvement from the union's point of view), a 1,250-hour eligibility requirement for vacations (the employers' offer), and a guarantee of four hours' pay when picked in the shape-up (a condition established by the 1945 arbitration award).

Rejecting these almost imperceptible gains as soon as they were announced, the members of Local 791 struck. Their business agent, Gene Sampson, had been one of three members of the negotiating committee to vote against the new agreement, and he presumably endorsed the men's action. Early the next day, Ryan was quoted as saying he would be very surprised if the membership failed to accept the contract. Significantly, however, he hedged by adding that "propagandists and disruptive elements have been peddling their stuff on the waterfront." Later in the day, he informed reporters that he understood the majority of the locals were voting against the agreement. By the next morning, half the port was idle.

Four days later, Ryan announced that the New York locals, as well as those in other Atlantic Coast ports, had been nearly unanimous in voting against the agreement, and he declared the strike, which was now coast-wide, to be "official." He announced his intention to resume the original demand for a 50-cent increase, and stated that he was also demanding an employer-financed welfare fund. This about-face was attributed by steamship officials "to the long-standing feud between Mr. Ryan and the so-called pretender to the 'Ryan throne,' John J. (Gene) Sampson."

A curious incident occurred on November 15, when about 800 longshoremen met at Manhattan Center to discuss the Supreme Court's overtime decision. As the men approached the meeting, they were confronted by a picket line which turned out to consist of Ryan and about one hundred officials of other AFL unions, who were distributing leaflets asserting that "the meeting has been called by the Communist Party to seek control of the ILA and to sabotage the Marshall Plan."

As the strike progressed, it became clear that both the employers and union officials expected the government to intervene, perhaps by setting up a fact-finding board with power to make recommendations, and they seemed to be waiting for the government to rescue them. Ryan commented, hopefully, "Well, the President will surely have to get into it. This is a national calamity. This harbor will clam up tight, even without a picket line. We realize this has to be settled sometime." The extent of the government's assistance was to send Cyrus Ching, director of the United States Conciliation Service, to help the parties reach a settlement. On November 24, the parties announced that still another agreement had been reached, this one providing for a 13-cent wage increase, a welfare fund (the details of which would be worked out by the parties), and one week's vacation for 800 hours worked (two weeks for 1,350 hours). The ILA negotiating committee cautiously sent this agreement to the membership without recommendation, and Ryan refused to predict how the men would vote on it. The contract was overwhelmingly accepted, and the 18-day strike ended on November 26. Sampson was reported to have urged acceptance of the new contract, and only five of the Atlantic Coast locals—four of them in Brooklyn—voted to reject it.

The significance of the 1948 strike could hardly be overemphasized. For the first time in the history of the ILA, officers of the international union had declared a strike of the membership to be "official." This recognition, plus the emergence of a respectable opposition leader,* demonstrated that the locus of power was definitely shifting. The 1948 strike was also significant in that it firmly established a pattern by which the men improved contract provisions by striking against the recommendations of their "leaders."

---

* Sampson had been a member of Local 791 for two years when Ryan first appeared on the waterfront in 1912. He had been business agent since 1919 of what was considered to be the most democratic local in the port. In his testimony before the Crime Commission in 1953, he stated that his salary was $75 a week, with $300 a month for expenses, and that the only gratuities he had ever accepted from employers had been a $100 gift from the Grace Line each Christmas from 1947 to 1951, which he had distributed among union members too old to work and for Christmas parties for the children of members. *New York Times,* Jan. 28, 1953.

When seeking an interview with Sampson in 1952, I was told by a longshoreman in the union office—a dingy room containing two desks and a filing cabinet—that Sampson came to the office only once a month or so, but could always be found across the street at Pier 61. The interview was conducted at Sampson's customary place of business, a bench in the corner of the stevedoring company's office at Pier 61,

(Note continued on following page.)

34

The Screening Program

Between 1948 and 1951, the port was untroubled by any major work stoppages, but in mid-1950 a development occurred which could have had far-reaching implications for the coalition of corrupt union officials, employers, and racketeers on the New York waterfront. This was the creation of the federal screening program in the maritime industry.

In July, 1950, not long after the outbreak of the Korean War, representatives of the maritime employers' associations and the maritime unions were called to Washington to set up a voluntary program to screen "security risks" from the industry. A program was agreed upon, and the unions and employers signed a statement of policy setting it up. Paul Hall, secretary-treasurer of the Atlantic and Gulf Coast District of the Seafarers' International Union, AFL, signed for the ILA and Thomas D. Morris for the NYSA.[60]

In August, Congress formalized the program in Public Law 679, authorizing the president to prescribe regulations to protect the security of the United States "against destruction, loss or injury from sabotage or other subversive acts, accidents or other causes of similar nature."[61] The Coast Guard was charged with enforcing the law under Executive Order 10173, issued October 18, 1950.

In enforcing the order, the Coast Guard in each port determines the waterfront facilities and vessels which require special "security measures," and following this determination, a Coast Guard Port Security Card is required to work in such an area. Applications for these cards are made to the Coast Guard security unit in the port, and "applicants must be sponsored by an authorized official of the employer or by an authorized official of his labor union." Applications are then sent to the commandant of the Coast Guard in Washington, D.C., who either grants or denies them.

Persons denied security cards have the right of appeal to a local appeal board, composed of one representative each of the public, management, and labor. The appeal board forwards a recommendation to the commandant in Washington, who may either affirm or deny the board's recommendation. If denied by the commandant or the local appeal board, the applicant may appeal to a national appeal board which is organized in the same manner as the local boards.*

---

where he had the use of the company's phone. He apparently kept the files on his 1,500 members "in his hat."

* Grounds for denial include acts of treason or sedition, espionage or sabotage, or advocacy of such acts; employment by, or being subject to the influence of, an unfriendly foreign government, advocacy of the overthrow of the government by force or violence; membership in, affiliation or sympathetic association with, any of

(Note continued on following page.)

The number of those denied security cards is not made public by Coast Guard officials, but they told me in 1952 that it was "less than one per cent."[62] After the elimination of this one per cent, all men who had been frequently described as the key figures in waterfront rackets were still active in the port—even in restricted areas. It is surprising that the screening program had so little impact in New York. If the employers or the ILA —or the Coast Guard—had been seriously interested in cleaning up the waterfront, the screening program would seem to have been a handy weapon. Some of the most notorious strong-arm men in the port were known to be "illegally present in the United States."* If men can be barred from the waterfront because at some time in the indefinite future they might, for political reasons, endanger national security, it would have been at least equally reasonable to use the screening program to bar men who have actually committed acts of extortion, larceny, and felonious assault; it could have been argued that they might also endanger the national defense by interfering with Army shipments and stealing from cargoes destined for our allies.

The Navy has maintained more rigid standards than the Coast Guard in barring men from loading or unloading ammunition in the port whose records show felony convictions during the past ten years, bookmaking or professional gambling, or theft from the government. It is possible that the Coast Guard may enforce the screening requirements more rigidly in the future.† As a result of testimony before the Crime Commission in December, 1952, several men who had passed the screening test had their security cards revoked.[63]

It is possible that the screening program can have unfortunate implications for the honest longshoremen. The program could be used by employers and union officials to eliminate "troublemakers" from the industry, because the application for a security card must carry the recommendation

---

the groups on the attorney general's list; mental disorder; previous conviction for arson; unlawful trafficking in drugs; drunkenness on the job; addiction to the use of drugs; illegal presence in the United States; and having been found subject to a deportation order by the U.S. Immigration and Naturalization Service.

Patrick Connolly, executive vice-president of the ILA, and David B. Roche, ILA legislative representative, were members of the New York local appeal board in 1952. Roche represented the union on the national appeal board.

* The ground of illegal presence in the country was added after considerable publicity had been given to the number of ship jumpers working on the waterfront. The ship-jumping racket is described in chapter 2.

† During a discussion of waterfront reform proposals in May, 1952, New Jersey Attorney General Theodore D. Parsons expressed a belief that the Coast Guard security program could materially aid in keeping racketeers off the docks. Parsons reported that state waterfront crime investigators had until then failed to obtain the Coast Guard's coöperation in identifying racketeers, but that he was hopeful of getting more help from them in the future. *New York Times*, May 29, 1952.

of an employer or union official, and cards may be revoked when such recommendation is withdrawn. In an industry in which individual workers have in the past had so little protection against arbitrary treatment, it would not be surprising if employers regarded as troublemakers any long-shoremen who vigorously insisted on their contractual rights. In view of the undemocratic character of the ILA and especially the penchant of some union officials for labeling their critics or competitors as "reds,"* one can only hope that the program will not be used to keep rivals for union office, or supporters of a rival union, off the waterfront.

The 1951 Strike

The 1948 agreement had been renewed without incident until 1951, when the fourth major wildcat strike within six years occurred on the New York waterfront. This strike—unlike those in 1945 and 1948—failed to pro-duce improvements over the contract originally recommended by the union officers, but one can only conjecture what the possible outcome might have been had not the State of New York intervened.

The union's negotiating committee and the NYSA reached an agree-ment on October 8, which was referred to the membership in Atlantic Coast ports for their approval. The agreement provided for a 10-cent wage increase, one shape-up a day, a reduction in vacation-eligibility require-ments, an additional employer contribution to the welfare fund, and a plan to set up small joint committees to deal with unauthorized work stop-pages. [64] On October 11, Ryan's office announced that the Atlantic Coast District had voted approximately two to one to accept the new contract. The negative votes were concentrated in several New York locals, and all four locals in Boston. On October 15, members of Local 791 struck in protest, and the strike soon spread to Local 1124 in Manhattan, and to Locals 808 and 968 in Brooklyn—the locals which were known to have voted against ratification of the agreement. The dissatisfaction of the strik-ers appeared to arise primarily from their distrust of the union's balloting procedure and the inadequacy of the wage increase.

In a vain attempt to persuade the longshoremen to return to work, Ryan toured the Chelsea piers (the jurisdiction of Local 791) and later an-nounced resignedly, "They won't listen. . . . They feel they have a griev-ance but they have no leader I can deal with. As for Brooklyn, that's strictly Communist-inspired."

---

* When I asked the head of one of the more democratic locals in the port, who was protesting that reports of hoodlumism on the waterfront had been exaggerated out of all proportion, "What about the murder of Pete Panto?" he dismissed the matter with the comment, "Panto wasn't a longshoreman at all. He was just a 'red,' trying to stir up trouble."

37

By October 19—the fourth day of the strike—well over half the port was shut down, the major exceptions being Staten Island and the New Jersey side, and Gene Sampson had announced that he had assumed leadership of the strike. Ryan repeatedly urged the men to observe the contract, asserting:

> Even if they manage to tie up the entire port, we still have a contract, and we must abide by it. If the majority go out then that is a question for the International and the District Office to handle, and we'll meet it if it comes. But it is now and would be then an outlaw strike. We wouldn't have any kind of an organization if we failed to carry out our agreement.

The NYSA stated its intention to "stand pat" on the contract, presumably expecting the ILA officials to regain control of the situation.

As the strike entered its sixth day, the press reported a series of confusing developments. After Sampson and the strike committee met with Ryan and ILA Executive Vice-President Patrick Connolly, a member of the strike committee announced, "We are not against Ryan. We want him to lead us out of this mess. He has already said he will follow the majority. We intend to show Ryan we are a majority." Ryan, in a statement reminiscent of O'Connor in the 1919 strike, denounced those who, as he put it, "ratified the agreement and then joined the strike," saying:

> I am President of the International and I shall carry out my duties as such. If these strikers, who are a minority group, continue their present tactics they may cripple this port, but I shall take no action whatever. Any action will have to be taken by port or Federal officials.

The strike spread to Boston on October 22, where Daniel J. Donovan, one of the ILA's innumerable international vice-presidents, described it as "a rebellion against the New York mobsters who have a stranglehold on the ILA and against a group who sold us out by accepting an unsatisfactory contract."

The Federal Mediation and Conciliation Service—setting a precedent by agreeing to mediate an intra-union dispute—appointed a mediation board on October 22. Its efforts were unsuccessful and the board withdrew from the dispute three days later. The ILA Executive Council then asked the Conciliation Service to appoint another commission "to hold hearings and take evidence of any grievances or complaints that may exist concerning the making of the contract or any conditions of work in the port." No such commission was appointed and when Sampson later asked President Truman (who had appealed to the strikers to go back to work two days before Sampson's request) to "set up an emergency impartial board to review this issue and our needs for honest balloting machinery" he received no reply. Apparently the federal officials felt that the problem of establishing communication between the "leadership" and the members was the responsibility of the ILA officials themselves.

Falling back on his traditional defense, Ryan described the pickets at many of the piers as "several thousand strangers . . . [who] are evidently being paid with funds contributed by various subversive organizations." The cause of the strike was more accurately pointed up by Spruille Braden, chairman of the New York Anti-Crime Committee,[65] who asked Governor Dewey on October 29 to take action against "inefficiency, crime and political corruption" on the New York waterfront.

The employers, who had been inactive for the first two weeks of the strike, finally entered the dispute on October 30 by requesting the NLRB to seek an injunction against Locals 791, 1258, 895, 808, and 975, on the grounds of failure to give notice of intent to strike—an alleged violation of section 8d of the Taft-Hartley Act. (Local 968 was not included because it had rescinded its earlier action and had gone back to work on October 24.) The NLRB dismissed the charge, stating that notice of intention to strike could not be required from the five locals because they did not constitute a majority bargaining representative of the employees. The employers in New Jersey were more successful. With the assistance of Ed Florio, international organizer in New Jersey, they secured an injunction on November 8 against picketing on New Jersey piers on the grounds that "no labor dispute exists."

In the meantime, some 200 members of the Commerce and Industry Association assembled at the city hall to ask Mayor Impelliteri to take action to stop the strike. The mayor sent word that he was "too busy to see them," and his secretary expressed surprise that "a group of business men should come over here like a bunch of Communists." When some of the men indicated a determination to enter the city hall anyway, police started closing the entrances and the group left in frustration.

Finally, Governor Dewey appointed a board of inquiry to investigate the dispute.[66] The board began its hearing on November 6, and persuaded the strikers to go back to work three days later, pending the board's findings and recommendations. Its final report was issued on January 22, 1952. The board found that the ILA had not given its members adequate notice of the final contract proposals before the vote was taken, that delegates to the negotiating committee were in many cases self-appointed rather than elected, and that ballot-box stuffing and other irregularities had occurred in connection with the ratification of the agreement. Nevertheless, the

39

board recommended that the contract be recognized as in full force and effect, since "these irregularities and acts of fraud were insufficient to have changed the final result."[67] Commenting on the causes of the strike, the report stated:

> . . . no single factor alone could account for the work stoppage . . . Whatever the conclusions as to the relative significance of the various issues as actual causes of the strike, it is clear not only that many issues played a part but also that the basic causes are of long standing. The stoppage was an outbreak of a long festering accumulation of complaints and dissatisfaction.*

A number of recommendations directed to the improvement of the internal administration of the union were included in the report, as well as proposals for a permanent arbitrator, and "a board of three public persons to receive complaints of union members and transmit them to union officials." The final recommendation was:

> The Industrial Commissioner should meet with representatives of the parties affected . . . to assist in putting the Board's recommendations into effect. It is also recommended that the Industrial Commissioner make progress reports public periodically, and at any rate that he prepare and publish a summary of such progress not later than 90 days from the date of this report.[68]

The insurgents were bitterly disappointed at having to accept the board's decision to uphold the contract, but dispirited as they were after their futile 19-day strike, they did not resume the walkout.† The strike was

---

* New York (State) Board of Inquiry on the Longshore Industry Work Stoppage *Final Report to the Industrial Commissioner . . . October-November, 1951, Port of New York* (New York: 1952), pp. 3–4, hereafter cited as *Board of Inquiry*. Ironically, a committee appointed by Mayor O'Dwyer in 1949 to investigate the reasons for the port's declining business had reported just two months before the strike began: "We have found that the labor situation on the waterfront . . . is generally satisfactory from the standpoint of the worker, the employer, the industry and the government . . . The morale of the men has been good." The report was signed by Hugh E. Sheridan (impartial chairman, New York City trucking industry); Joseph Papa (president, Local 202, International Brotherhood of Teamsters); Martin T. Lacey (president, New York City Central Trades and Labor Council, and president, Joint Council of Teamsters of New York City); William J. McCormack (a prominent waterfront employer); and Joseph Ryan. New York (City), Mayor's Joint Committee on Port Industry, *Labor Conditions Affecting Waterfront Commerce*, Report of Subcommittee No. 5 (New York: 1951), p. 38.

† On the day the report was issued, I was in the office of Father Corridan, a Catholic priest who had been working with the longshoremen for years to help them improve conditions on the docks. When the news of the board's decision reached the longshoremen, many of them came to Father Corridan's office or called him on the telephone to "let off steam." A few were so frustrated at having been sold out again, as they saw it, that they were openly weeping.

40

a failure in the sense that it did not secure any immediate gains. In the longer view, the walkout paved the way for real and sweeping reforms. The appointment of the board of inquiry to end the work stoppage and air its causes was only the first step in the state officials' program for attacking the basic causes of the decline in port business. Even while the board of inquiry was sitting, Governor Dewey instructed the New York State Crime Commission to make a thorough investigation of waterfront crime, with special emphasis on the relationship between the shape-up, racketeering, and diversion of cargo from the port. The disclosures of the Crime Commission were to result in the outlawing of the shape-up and to cause the AFL such embarrassment that they, too, were forced to take action against the ILA. Before discussing these developments, I shall describe another incident which followed close after the 1951 strike.

Thieves Fall Out

The storm of public criticism aroused by the 1951 strike and Ryan's inability to control some elements in the union created a power vacuum on the waterfront. An attempt to take advantage of this situation—an attempt which may be of lasting importance—was made in Brooklyn shortly after the waterfront settled back to work. Anthony Anastasia, a hiring foreman for the Jarka Stevedoring Corporation and, in the past, a stanch supporter of Ryan's leadership, announced that he was undertaking a "crusade against Communism" in the port, and was setting up the Longshoremen's, Checkers' and Clerks' Social Club in Brooklyn. The purpose of the club would be to "educate longshoremen to the menace of communism," and Anastasia was reported to be charging new members a $5 initiation fee (later denied by Anastasia) and monthly dues of $1. When informed of this "crusade," Ryan declared he would urge the New York District Council to disband the club, pointing out:

> Every local of the ILA is a club engaged in a crusade against communism on the waterfront. Therefore, there is no need to have an additional organization charging dues and initiation fees to our members.[69]

Anastasia refused to disband his "patriotic organization" and Ryan was forced to withdraw his objections. Shortly thereafter, Anastasia, who was a member of Local 1199-1 (but had never held a union office), announced the establishment of the Independent Longshoremen's Committee, Port of Brooklyn—an affiliate of the social club—which called for the unification of seven Brooklyn locals under a single banner and presented a reform program. Included were proposals that Brooklyn long-

41

shoremen be allowed to choose between the shape-up and a hiring hall, and that the Brooklyn locals be made more democratic. On April 27, the committee threatened to tie up the port if the ILA did not meet its demands "within a reasonable time."

The Maritime Trades Department of the AFL* came to Ryan's aid immediately by setting up its own Brooklyn group and announcing a reform program embodying all of Anastasia's major proposals. Lloyd Gardner of the Seafarers' International Union declared at a meeting of the new AFL group, "I would like to give warning to anyone who tries to disrupt the Brooklyn waterfront that such an attempt will be met by the Maritime Trades Department with all the power at its disposal." Paul Hall, another SIU official, presided at the meeting and added, "We're in the boat with you longshoremen, and we don't like to ride with traitors who try to rock or upset the boat." Ryan was present but took no part in the meeting except to announce that the reform program had been largely suggested by him.[70]

It is significant that during this period neither Ryan nor the ILA Executive Council issued any public statements. Within a week, however, a truce was arranged and Ryan resumed the role of spokesman for the ILA. He announced that Anastasia had agreed to disband the Independent Longshoremen's Committee and to limit the jurisdiction of the club to social activities. On his part, Ryan agreed "to consider the reform demands of the Brooklyn locals and to work on improving conditions in the Port." Bringing the dispute to an end on a happy note, club officials promised to do all in their power "to protect our leader, Joseph P. Ryan."[71]

This truce lasted about a year, during which Ryan did nothing to make good on his promise to improve conditions in the port. In fairness to the international president, he had little time during that year to ponder internal reforms—he was busy testifying before the Crime Commission, preparing his defense against an indictment for stealing union funds, and attempting to persuade the American Federation of Labor not to act on their threat to expel the ILA. As Ryan's position became less and less tenable, Anastasia bided his time. Finally, in April, 1953, Anastasia reiterated his intention to champion a hiring hall for Brooklyn dock workers and announced plans for a $400,000 building to house the hall.† Three

---

* The Maritime Trades Department had been established in 1946 with Ryan and Harry Lundeberg, president of the Seafarer's International Union, as its chief officers. It included the ILA, the SIU, the Masters, Mates and Pilots, the Operating Engineers, and the Commercial Telegraphers. In 1953, Ryan was president, and Lloyd Gardner, a New York SIU official, was executive secretary.

† Anastasia said the building fund had already received contributions of about $7,000, mostly from dock workers. Letters of solicitation had been sent to 250 steamship and stevedore company officials. *New York Times,* April 19, 1953.

months later he announced again his plan to amalgamate the Brooklyn locals. Originally, he had had only the Camarda locals primarily in mind; this time, he planned to merge all ten locals. Representatives of the locals involved met with Ryan and Anastasia, and Ryan gave his blessing to the plan, saying, "We always welcome amalgamation of locals because there are too many locals now." Four "non-Camarda" locals—808, 1195, 968, and 975—served notice that they intended to resist being absorbed in the merger.[72]

Anastasia had begun his campaign for amalgamation by quitting his $13,500-a-year job as hiring boss at the Erie Basin and transferring from his old local into Local 327-1, one of the Camarda group. A quick meeting was held, the incumbent business agent was deposed, and Anastasia was installed instead. Shortly after, the ILA Executive Council gathered in Washington, D.C., to appeal to AFL President George Meany for an extension of time in which to meet the federation's ultimatum that the ILA "clean up or get out." The executive council decided that Anastasia could be used as an example of their intention to insist on democratic procedures, and announced his suspension on the grounds that he had used strong-arm methods to become business agent. This time, Anastasia was not interested in a truce. He immediately demanded that he be reinstated and that the local hold another election supervised by the Police Department and the ILA. "And if they don't go along with my proposal," he threatened, "we'll go independent. We don't need Meany and Ryan in the port of Brooklyn."[73] This was enough for the ILA Executive Council. It made a half-hearted attempt to take over the local's books but when Anastasia resisted, it retreated. Finally, on August 26 (shortly before the ILA was expelled from the AFL) the suspension order was rescinded and Anastasia was accorded full recognition as an ILA official.

It is possible that Anastasia's reform program will have as little impact as the many Ryan-sponsored reforms. But it is becoming increasingly clear that Anastasia and the Brooklyn group constitute the nucleus of a permanent force on the waterfront. Anastasia himself is a rather enigmatic person,* but he appears to have strong support among many Brooklyn longshoremen who have for many years considered themselves a separate and unique group within the ILA. Anastasia, who alone among ILA officials proposed a rotary hiring hall, may be voicing the real desire of many longshoremen, and he seems to possess the ruthlessness and tenacity necessary to become a powerful figure in the port.

---

* He has never been convicted of a crime. Although he is constantly identified by public officials and the press as "the brother of the notorious Albert Anastasia of Murder, Inc.," no evidence has been presented that he was part of that group or that

(Note continued on following page.)

Even before Anastasia had begun his efforts to carve out a domain for himself, the attention of ILA officials was occupied by a threat which made the menace of the Brooklyn challenger seem insignificant by comparison. The 1951 strike had hardly ended when the New York State Crime Commission began quietly but efficiently investigating waterfront conditions, interrogating union officials and employers, and subpoenaing company and union records and personal bank accounts. As the date of the Crime Commission's public hearings neared and it became increasingly clear that few ILA officials would be spared, signs of dissension and distrust began to appear within the ranks of the union hierarchy. In November, 1952, Ryan attempted to form a united front, urging all officials to be represented at the hearings by Louis Waldman, the ILA legal counsel. Remembering Waldman's treatment of Spencer in the 1951 board of inquiry hearings, few of them concurred. The majority asserted that "little guys, especially those with prison records" were to be sacrificed "to protect the higher-ups."[74]

As soon as the public hearings began in December, it was apparent that the Crime Commission's preparation had been extraordinarily careful, and that this was to be the most thorough, if the most ruthlessly conducted, of a long series of investigations and exposés which had begun in 1914. The hearings crowded other news off the front pages of the papers and provided New Yorkers with page after page of dramatic and shocking testimony. In the two weeks of public hearings, witnesses described case after case of collusion between employers and union officials, bribery of steamship company agents by stevedores in order to gain contracts, exploitation of longshoremen by ILA officials, assault, organized theft, extortion, kickbacks, loan sharking, gambling, payroll padding, and murder—all of which were attributed to the shape-up. For the first time, the role of the

---

he participated in his brother's coup in the Camarda locals in 1940. During World War II, he operated his own stevedoring company on Pier 1 in Brooklyn. In 1947, he was employed by the Phelps-Dodge Corporation at a retainer of $1,000 a day to break a strike at their plant in Elizabeth, New Jersey. U.S. Congress, Senate Special Committee to Investigate Organized Crime in Interstate Commerce, *Third Interim Report . . .* p. 172, hereafter cited as *Kefauver Committee Report*. The only evidence produced against him by the Crime Commission was that he obtained his job as hiring foreman for Jarka, over Jarka's objections, by causing a strike at their piers first in 1948 and again in 1950. *Fourth Report of Crime Commission*, pp. 42–43. On the other hand, four steamship companies whose vessels used the Erie Basin, where he was hiring foreman for six years, stated that he was dependable and capable and that his piers "were among the cleanest on the Brooklyn waterfront." He has also been accused of coöperating with stevedoring officials in hiring ship jumpers to work under speed-up conditions, but he has vigorously denied this charge. *New York Times*, Jan. 17, 1953.

employers and public officials in perpetuating the shape-up was made clear.

The longshoremen, made wary by the failure of earlier investigations to bring reforms, seemed to have a fatalistic attitude toward the probable effect of the hearings.* But this time the waterfront was not permitted to sink back into oblivion. The commission's findings and recommendations for remedial legislation were submitted to Governor Dewey on May 20, public hearings on the proposed legislation were held on June 8 and 9, and by June 25 the governor had called the state legislature into special session and had persuaded the State of New Jersey to take similar action. Bills based on the Crime Commission's recommendations were passed by the two legislatures within two days. Since the legislation involved the creation of a bistate agency, congressional approval was necessary, and the Congress moved to pass enabling legislation with almost unheard-of dispatch. The Senate acted on July 17, the House on July 30, and by August 12 President Eisenhower had signed a bill into law which proscribed the shape-up.

The commission had proposed two separate bills. The first provided for the establishment of state-operated hiring halls in which all dockworkers would be registered and through which all hiring would have to be done.† To ensure that business on the docks would be conducted "in accordance with fundamental standards of business morality," the commission proposed that all stevedoring companies, hiring agents, pier superintendents, port watchmen, and public loaders be issued licenses which could be revoked for cause. The bill finally passed by both legislatures incorporated all these recommendations except that public loaders, instead of being licensed, were outlawed.

The second bill proposed by the commission was aimed at safeguarding the rights of longshoremen within their union, and required that all labor unions in the state meet specified standards in their internal administration.‡ Reluctant to draw the state into this dangerous area merely because

---

* When a *New York Times* reporter asked longshoremen how they felt about the investigation, one of the few responses he was able to elicit was, "Half a dozen guys will probably go to jail . . . then the whole thing will be forgotten and things will be as bad as ever." Jan. 30, 1953.

† The NYSA had proposed in their testimony that they set up a series of employer-operated hiring halls. Later, the ILA had proposed the establishment of joint employer-union–operated halls. The proposals of the parties and the law that was finally passed are discussed in chapter 7.

‡ The commission apologized to New York unions for proposing a law of this kind. "While the purpose of this proposed statute is to safeguard the rights of waterfront workers, it would have to be drawn in general terms applicable to all unions. The end sought is merely to give legal sanction to certain fundamental requirements now voluntarily observed by most labor unions, and to aid such an endeavor as has already been evidenced by the American Federation of Labor." *Fourth Report of Crime Commission*, p. 74.

of the derelictions of one union, the commission urged that this bill be held over until the 1954 session of the legislature, "thus affording ample opportunity for voluntary action by the unions concerned." The special sessions of both legislatures deferred action accordingly, but included in the laws they passed one provision dealing exclusively with unions in the port. Any waterfront local was prohibited from collecting dues from its members if any local officer was a convicted felon who had not received a pardon or a certificate of good conduct.

Thus, after forty years of ineffectual attempts to clean up the waterfront, the Crime Commission achieved what seemed to be the impossible—the abolition of the shape-up. The speed with which this reform was carried through, once the wheels were put in motion, is truly remarkable. In less than three months the recommendations of the Crime Commission became law.

Expulsion from the AFL

While the government was taking action, the American Federation of Labor moved to clean its own house. Acting on the strong hints during the Crime Commission's hearings that such a clean-up was long overdue, the AFL Executive Council wrote the ILA four days after the hearings ended in January, 1953, expressing shock at the Crime Commission's disclosures and deploring "the clear and definite indication that these workers in the Port of New York are being exploited in every possible way and that they are not receiving the protection which they have every right to expect as trade unionists and members of your organization."[75]

The AFL then made the unprecedented threat to expel the ILA if it did not institute sweeping reforms.* Briefly, these reforms included putting into operation "recognized democratic procedures" in internal government and removing all officials with criminal records and those guilty of accepting bribes from employers. The AFL further demanded that "the so-called shape-up, which encourages the kick-backs and other objectionable practices, must be supplanted by a system of regular employment and legitimate hiring methods."

The Crime Commission had not been able to shake the ILA's determination to preserve the old hiring system, but the AFL's ultimatum induced the union to announce that they had worked out a plan for setting up hiring halls. Ostensibly to test the sentiment of the men on this proposal, the ILA

---

* One of the cardinal principles in the philosophy of the AFL has been that international unions making up the federation should be autonomous, and the AFL has always maintained a hands-off policy with respect to its affiliates. In the history of the federation, this was the first expulsion threat based on a criticism of an affiliate's internal affairs.

46

conducted a referendum among its members two months later on the question, "Are you satisfied with the present method of hiring?" The results were announced as 7,000 in favor of retaining the shape-up, and 3,920 opposed to it. Considerable confusion was involved in the balloting— no alternative was presented—and the ILA itself must not have put much faith in the verdict, because Ryan notified the AFL a few days later that plans were under way to abolish the shape-up. On receiving this assurance, the AFL gave the union until August 10 to meet the terms of the ultimatum.[76]

As the August deadline approached, the problem of the shape-up had been taken out of the ILA's hands by the government, but it was evident that the union was making no effort to meet the other requirements of the ultimatum. AFL President Meany's patience began to wear thin, and when asked on July 27 if he felt that the suspension of Anthony Anastasia represented a step toward restoring the ILA to AFL favor, he responded, "I don't know whether their kicking out Anastasia is any more significant than if Anastasia had kicked them out."*

The ILA met with Meany in Chicago early in August and submitted a plan to eliminate objectionable officials. The ILA reported that a committee of three vice-presidents from outside the New York area had been appointed to prepare charges based on evidence contained in a report by Louis Waldman and evidence obtained from the Crime Commission. These charges would be turned over to an ILA trial committee whose recommendations would then go to the ILA Executive Council for final action. Meany was unimpressed by a procedure in which some of the worst offenders were to sit in judgment on themselves. Thus, on August 10 Meany and the other AFL officials gathered at Chicago voted to suspend the union pending formal expulsion by the entire federation at the September convention.†

Toward the end of August, the ILA took two actions which practically ensured expulsion by the AFL convention. The first was withdrawal of the suspension of Anthony Anastasia and his reception back into the ranks of the ILA. The second was the executive council's vote to abandon the

---

* Although Ryan was by then under indictment for theft of union funds and had admitted serious abuses of his office, he still enjoyed the confidence of his colleagues in New York. On the same day that Meany made his caustic remark, the executive council of the State Federation of Labor announced that it had voted unanimously to support reëlection of the incumbent slate of 15 vice-presidents "including Ryan." *New York Times,* July 28, 1953.

† For the first time in slightly more than a decade, Ryan was deprived of the advice of Louis Waldman, who did not make the trip to Chicago. Waldman had accompanied Ryan to an earlier meeting with Meany in Washington but had been excluded from the meeting by Meany who told him that the AFL was interested in meeting with union officials only. *New York Times,* March 30, 1953.

plan submitted to the AFL for eliminating criminals and racketeers from the union. Ryan and Waldman had been attempting to implement the plan despite the lack of enthusiasm for it evinced by Meany and other federation officials, but were forced to abandon it by a majority vote of the ILA executive council, who felt they could ride out even this storm.*

The AFL convention met on September 21. In a final desperate bid Ryan addressed the full convention offering to submit the ILA to receivership by the AFL. The delegates heard him in silence and then voted 72,362 to 765 to expel his union.† The convention authorized the formation of a new longshore union, to be called the International Longshoremen's Association (AFL). Trustees of the new group were George Meany; William C. Doherty, president of the National Association of Letter Carriers; Al J. Hayes, president of the International Association of Machinists; Paul Hall, secretary-treasurer of the Atlantic and Gulf Coast District of the Seafarers' International; and Dave Beck, president of the International Brotherhood of Teamsters.‡ The ILA-AFL announced that an organizing drive would be immediately undertaken, backed by the full resources of the AFL.

In September, 1953, New York longshoremen seemed to be on the threshold of a new era. Not only had they been given an alternative to the old ILA in the form of a new union, but the basic cause of their difficulties —the shape-up on the piers—was to be supplanted by state-operated hiring halls.

---

* This precipitated the dropping of the pilot. Shortly thereafter, Louis Waldman announced his resignation as counsel for the union. *New York Times,* Sept. 3 and 10, 1953.

† Each vote represented 100 members. Aside from the ILA itself, the only votes against expulsion came from the Masters, Mates and Pilots, which had a membership of 9,000.

‡ Beck had been giving close attention to developments on the waterfront. When it had come out in the Crime Commission hearings in January that Joseph Papa and another Teamster official had been engaging in racketeering practices in the New York produce market, Beck had dramatically announced that he had given them until noon the following day to resign or be removed. Several weeks before the AFL convention, a New York ILA lumber handlers' local with 2,500 members had seceded from the ILA and obtained a charter from the Teamsters.

2

The Shape-up

The shape-up has been found by both the employers and employees in this Port to be best fitted to their needs.—Mayor's Committee on Port Industry.[1]

As the history of labor relations in the Port of New York makes clear, the shape-up had a profound influence on all parties and institutions affected even remotely by conditions on the waterfront. What gave the shape-up such key importance that two state legislatures felt required to abolish it by law in order to restore the reputation of the port?

To put the New York hiring system in perspective, the waterfront should perhaps be viewed as a typical example of a casual-labor market. A casual-labor market is one in which the need for workers varies frequently and widely at a number of different points (in this case, at a number of pier areas). Workers are hired for a few hours or for a short period, some of them picked at random when the employer is hard-pressed to complete the job quickly—a condition typically found on New York piers. It is a labor market in which, in addition to the relatively small core of workers who regularly offer their services, there are always many newcomers competing with them for jobs. Previous experience in the industry is not always required, so both regular workers and newcomers have some chance of being hired. Thus, it appears worth while to everyone to try for a job and continue trying—the man not hired today may be taken on tomorrow.

The ease with which men can qualify for work in a casual-labor market attracts all those unwilling or unable to obtain regular employment—those who wish to supplement earnings on other jobs by working after hours, students interested only in part-time work, men who prefer the freedom of not having to report for work at the same hour day in and day out, and those who enjoy the variety of casual work. In addition to those who *voluntarily* choose casual employment, casual-labor markets attract also the rejects of industry and society—recent immigrants and members of minority groups who typically experience difficulty in obtaining more desirable jobs, the temporarily unemployed, and the unstable element in society who may have been regularly employed in the past but who for one reason or another have descended the occupational ladder to drift about in the casual market. Little detailed information about the composition of the labor force on the New York waterfront has been available, but the report of the board of inquiry showed that this definition fitted the "floaters" in New York:

> Various people familiar with the situation have mentioned the following types of people who make up this group: City of New York employees, such as policemen, firemen, sanitation department workers; shenangoes (loaders and unloaders of railroad cars and lighter workers); warehouse workers; truck drivers; construction workers; and unemployed workers with a variety of backgrounds.[2]

The unique character of casual-labor markets is produced by the constant fluctuation in employers' needs for workers and the unrestricted movement in and out of the market by the workers themselves. This results in the chronic labor surplus which typifies such markets. The process by which this surplus is accumulated and retained may be illustrated by an example. Suppose a casual-labor market—such as the Port of New York —comprises ten submarkets (or pier areas), each of which operates largely independently of the others; and that in each submarket the need for workers can reasonably be expected to increase at one time or another up to three times the normal requirements, while for the labor market as a whole (the Port of New York), peak needs are not expected to exceed twice its normal demand, because labor requirements in each submarket fluctuate in different directions. One submarket will have a shortage of workers while another has a surplus. If the normal requirement in each submarket is 1,500 workers, the normal requirement for the market as a whole would be 15,000. If employers in each submarket accumulate a labor force equal to their peak needs, or three times 1,500, the labor force in the market as a whole grows to 45,000. This figure contrasts with the labor force which would be needed to handle peak loads if the submarkets were integrated into one employing unit, that is, two times 15,000, or 30,000.[3]

These circumstances caused the labor surplus on the New York waterfront. Since longshoremen's pay did not start until they were picked in the shape-up, employers were free to use both negative and positive methods to ensure that workers would always be available without having to pay men for idle time. By having their hiring foremen make it clear that they looked with disfavor upon longshoremen who sought work at other piers, even when work was not available on their own, employers forced regular workers to be always on hand at the times specified for hiring. A positive inducement to be on hand was embodied in the collective agreement. While the employers were never willing to sign a closed-shop agreement with the union, the contract did provide that "men who regularly work on a pier should be given preference in hiring."

In addition to the conscious desire of employers to have a labor surplus available for their use, the very nature of a casual-labor market adds to a poor distribution of workers among the submarkets, causing surpluses at some while at the same time shortages exist at others. Most workers in such a labor market are prevented from moving freely among the sub-markets simply because they don't know where they are needed. This was the situation in New York before the establishment of regular shaping times. The hiring places were located at some distance from each other around the port and the need for workers at the different piers fluctuated so rapidly that it was virtually impossible for the regular men to get advance notice of where and when shape-ups were going to be conducted. On the other hand, the problem was not solved when a uniform time for shaping was set throughout the port. A man still had to guess the probable number of workers who would turn up at a particular shape, as well as the number the stevedore would need. If he were not hired at one shape, he was out of luck because he could not get to another shaping place in time to be taken on there.

TABLE 1

HOURS WORKED BY LONGSHOREMEN EMPLOYED BY MEMBERS
OF THE NEW YORK SHIPPING ASSOCIATION[a]
1949–1950

Hours Worked	Number of men	Per cent of total
2,000 and over	1,971	5.4
1,200 to 1,999	9,140	25.0
700 to 1,199	4,881	13.4
200 to 699	5,431	14.9
100 to 199	2,340	6.4
Under 100	12,777	34.9
Total	36,540	100.0

[a] The year begins October 1 and ends September 30. Hours worked include both regular and overtime. Overtime hours constituted 26 per cent in 1949-50. *Board of Inquiry*, p. 53.

All these factors taken together, then, produce the over-all surplus which gluts a casual-labor market. The process is intensified if the job offers a high hourly wage rate, since the market then assumes the character of a lottery. The possibility of high earnings for a few hours' or a few days' work, some of it at overtime rates, appears to many workers a prize worth taking a chance on. Under these circumstances, a small proportion of workers are more or less regularly employed, with the remainder taken on in a haphazard fashion. Table 1 shows that the typical employment pattern of a casual-labor market existed on the New York waterfront. The distribution of the longshoremen's annual earnings (the hourly rate was $1.88) reflected the employment pattern:

TABLE 2

ANNUAL EARNINGS OF LONGSHOREMEN EMPLOYED BY MEMBERS
OF THE NEW YORK SHIPPING ASSOCIATION[a]
1949–1950

Annual earnings in dollars	Number of men	Per cent of total
7,000 and over	32	0.1
5,000 to 6,999	660	1.8
4,000 to 4,999	2,519	6.9
3,000 to 3,999	5,636	15.4
2,000 to 2,999	4,958	13.6
1,000 to 1,999	4,208	11.5
500 to 999	2,822	7.7
Under 500	15,705	43.0
Total	36,540	100.0

a The earnings figures include only gross wages paid by members of the NYSA to longshoremen. Board of Inquiry, p. 54.

These hours and earnings data point up the cardinal feature of the shape-up—unstable and insecure employment. The way men were picked in the shape-up varied from one section of the port to another and from one time to another, but never was there a firm commitment from the employers that if a man always made himself available to one employer he could build up a real property right in his job.

Mechanics of the Shape-up

The most primitive form of hiring was the "open shape," in which the hiring foreman made up longshore gangs by picking each man individually from the shape-up.* In recent years, the open shape was seldom used continuously, but where some other form was used the men would sometimes call for a "new pick," and the open shape would then exist for a time.[4]

---

* A standard longshore gang consisted of 21 men: 1 gang foreman; 4 deck men (2 winch operators, 1 hatch tender, 1 extra man to handle gear on deck); 8 men to work in the hold; 8 men to work on the dock.

The most commonly used variant of the shape-up involved hiring by "regular gang." Gang members were classified in three different groups: the deck men, who were the most highly skilled; the hold men; and the dock men. At the shape-up, the hiring boss called out "Number-1 deck gang! Number-1 hold gang! Number-1 dock gang! Only you regular men step out!" The gang foreman then took them to the Number 1 hold of the ship. The necessary number of gangs were hired first, then supplemented with men picked as individuals. The ILA and NYSA asserted that 80 per cent of hiring was carried on in this way, and that membership in a regular gang assured a man reasonable continuity of employment, but the findings of the Crime Commission greatly discounted this assertion.[5] Indeed, if 80 per cent of hiring were actually done through regular gangs, the hours and earnings data show that considerable shifting in and out of these gangs took place and it is a reasonable inference that many workers who were replaced relinquished their positions involuntarily. In some sections of the port the gang foreman—who was appointed by the company on the recommendation of the hiring foreman—could replace the men in his gang at his discretion. In other sections, gang members were chosen by the hiring foreman. In either arrangement, a gang member had no formal guarantee of a "right" to his position in the gang, and could be replaced by a casual at any time.

Two other forms of hiring deserve only passing comment because they were used only infrequently. Sometimes, when the shape-up failed to provide enough men, a hiring foreman would call a local union office for traveling gangs. This occurred on the East Side of Manhattan, where the piers are scattered; in the Columbia Street area of Brooklyn; and in Jersey City when gangs were needed at Navy bases located some distance from the main piers. To a lesser extent, the hiring foreman who knew that a ship would be at his pier the following day would notify the business agent of a local that a certain number of men would be needed. In both cases, the shape-up took place in the union office with the union official substituting for the hiring boss. In view of the character of the union, this arrangement was no better than shaping-up on the pier.

Whatever form the shape-up took, the power in the hands of the person doing the hiring—whether hiring boss, gang foreman, or union official—is apparent. In any casual-labor market, the chronic surplus of labor, the low earnings of most workers, and the intense competition for jobs combine to give the man in charge of hiring extraordinary power. When he has three hundred jobs to dispense daily and sees four hundred or five hundred men waiting to be hired each morning, it should not be surprising if he succumbs to the temptation to abuse his power by extorting bribes from workers in return for jobs. In time, the hiring agent—even when he is a representative of the employer—is likely to become an intermediary between the workers and the employer, putting his own interests first. The labor movement has long recognized this danger. When workers whose employment is casual or intermittent organize a union, usually the first item on their agenda is to establish a hiring system in which this intermediary function has no place. This typically involves restricting the entry of new workers into the labor force and developing some device for a fair and impersonal distribution of jobs among the regular workers.* The ILA's course of action in this respect was almost unique among such unions. Even though the ILA was able to assure its members preference in employment as early as 1916—indeed, the hiring foreman was a fellow union member—the union's failure to protect its members against competitors in the shape-up enabled the hiring agent to retain his arbitrary power. This, in turn, gave rise to abuses of that power. The extent of these is unknown because of the clandestine atmosphere in which they took place, but evidence of an amazing variety of abuses has been brought to light.

Kickbacks

Testimony about kickbacks on the New York waterfront has been contradictory. In 1951, the chairman of the employers' association dismissed the matter as follows:

> Accusations have been made for years that the kickback exists on the waterfront and is associated with the shape-up. I do not know whether this is true or not. If it is true, the properly constituted authorities should have prosecuted the guilty persons and thus gradually eliminated the practice. I cannot recall any instance in which it has been proved that the kickback exists.[6]

Union officials expressed a similar attitude:

> The problem of kickbacks, which has received a great deal of publicity is, in this industry at least, largely a thing of the past. With a strong union representing his interests, no longshoreman need pay a kickback for a job.[7]

On the other hand, official studies from 1914 on reported the extortion of kickbacks in one form or another. Taken together, the bits and pieces of evidence which have been turned up suggest that the payment of kickbacks was widespread either in direct cash payments or in some other form.

---

* This has been widely practiced by the maritime, building-trades, and printing-trades unions, either through a union hiring hall or some similar device.

One ingenious device for obtaining kickbacks was the "hiring club."* The way the clubs operated is best described in the words of a longshoreman:

> I once belonged to a club. I had to give the club a dollar a week. The club operated from an apartment where some sharp operators had a phone. Some clubs worked out of a saloon or a store front.
>
> Well, anyhow, we would get to the club at 6 A.M. By that time the fellow who ran it had been tipped off by some boss-friend of his. He knew where there was work. Then he shaped us in the street. He made up gangs and sent us to a pier for work. There you pretend to shape-up again and the other fellows waiting there think they have a chance. But they don't.
>
> They just wasted their time and carfare. The boss calls for your gang and you go out. Then at the end of the week the boss splits the fees with the fella who runs the club.[8]

When the hiring clubs sent men to the piers to be hired as individuals, various means were used to identify them to the hiring boss. One was the "toothpick gimmick" where men who were set up by the club held a toothpick in a particular way in their mouth or placed it behind their ear. One hiring club reportedly catered to nonunion men "because they will pay the highest sums."[9]

Sometimes hiring clubs were operated by the hiring foreman himself. He met men at some off-pier rendezvous to collect their "dues," then went through the motions of picking them again in the shape-up on the dock. Less direct payments to the hiring foreman included, for example, buying him a pint of whiskey now and then, or taking him to a waterfront bar for a few drinks at the end of the shift. On some piers, the hiring boss periodically took up a collection for his "favorite charity." Gang foremen, as well as hiring foremen, extorted kickbacks in various ways, sometimes mixing business with pleasure:

> A hatch-boss (gang boss) . . . may have a gambling game in his home. The fellows who work in his gang must play the game. The fellows who play most, lose most, and buy most of the boss's booze—well, that man is sure of a steady place in the shape-up.[10]

Another practice which was often a thinly disguised kickback was that of loan sharking on the piers. Because of low earnings and unstable employ-

---

* The use of hiring clubs was exposed when charges that the clubs discriminated on racial grounds were filed a few years ago with the New York State Commission Against Discrimination. The commission investigated them under its power to regulate employment agencies, but the matter was dropped for lack of evidence that the clubs actually discriminated.

ment, many longshoremen periodically needed to borrow money. Regarded as poor credit risks by banks, they became the prey of waterfront loan sharks whose rate of interest was typically 10 per cent per week— 520 per cent per year.* On some piers, the hiring foreman awarded the lending concession to a particular loan shark in return for an agreement that he would kick back part of his income to the foreman. The foreman then had a vested interest in hiring men who had borrowed money from the loan shark, and some longshoremen purposely borrowed money even when they didn't need it to ensure being picked in the shape-up.

Still another form of tribute was the requirement that men place bets with the man who had the bookmaking or numbers concession. A longshoreman has described this practice:

> The pier steward's brother is a checker, has never checked in his life but does get placed. From the time he goes on the pier all he does is make book. Believe me, it is just too bad if you do not place a bet. Then at noon hour as we check out there is another criminal standing at the gate and he takes the numbers. You have to play at least $1.00."[11]

In some instances, loan sharks and bookmakers enlisted the coöperation of higher company officials as well as the hiring foreman. One bookie testified in 1953 that he had arranged with supervisory personnel to be put on the payroll, although he performed no work, so that he would have the run of the docks and an alibi if police questioned his presence there. Subsequently, he made arrangements with the dock manager to pick up the pay envelopes of longshoremen who owed him money.[12]

Still another thinly disguised kickback was the "testimonial dinner." Through collusion between hiring foremen and union officials, tickets for banquets in honor of ILA officials were sold to longshoremen (and employers) at prices which left a comfortable margin of profit. The annual affairs of the Joseph P. Ryan Association were mentioned in the preceding chapter, but the practice was not confined to Ryan. Other such affairs received little publicity, but in the late 1930's and early 1940's such ILA officials as Gene Sampson and Thomas Gleason, business agent of Local 1346, ran their own testimonial dinners.[13] More recently, Anthony Marchitto, then business agent of Local 1247, organized a dinner for which 2,800 tickets were sold at $7.50 each.†

---

* In 1950, a Brooklyn longshoreman testified that he had borrowed $100 from a loan shark in February. By October, he had paid $360 in interest and still owed the principal. *Brooklyn Eagle*, Oct. 28, 1950.

† *Jersey Journal*, Oct. 8, 1951. One of the guests at the dinner was Jersey City Mayor Kenny who included in his speech a testimonial to Marchitto as "the type of labor leader I'd like to see in all labor organizations." *New York Times*, Oct. 8, 1951.

56

Payroll Padding

The chaos of the shape-up, coupled with the method of wage payment used on the waterfront, facilitated another highly lucrative scheme—padding the company payroll with fictitious names. When longshoremen were picked in the shape-up, they were given a brass check about the size of a quarter with the name of the stevedoring firm and a number stamped on it. As they filed through the dock gate on their way to work, they showed the check to the timekeeper who recorded that they were working. Checks numbered within a certain range were used for particular ships. There was no central paying office, so on pay days the men went to the piers where they had worked and turned in the brass checks in exchange for their pay envelopes. Payment was in cash, with any deductions itemized on the envelope. The brass checks could be presented by the longshoreman himself or by some other person.*

Payroll padding seems to have been of three main types. The type which received the most attention from the Crime Commission involved top company officials putting "phantoms" on the payroll who guaranteed to keep them out of trouble with the union. This was merely one method of buying off union officials and can hardly be attributed to the hiring system —an employer can engage in this practice regardless of the hiring system in use.† The second type of payroll padding was described in the discussion of loan sharking and bookmaking. The hiring of loan sharks and bookies with the approval of top company officials was not directly related to the hiring system, but where the arrangement was restricted to the hiring foreman and the concessionaire it was clearly made possible through the hiring foreman's broad powers in choosing the work force. The third type of payroll padding—"short-ganging"—depended for success completely on the shape-up. Short-ganging required a close working relationship between the hiring foreman and the timekeeper; and the union representative, who closed his eyes to the fact that the contract called for gangs of 21 men. The hiring foreman picked less than a full gang—usually 15 or 16 men— but the timekeeper recorded a full 21 names on his records, using spurious social security numbers.‡ On pay day, the extra brass checks were turned

---

* Recognizing that the looseness of this method of payment encouraged payroll padding and other irregularities, the Crime Commission recommended in its proposed statute that all dock workers be paid by check.

† The Crime Commission reported the cases of two such phantoms on the payroll of the Huron Stevedoring Corporation: James O'Connor, a business agent of Local 791, who received $18,000 over a six-year period; and Timothy O'Mara who received more than $25,000 in eight years. O'Mara was not a union official but was reported to have been "fairly successful in preventing strikes."

‡ Some longshoremen carried as many as half a dozen different social security cards taken out in the names of members of their families. These extra numbers could be used by the timekeeper.

57

in and the money in the extra pay envelopes divided among the foreman, the timekeeper, and the union official. Short-ganging seems to have been most prevalent in the Hoboken area but examples of the practice were reported in other sections of the port as well.

Ship Jumpers

Another profitable operation made possible by the shape-up was the hiring of ship jumpers—the waterfront counterpart of the "wetback" in agriculture. For more than two decades a trickle of men entered the United States illegally by jumping ship in New York, many of them finding work as longshoremen. A substantial percentage of the ship jumpers came from one town in Italy, and there are indications that before their departure they were given assurances that they would be able to get jobs on the Hoboken docks where Italian was the common language among most of the workers. Upon arrival in New York, the men contacted an ILA official in Hoboken who took them to prearranged lodgings and, within a day or two, escorted them to a pier where the hiring foreman was alerted to pick them in the shape-up.[14]

The hiring of ship jumpers was lucrative in several ways. When they received their brass checks, they turned them over to the contact man who collected their pay for them and gave them what was left after making deductions for "room and board." Ship jumpers also provided him with a market for the illicit sale of union memberships in a local which had not held a meeting for the preceding ten years.* When a group of ship jumpers were picked up on Hoboken piers in June, 1951, all of them—including one man who had been in the country only three days—were wearing union buttons.† But the most lucrative source of income provided by ship jumpers came from using them in short gangs where they could easily be subjected to speed-up conditions through threats of exposure and deportation. When carried on for any length of time, their use in short gangs could be highly profitable.‡

Political Patronage

The high turnover of workers on the waterfront made possible another practice which normally would not be considered in a discussion of a hiring

---

* The official set $59.50 as the standard initiation fee. The regular fee was $50.

† The raid was conducted by New Jersey police with the support of the U.S. Immigration Service. The director of the immigration service was reported as saying that he did not initiate the raid but had been asked by New Jersey officials to aid in the roundup. *New York Daily Mirror,* June 13, 1951. No roundups were reported in 1952, but two successful raids were made in Hoboken in 1953.

‡ For example, if five regular gangs of 21 men each were used to load a ship, 105 men would be required. But if each gang were five men short, the wages of 25 men ($420) would be "saved" a day. Over a five-day week, the "saving" would be $2,100.

system. This was the use of waterfront jobs for political pay-offs. The extent to which the waterfront served as a source of political patronage is uncertain, but there is no doubt that it did serve such a function. The Joseph P. Ryan Association operated partly as a medium through which policemen were given weekend work on the waterfront, and in Hoboken public loading concessions were at one time awarded by the mayor and the public-safety commissioner. In 1952, a senate committee investigating the preparedness program found hiring foremen at the Claremont Terminal in Jersey City helping public officials pay off their political debts in a wholesale manner:

> They would select almost anyone recommended by local politicians without regard to qualifications. The committee has received from the New York City Anti-Crime Committee, Inc., a list of approximately 500 names, indexed by wards, alleged to have been given to one Tony Marchitto, a hiring boss, by an official of Jersey City. We were also furnished by the Anti-Crime Committee copies of approximately 100 calling cards of local officials with inscribed messages introducing their friends to the hiring bosses. The cards in nearly all instances were addressed to Marchitto or one August D. Acuitis, hiring bosses, recommending the bearer as "O.K."[15]

One recipient of this patronage testified that he received a job paying $125 a week. Jobs at Claremont Terminal were used for patronage purposes throughout 1951, but the arrangement was terminated in the spring of 1952 because of a disagreement between New Jersey politicians and local ILA officials.[16]

Organized Theft

Some pilferage seems to be inevitably associated with longshoring, warehousing, and trucking, but the volume of cargo stolen on New York piers reached proportions which could only be explained by the operation of organized gangs engaging in large-scale theft. New York employers and insurance companies have declined to make public statistics on the extent of theft on the New York waterfront but the Crime Commission reported that conservative estimates were $5,186,465 for 1948; $3,942,428 for 1949; and $3,995,130 for 1950.* A statement by the president of the NYSA indicates the magnitude of the problem:

> Theft and pilferage in this port reached such proportions that steamship operators, insurance companies and other allied

---

* *Fourth Report of Crime Commission,* p. 59. According to a 1953 report of the Senate Committee on Preparedness, insurance rates "are 25 per cent additional on cargoes consigned to the New York area." U.S. Congress, Senate Subcommittee on Preparedness . . . *Investigation of the Preparedness Program,* p. 14.

industries found it necessary to establish a bureau, known presently as the Security Bureau, Inc., to aid in the suppression of these unlawful activities.[17]

The Security Bureau was established in 1947, and the task which confronted it is reflected in the following examples: In 1948, after suffering heavy losses from theft, the Grace Line moved its operations from Pier 3 in Hobokken to a Manhattan pier. The Isbrandtsen Line subsequently occupied Pier 3 but moved out in 1950, also giving excessive pilferage as the reason. An investigation into waterfront conditions was touched off in 1948 when it was discovered that the reason for New York City's inability to rent Piers 42, 45, and 46 in Manhattan was the extraordinary amount of cargo stolen on these piers.[18] The very nature of some of these thefts places them well outside the normal losses usually suffered by shipping concerns. For example, an official of the United States Lines who was testifying about pilferage on Pier 46 was asked:

> Q. How about steel; were there ten tons of steel stolen from that pier?   A. That was the most remarkable case of pilferage. It was remarkable how one could get away with it.[19]

No clear connection can be established between the shape-up and the apparent ease with which ten tons of steel were spirited off a pier, and I am not familiar with any actual proof that any hiring foreman in New York was involved in any such thefts. Nonetheless, it is reasonable to assume that a man who was attracted to the job of hiring foreman because of the many opportunities to get his cut from kickbacks, loan sharks, payroll padding, and working illegal immigrants under speed-up conditions, would not draw the line at working with a gang organized to commit robbery on the piers. Hiring foremen were in a key position to give criminals access to the cargo, and it is difficult to picture how some robberies could have been carried out without coöperation from such key men.

It is also reasonable to assume that the demoralizing effect of other waterfront practices on the longshoremen made them feel no personal responsibility for trying to prevent any thefts they saw taking place. The atmosphere of lawlessness which the shape-up brought into the industry would appear to have encouraged organized theft and to have placed no social strictures on men engaging in as much pilferage of cargo as they could successfully manage.

The total picture of the shape-up and the intolerable conditions associated with it make it abundantly clear that the old hiring system had to be discarded before any real reforms were possible. But a question as yet not fully answered is, why wasn't the shape-up abolished long ago?

60

3

Who Wanted the Shape-up?

The Frauds of New York and the Aristocrats Who Sustain Them.—Waterfront exposé[1]

To survive, a social institution must satisfy the interests of some group or groups. Obviously the employers and workers have an interest in how a hiring system works; further, a union has institutional needs of its own which can be affected by the hiring system; and, finally, the community has an interest in the result produced by the system.

One way to discover why the shape-up survived as long as it did, is to set up a check list of what each of these groups expects from a hiring system and then see how close the shape-up came to meeting these requirements. This test will reveal who had a vested interest in preserving the shape-up.

The Employers

Employers are primarily interested in operating as efficiently and economically as possible. To satisfy their interests a hiring system should provide them with an adequate supply of labor. In a labor market where the labor requirements of particular employers fluctuate widely and at different times from those of others, the hiring system either should provide a labor force large enough to meet peak needs of all employers at all times, or it should permit enough mobility so that shortages of labor do not exist in some sections of the market concurrently with surpluses in others. An adequate supply also requires a labor force of enough workers with different skills and abilities to fill all jobs. Besides, employers want to hire their workers on terms which are not laid down unilaterally by somebody else, but on terms which are at least the product of joint employer-union determination.

The first question to be considered is whether the shape-up provided

61

New York employers with enough workers in both normal and peak periods. It clearly did—the most striking feature of the system was its chronic surplus of labor. In 1951, the chairman of the NYSA reported the employers' essential satisfaction with this aspect of the shape-up:

> The shape-up in this Port has been found by the Employers and the Union best fitted to meet the needs of the industry . . .
> There is an adequate and experienced group of longshoremen, clerks, checkers, *etc.,* to supply the ordinary needs of this Port. Employers prefer to employ these men because they are familiar with the waterfront industry.
> There are peak periods, however, when the number of these men is insufficient and it becomes necessary to employ additional men from any source available. The International Longshoremen's Association recognizes this employer problem.[2]

It is difficult to determine whether the shape-up provided enough mobility of labor to preclude shortages in some sections of the port while a surplus existed in others. Various outside investigators reported that the labor force would not be efficiently distributed when port activity was unusually heavy. On the other hand, none of the employers themselves considered local shortages to be a problem. Evidently the methods they used to induce longshoremen to make themselves available at the same pier were reasonably effective under most circumstances. In the few sections of the port where piers are located at some distance from each other, any temporary labor shortages seem to have been adjusted by the employment of traveling gangs, and the limited need for these gangs indicates that local shortages occurred only infrequently. Apparently, the shape-up created not only a chronic surplus in the port as a whole but also a surplus in each separate area large enough to meet most peak needs. These circumstances made it unnecessary for the hiring system to provide any additional machinery for allocating the labor force throughout the port.

One might expect that a shape-up should fail to provide employers with enough skilled workers, but this is contradicted by the evidence. Employers were able to obtain enough men in the various skilled categories —hatch tenders, winch drivers, even gang foremen—to obviate the necessity of hiring them on a more permanent basis than by the day. These men must have been assured more consistent employment in the "regular gangs" than the unskilled men who worked in the hold and on the dock, and were undoubtedly the group the chairman of the employers' association had in mind when he spoke of "regular employees who obtain steady work throughout the year." It would appear that the shape-up produced gradually enough skilled men to meet all emergencies merely through their learning on the job, because New York employers never found it necessary to institute any sort of training program—not even during World War II when most industries were confronted with shortages of skilled workers and met the problem by setting up training programs. In any event, the employers never expressed dissatisfaction over the number of skilled men they were able to obtain through the shape-up.

Most employers are vitally interested in hiring dependable workers. Here at least we would expect to find in the record severe indictments of the shape-up by the NYSA, or at least by individual employers. Surprisingly, it was not until 1951 that they protested against the quality of workers they were forced to hire. In his minority report as a member of the mayor's joint committee investigating the decline in port business, the head of the employers' association qualified his over-all satisfaction with the shape-up in these remarks:

> Under existing collective bargaining agreements foreman stevedores shall be selected solely by the employer. Despite this provision, the Union insists that the foreman stevedore and key men, before being employed, be approved by them. Thus the employee actually becomes the selectee of the Union.
>
> The Employer should not be deprived, under any circumstances, of the right to select his foreman stevedore . . .[3]

This criticism suggests an ambivalent attitude. Employers supported the shape-up apparently because it kept their labor costs low—assuring a high rate of production from the men who were hired because of the constant threat of "the men at the gate." Employers apparently felt that this advantage more than offset the disadvantages of placing so much arbitrary power in the hands of the hiring boss that the job attracted men who used it for their own personal gain—foremen picking workers who paid the biggest kickback rather than those best able to do the job. The employers' cordial coöperation with the ILA was presumably based on a belief that such action would also keep their labor costs low, even though they saw the union falling more and more under the influence of hoodlums and racketeers. Even where foremen were forced on stevedoring concerns, employer representatives later commented favorably on the way such foremen "get work out of the men."* And by voluntarily recruiting as foremen men whose principal qualifications seemed to be their criminal rec-

---

* Frank Nolan, then president of the Jarka Stevedoring Corporation, who had originally protested against hiring Anthony Anastasia, told the Kefauver Committee in 1951: "I am quite satisfied with his services and ability. He is resourceful and tireless on the job. He preserves discipline and good order on the part of the men." *Compass,* Dec. 4, 1951

ords, employers further contributed to the possibility that hiring foremen would become key figures in the operation of petty rackets and large-scale thefts. Because of these conditions—which were in part, at least, of their own making—it was inevitable that employers would be increasingly circumscribed in their freedom to select their hiring foremen. Since the NYSA did not publicly criticize the union for this usurpation of management functions until the ILA hierarchy lost their effectiveness at "keeping the men in line," it must be concluded that most employers considered the disadvantages of not being able to select their own hiring foremen to be of relatively minor importance.*

Employers naturally don't wish to have wage rates and other labor costs imposed upon them by someone else. Their first preference would be to set these terms themselves but, where collective bargaining exists, most employers are reasonably satisfied with joint union-employer determination. Between 1916 and 1945, the amicable nature of collective bargaining and the union's modest demands resulted in contract provisions eminently satisfactory for the employers on the New York waterfront. In 1945, a leading stevedore in the port described the bargaining relationship: "We call Ryan in once a year or so and say, 'Joe, how much of a raise do you need to keep the boys in line?' "[4] It is true, of course, that the contract contained a clause which as a practical matter gave union members preference of employment, but the ILA did not insist on its enforcement. Without job security, rank-and-file longshoremen were unable to insist on their rights under the contract. Consequently, no effective pressure was exerted on employers to establish grievance machinery or strictly observed safety procedures (indeed, the union insisted that a safety code did not belong in a collective bargaining agreement[5]), or even to live up to the contract by hiring full gangs. Insistence on all of these would, of course, have increased the employers' labor costs.

After World War II, however, the balance of power began to shift against the employers. On top of their increasing inability to select their own hiring foremen and the necessity of making substantial expenditures for protection against theft, they were subjected to the harassment of a rash of wildcat strikes, the causes of which were traceable directly to the shape-up. Taken together, these work stoppages constituted a severe curtailment of the employers' ability to control their operations. It is significant that one of the few criticisms of the collective bargaining relationship ever voiced by the NYSA was concerned with these work stoppages:

* I interviewed one employer in 1952 who was seriously concerned about this problem and criticized other practices associated with the shape-up. When asked what he had done to correct the situation, he threw up his hands and replied, "What can one man do?"

64

The employers are alarmed at the increasing number of work stoppages. Men have walked off piers in all parts of the Port in an effort to win concessions or correct alleged grievances without utilizing the adjustment machinery provided for under the agreement. Employers have suffered serious losses because of such work stoppages and the reputation of the Port has been considerably injured . . .[6]

This complaint was made to the board of inquiry investigating the 1951 strike. Actually, the remedy for these strikes was at least partially available to the employers had they been willing to participate in collective bargaining as fully as have employers in other unionized industries. As the board pointed out, it is not enough merely to include a clause in an agreement—adjustment machinery to be meaningful must be put into practice by setting up grievance committees, composed of union and employer members, which really function.

The Board's investigation reveals that there has been a long-standing complaint that individual union members are unable to assert their rights under the contract with respect to having their grievances taken up in the proper manner . . . The history of work stoppages caused by grievances appears to confirm this . . . The evidence shows that one of the causes and circumstances surrounding the recent strike is the inadequacy of grievance machinery.[7]

Table 3 shows some strikes to which the employers referred. It is notable that, of all disputes listed on the table, the only work stoppage which was termed "official" by the union was the strike in November, 1948.

Another aspect of the environment which became increasingly annoying to employers was their custom of making sizable financial contributions to ILA officials. According to the Crime Commission, the total amount paid by employers to these union officers from 1947 to 1952 was at least $182,000.* This raises two questions: (a) Did these payments represent extortion from employers by union officials, or domination of the union by employers? (b) Was the practice traceable to the hiring system? The second question is particularly pertinent for our purposes.

Some employers admitted that their motives in making these payments were to buy off the union, and it must be conceded that $36,000 or so a

---

* *New York Times,* Dec. 28, 1952. Even the U.S. Treasury made a modest contribution. In 1953 the federal maritime administration disclosed the fact that "three subsidized shipping lines paid $64,824 to New York waterfront labor racketeers during the period in which the companies received about $54,000,000 from the Government." *New York Times,* March 11, 1953.

TABLE 3

Work Stoppages on Piers on the New York Side of the Port of New York Involving Longshoremen, Checkers, and Maintenance Workers January, 1946, to December, 1951

Date	Party affected	ILA locals involved	Issues	Man days lost
1946 July 10–15	Staten Island Piers 16–21 and North River Piers 56–62	Various	Jurisdictional dispute between ILA locals	12,000
Sept. 8–10	Piers 60–62, North River	791	Wildcat strike	800
Sept. 20–22	NYSA, New York City	Various	Vacations (wildcat)	5,000
1947 Sept. 6–8	Atlantic Gulf and West Indies Company	Various	Working conditions	700
Sept. 20–25	ILA, later NYSA, New York City	791	Insurgent protest against terms of agreement	16,300
1948 June 6–8	Yugoslav vessel *Radnik, New York City*	327, 338	Don't know	189
Nov. 10–27	ILA, New York City	All	Insurgent protest against new agreement	270,700
Dec. 8[a]	Piers 84, 86, 88, 92	824	Two men questioned by district attorney about murder of hiring foreman	150
1949 May 31 to June 2	U. S. Maritime Commission, Luckenbach Steamship Company, Brooklyn	Various	Don't know	300

Date	Company, Location	Local	Cause	Number
Aug. 4–8	Hercules Maintenance Company, Brooklyn	338	Number of men to be employed on job	45
Aug. 29	John L. McGrath Corp., New York City	824	Attempt of company to split one gang	150
1950				
Feb. 2–5	Cunard Line, New York City	791	Protest against proposed shift of company operations from one pier to another	200
Sept. 29 to Oct. 3	Cunard White Star, Ltd., New York City	791	Assault charge against union member by company guard	450
Nov. 7–9	T. Hogan & Sons, Inc., New York City	791	Assignment of certain work to steward; settled by taking work away from steward	100
1951				
Jan. 2–3	Isthmian Line, Brooklyn	Various	Protest against article in *Brooklyn Eagle* about Anthony Anastasia	110
Jan. 13–16	T. Hogan & Sons, Inc., New York City	791	Work assigned to superintendent	400
March 20–25	Grace Line, New York City	895, 1346	Company moved to another pier; jurisdictional dispute between ILA locals	1,200
June 26[b]	31st Street Pier, Brooklyn	1195	District attorney took pictures and questioned men about thefts on pier	150
Sept. 18	Bull Lines, Brooklyn	Various	Jurisdictional dispute between ILA locals	400
Oct. 15 to Nov. 9	Stevedoring Industry, New York City, Staten Island, Brooklyn	All	Insurgent protest against terms of agreement.	203,700

Source: *Board of Inquiry*, pp. 33–34, unless otherwise indicated.
[a] *New York World Telegram and Sun*, Dec. 8, 1948.
[b] *Brooklyn Daily Eagle*, June 26, 1951.

year would have been a low price to pay for a union as coöperative as the ILA.* Other employers testified that payments were extorted from them "to assure a sufficient supply of labor," "to prevent quickie strikes," "because I want peace on the waterfront."† Whether this practice is a result of the hiring system depends upon the interpretation one accepts of the nature of these payments. If they did represent company domination of the union, the practice was clearly related to the shape-up, because the hiring system had contributed to the corruption of the union and made officials more susceptible to accepting bribes from employers. But if the second interpretation is correct—that the payments were extorted by powerful union officials—the practice was not necessarily related to the shape-up, because a powerful but unscrupulous union official in any industry might be able to extort such payments regardless of the hiring system used in the industry. To know with certainty which interpretation is correct would require a more intimate knowledge of how the employers themselves viewed the matter. Nevertheless, it can be surmised that even when these payments were added to the industry's payroll (in proportion to which they were, after all, a negligible fraction), the shape-up for many years provided New York employers with low labor costs—which was their *primary* interest. It is likely that the employers began to regard these payments as exorbitant only when they failed to keep labor costs down and to prevent "quickies" and port-wide strikes.

When the shape-up was outlawed in 1953, it was still providing employers with an adequate supply of labor, both quantitatively and qualitatively, although the terms on which men could be hired were increasingly being imposed on employers unilaterally. It is significant that even though the system was beginning to break down, and despite the growing diversion of cargo from the port, New York employers insisted on keeping the shape-up; and it was not until threatened with government intervention that they proposed basic changes. We can safely conclude that, in general,

---

* In the parlance of economics, it might even be argued that ILA officials were "exploited" by the employers in the sense that the payments were less than the value of their marginal product.

† The case for extortion is weakened by the failure of employers, either individually or through their association, to bring any complaints to the attention of law-enforcement officials. Only after the Crime Commission's investigations were under way did one stevedore charge an ILA official with extorting $2,000—the total wages paid a hiring foreman the union had forced on him. *New York Times,* Dec. 22, 1952. Another case clearly involving extortion was aired in the Crime Commission's hearings. In 1950, a group of importers had been forced to pay $70,000 to certain ILA officials in order to secure delivery of two shipments of furs from Russia. Unloading of the $2,000,000 cargo had been held up by the ILA officials who had persuaded the longshoremen not to handle shipments of Russian furs for "patriotic reasons." *Fourth Report of Crime Commission,* p. 25.

the shape-up was satisfactory to them and that they had a vested interest in preserving it.

The Longshoremen

For workers, the performance of a hiring system is a much more personal and intimate matter than for employers. Workers are vitally interested in economic security, so they want to know in advance how much they will be able to earn on a job and how permanent they can expect it to be. If a hiring system is to meet these needs, it should provide workers with enough information about the jobs available in the labor market to enable them to make reasonable choices. Also, since workers spend so much of their lives on the job, they want to find their work also subjectively rewarding. Because they want to be treated fairly and impartially by their employers, it is important to them to have some control over their working conditions both individually and through their union. To preserve their self-respect, they prefer a job on which special abilities and skills will be put to the best use. A job where one's fellow workers are compatible and where the work is viewed by the community with approval is naturally preferred. In industries where people are hired on a relatively permanent basis the hiring system has little effect on these subjective desires of workers, but where men are hired anew each day the hiring process can vitally affect workers' chances of finding these satisfactions in their jobs.

New York longshoremen had only the most limited opportunity to choose among alternative jobs because they got so little information in advance about what jobs were available. When hiring foremen were told of jobs in advance they sometimes told the foremen of regular gangs, who in turn told regular gang members, but men not notified in this way had to depend for news of ship arrivals on notices on bulletin boards at the various piers or on checking the newspapers and trade journals. Since men were encouraged always to shape at the same pier, they were not really free to show up in another section of the port when they did hear of extra jobs elsewhere. The immobility of the men, coupled with their inability to build up property rights in jobs on their regular piers, resulted, as would be expected, in many of the men working irregularly and earning far less than they would have been able to on a regular job. (The earnings data for 1949–1950 show that more than 60 per cent of the men earned less than $2,000.) But the most frustrating aspect of appraising the shape-up is the impossibility of proving that men who made themselves regularly available were kept from working as much as they wished to. No reliable survey was ever made among men working on the waterfront to find out how many of them wanted to work full-time and how many were satisfied with part-time or even occasional work.[8] Consequently, there is no specific evidence to refute the repeated assertions by NYSA and ILA officials that the system gave "regular men" steady employment. Every investigation of waterfront conditions resulted in vigorous demands for stabilizing employment for regular workers, but who the "regular workers" were was never established.

One measure of the adequacy of workers' earnings is the City Workers' Family Budget, compiled by the U.S. Bureau of Labor Statistics. As the bureau has stated, this budget is based on a modest standard:

> The Budget represents the estimated cost in dollars for a city worker's family of four persons to maintain an adequate level of living according to prevailing United States standards of the needs for health, efficiency, nurture of children, and participation in community activities. It is neither a "subsistence" nor a "luxury" budget. It provides a modest but adequate American standard of living based upon the kinds and qualities of goods and services that workers actually select.[9]

In 1950, the BLS budget in New York City was approximately $3,500. On the assumption that a longshoreman's earnings were adequate if they met this budget, the 1950 earnings data show that perhaps 8,000 (or 22 per cent of the men) earned adequate incomes. Assuming that more than 8,000 of the 36,500 men *had* wanted to work regularly enough to earn adequate incomes, would it have been possible for them to do so if an alternative hiring system had been in use? Because of the crudeness of available data, only a rough answer can be attempted.

In 1950, the straight-time wage was $1.88. The total man-hours worked in the port were 34,910,675, of which 26 per cent were overtime.[10] Unfortunately for our purposes, the figure for total man-hours worked includes 5,500 checkers, dock bosses, clerks, and carpenters, as well as the longshoremen.[11] On the assumption that a 35-hour week was normal for the latter relatively specialized group, a figure of 1,800 hours per man per year may be subtracted from the total man-hour figure in order to arrive at an estimate of the man-hours worked by longshoremen only— 25,000,000. Thus, if the labor market were organized in such a way that the average number of hours worked by regular longshoremen were 1,800 (roughly, 35 hours per week for 52 weeks), the industry could have provided annual earnings of approximately $3,700 to about 14,000 longshoremen (6,000 more than under the shape-up);* Thus, if a survey of the

---

* This estimate of 14,000 approaches the number (15,000) denominated by the head of the employers' association in 1952 as "regular longshoremen."

labor force had clearly shown the existence of involuntary underemployment, it is evident that a hiring system which shared the work among the men for whom longshoring was a primary occupation could have enabled almost twice as many longshoremen to earn adequate incomes as did under the shape-up.

In addition to the effect of irregular employment on their earnings, longshoremen had little protection against being paid less than they were entitled to. Their wages were determined by collective bargaining, and it would seem that a worker should at least have been able to insist on the wage rate set forth in the contract. As it was, one longshoreman who had worked on the docks for twenty years told me that he had been paid less than the standard rate on more than one occasion, and that his was not a unique experience on the New York waterfront. This could have arisen, of course, because of a difference of opinion as to whether a particular penalty rate should have been paid.* In longshoring, the possibility of honest differences on such matters is so great that vigilant policing of the agreement is imperative if equitable compromises are to be ensured, but where the union was so little concerned with protecting the rights of its members and the method of wage payment so archaic, wage-cutting could easily be practiced. Furthermore, the variety of kickbacks extorted by hiring foremen and their henchmen made uncertain how much of the money in a longshoreman's pay envelope could appropriately be described as take-home pay.

Where a union plays an important role in the operation of a hiring system, the workers exert control only according to the degree to which they participate in framing the collective-bargaining agreement and according to their ability to influence the union officials who police the agreement. The extent to which the longshoremen had been disenfranchised in deciding what their agreement would contain was uncovered in the investigation following the 1951 strike. ILA officials had announced that the men had voted two to one in favor of accepting the agreement, but it was discovered that many of the delegates to the committee which had formulated and negotiated the agreement had appointed themselves without holding elections or even consulting the membership of the locals they represented. The terms of the proposed contract were summarized and distributed to the locals on one day and voted on the next day. Ballots were not numbered and members could vote either at their own local or at another if more convenient.[12] After ballots were "counted" at the locals, the results

---

* The contract specifies that premium, or "penalty," rates shall be paid when the cargo is exceptionally dangerous, dirty, or hard to handle. There are seven categories of such cargo, and the hourly wage paid for handling two of them—damaged cargo and explosives—was just under twice the regular hourly rate.

were telephoned to ILA headquarters. None of these phone calls was confirmed in writing.[13]

The ballots of several locals examined by the board of inquiry looked suspicious, so Albert D. Osborn, an examiner of questioned documents, was called in. The examiner found that the ballots of seven locals showed some evidence of fraud. The worst example, Local 920 (Staten Island), had submitted 286 ballots of which 264 were Yes, the remaining 22 No. Osborn found nothing suspicious about the No ballots, but concluded that 89 of the Yes votes were fraudulent, stating ". . . it would appear to me that one person, or more than one, sat down with the ballots stacked on top of each other and marked the 'X' in the 'yes' box on many of these ballots."

The conclusion is inescapable that rank-and-file longshoremen had little to say about the contents of their collective-bargaining agreement—the workers' Bill of Rights in any unionized industry. The members had even less control over the officers whose duty it was to enforce the contract. In 1953, officials of almost a dozen locals admitted they had not held elections for ten to fifteen years (one local, for thirty years) and other officials testified that when "elections" were held, incumbents were continued in office on a motion passed by a handful of members. In a few locals, union offices had been taken over by force. Add to this sordid record Ryan's election "for life" and the coercive actions taken against men who opposed the hierarchy, and it is clear that the men could not look on the union as an instrument for improving their working conditions.

Workers also want to use to their best advantage any special skills they may possess. If they are to do this, their ability to obtain jobs must not be affected by such arbitrary factors as race, color, or creed. The possibility that workers will be denied employment on these grounds is present in any labor market, and a charge of discrimination is difficult enough to support in industries where orderly, systematized hiring procedures are used. Under the shape-up, it was virtually impossible to prove charges of discrimination, but some evidence indicates that it was practiced. During World War II, ILA officials organized a Jim Crow local (824-1) for Negro longshoremen to whom Local 824 refused membership.[14] Local 968, largely composed of Negro members, in addition to (unsuccessfully) filing charges of discrimination with the New York State Commission Against Discrimination, pointed to the fact that it was the only ILA local in the port which did not have exclusive jurisdiction over a pier.[15] In 1949, ILA officials circulated a petition urging longshoremen to go on record opposing a hiring hall because, among other things, a hiring hall would "break the morale of the union through the wholesale hiring of Negro longshoremen.""[16] On the other hand, charges of discrimination against Negroes were repeatedly denied by ILA officials who called attention to the fact that Negroes were employed in various sections of the port, and Joseph Ryan made a number of public statements condemning racial discrimination. Nevertheless, it is easy to understand that a sense of insecurity would be felt by members of any minority group who stood in the shape-up, because no safeguard was provided against a hiring foreman acting on any prejudice which he might happen to hold. Interestingly enough, some groups were treated with "reverse prejudice" in parts of the port. At some piers, Italian-Americans were almost exclusively picked; at others, Irish-Americans were the favored group. As a consequence, if a longshoreman with either of these ethnic backgrounds lost favor in the eyes of his regular hiring foreman, other sections of the port where he might be able to establish himself were limited.*

The attainment of status in the community is another important objective of workers, and it is obvious that the shape-up prevented longshoremen from achieving this goal. Through a process of guilt by association, the bad reputation deserved by some longshoremen was applied to all. This reputation was reflected in the unwillingness of banks and finance companies to give personal loans to longshoremen, and the reluctance of many inland employers to hire former longshoremen on the ground that they were unstable. After the description of the waterfront, nothing more need be said about the impact of the shape-up on the ability of longshoremen to preserve their self-respect. By 1953, the longshoremen had indeed come a long way from the day when Barnes could say of their proud, independent spirit: "Having no steady job to jeopardize, they take bad treatment with less grace than do men in other trades."[17]

The shape-up prevented workers from achieving even the elementary goal of reducing the physical discomfort of waiting in the street regardless of the weather. In almost any other industry, the elimination of this inconvenience would be so obvious as to preclude the need for discussion, but the stultifying effect of the hiring system was so great that as recently as 1953 men waited for the shape in the open just as they had done a century before.

In evaluating the effect of the shape-up on longshoremen's earnings, it has only been possible to draw the inference that the hiring system prevented many longshoremen who regularly sought work from even approximating full-time employment and thus from earning adequate incomes. With respect to the impact of the shape-up on other desires

---

* In the past, these ethnic barriers were mentioned by several students of the port as an important obstacle to the establishment of a centralized hiring system.

of workers, however, the record is clear. The shape-up served their employers very satisfactorily, but for the longshoremen it was a monstrous obstacle to the achievement of their goals. The frustration of the workers explains the random character of the strikes which began breaking out in 1945, but the inconclusive character of these strikes showed how badly the longshoremen had been demoralized by the shape-up.

The Union

Primarily, a union is an instrument for the achievement of its members' objectives. But a union is more than this—it is a political entity having as a separate objective its own survival as an institution. In any type of labor market, these dual aspects of a union may come into conflict to the detriment of one or the other. In an industry where employment is stable, this conflict is reconciled without great difficulty because the union can easily ensure its own survival by controlling the jobs over which it claims jurisdiction—by a union shop agreement, for example. This achieved, the union is free to serve efficiently as a medium for satisfying the interests of its members. When workers are hired on a casual basis, however, serious obstacles are placed in the path of reconciling this conflict of objectives. To survive in such a labor market, a union is faced with two alternatives. Either it must control the job market by restricting entry of newcomers and thus serve its own and the individual members' interests at the same time, or it can forgo any attempt to control the job market, maintaining its existence instead by controlling the workers themselves. A union which chooses the latter course can no longer be considered an instrument for the achievement of its members' objectives. Under these circumstances, the "union" becomes identified with the interests of its officials. Since the ILA clearly fell in this category, the relevant question to ask is: How did the hiring system affect the ability of ILA officials to satisfy *their* interests?

For them, preservation of the shape-up became an imperative necessity. As early as the 1930's, the union hierarchy perceived that they could easily keep the entire labor force under control by establishing coöperative relationships with the hiring foremen, because the foremen could keep "troublemakers" off the waterfront simply by not picking them in the shape-up. Any alternative hiring system which diffused the hiring power would have made the job of controlling the workers more difficult for union officials.

Another technique of control facilitated by the shape-up was the traditional method of "divide and rule." With a high turnover of members in a port the size of New York, ILA officials were able to keep the membership segregated in small units, ignorant for the most part of what was happening in other areas of the port, and consequently unable to challenge the hierarchy's control. By design, the union was ". . . politically gerrymandered. . . . As a result, any dissident locals [could] be easily outvoted in the district council."* But ILA officials were too careful to put their trust in these administrative arrangements alone. They saw to it that their power was preserved by appointing men to jobs in the union who would use strong-arm methods to intimidate the rank and file and perpetuate the hiring system.

Having securely established themselves in power, union officials made the most of their opportunities. Appropriately enough, the international president was in the forefront. It was brought to light in 1953 that although Ryan's salary was $20,000 a year, he had withdrawn $241,097 from the ILA treasury between 1947 and 1951. Of this amount, $126,000 was for expense allowances. Ryan's interpretation of what should be included as expenses was broad—$10,774 was used for premiums on his life insurance, $1,332 for dues and other charges at his golf club, $12,494 for Cadillacs, $460 for a cruise to Guatemala, and $220 for new shirts. Other items for which he drew on ILA funds included expenses incurred in burying a sister-in-law, taxes on his personal real estate, and his dental bills. Ryan admitted he had kept improper accounts, and that he had received substantial sums from steamship and stevedoring executives for his private "anti-Communist fund." He explained his use of ILA funds for his own purposes by saying that on occasions when the union was short of cash he drew on his own personal bank account or took money from the "anti-Communist fund" to pay ILA expenses, later using ILA funds to pay his personal bills.†

Not far behind Ryan were some of the other top figures in the hierarchy, who turned the necessity for political gerrymandering to their personal advantage. One such official was John J. Gannon, who held the following

---

* Daniel Bell, "Last of the Business Rackets," *Fortune,* 43 (June, 1951), 196. In 1952, Louis Waldman reported that some locals in the port were almost inactive. One had about 16 members. The Crime Commission reported in 1953 ". . . four locals are actually inactive; yet the vote for each is cast at conventions and other union conferences." *Fourth Report of Crime Commission,* p. 32.

† *New York Times,* Jan. 31, 1953. For these acts Ryan was indicted shortly after the Crime Commission hearings. In the original indictment, Ryan was charged with 51 grand larceny counts amounting to $48,000. When his trial began in April, 1954, the court reduced the number of counts against him to 42, which amounted to $17,000. On May 14, after the jury had been deadlocked for 18 hours, the judge declared a mistrial. At the time of writing, the district attorney had not moved for a retrial. In January, 1955, however, Ryan was convicted of having accepted $2,500 from a stevedoring firm in violation of the Taft-Hartley Act. He was fined $2,500 and sentenced to six months in prison.

posts: president of the New York District Council; vice-president of the Atlantic Coast District; secretary-treasurer of Local 901-1; secretary-treasurer of Local 824-1 (the Jim Crow local); and "labor adviser" of Local 1456 (the port watchmen's local). Gannon estimated in his testimony before the Crime Commission that the combined salary from his various union offices totaled $225 a week, plus a monthly expense account of $440—approximately $17,000 a year.* Gannon noted, however, that he did not always receive the full amount because sometimes the locals did not have enough funds to pay his salary.[18] Another example was Thomas Gleason, acting president of Local 783, business agent of Local 1346 (both in Staten Island), financial secretary of Local 1730 (in midtown Manhattan), and international organizer. In 1951 alone, Gleason received a total of $26,025 for his services to the ILA.[19]

Union treasuries proved to be bonanzas for lesser luminaries as well. Unlike the practice in most unions, some ILA locals rendered no financial reports whatever to their members, and officials appropriated funds for their personal use almost at will. This came to light after the 1951 strike, when Ryan and Waldman attempted the last of their clean-up campaigns, which like the other efforts at reform, was abortive and received less and less attention as the Crime Commission investigation got under way. As part of the campaign, Waldman made a survey of the internal practices of all locals in the port and reported the following:†

> 53 locals have checking accounts in the name of the local for the deposit of local funds.
> 5 locals maintain savings accounts in the name of the local for the deposit of surplus local funds. The financial transactions of these locals are conducted on a cash bookkeeping basis.
> 9 locals, at the time of our examination of their officers, did not maintain any bank account for the deposit of their local funds. Subsequently, we were informed that some of the locals, pursuant to recommendations in interim reports by us, had already opened a bank account.[20]

One local to which Waldman may have been referring in the third category was Local 920. The financial secretary of the local presented a bizarre picture of the local's financial processes in his testimony before the Crime Commission. The president, Alex Di Brizzi, periodically picked

---

* Gannon's advice to the port watchmen must have been valuable indeed. For it, he received a salary and expense allowance of $155 per week, an automobile, and $20 in expenses for every monthly meeting. Not counting the car, this was more than $8,300 a year. The local claimed a dues-paying membership of 1,600.

† Because the survey covered all ILA locals in the port, it included more than just the 31 longshore locals.

up the dues money received by the local, deducted whatever he needed for expenses, and turned the balance over to the financial secretary. The two officers adopted a cavalier attitude toward the matter of receipts and vouchers for disbursements as well as other financial records.* The financial secretary described his method of handling the local's cash as follows:

> Q. Mr. Di Brizzi on Saturday sometimes would hand you quite a roll of bills, would he not?   A. Yes, he would sometimes.
> Q. And you would take those bills home and put them in a jar?   A. In a sort of novelty jar. I learned to discontinue that.[21]

Even petty officials of the union derived substantial benefits from the system. In addition to extorting kickbacks from longshoremen in return for a good word to the hiring foreman, they got their cut from loan sharks, the numbers racket, short-ganging, employment of phantoms, public loaders, selling union books, and "Christmas gifts" from employers. There was something for everybody in the system—as long as he was on the inside.

Like the employers, the ILA hierarchy were well satisfied with the shape-up and fought hard to keep it. Unlike the employers, for whom the usefulness of the shape-up was beginning to break down in the 1950's, the union officials were unshaken by the strikes and investigations which followed the war. It seems likely that if the New York and New Jersey legislatures had not taken drastic action, the ILA would have been able to ignore public criticism after the Crime Commission's hearings just as they had ridden out other storms in the past. But when the two states outlawed the shape-up, they struck at the very heart of the system by which ILA officials had maintained themselves in power.

The Community

Until 1953, the New York waterfront furnished the fascinating spectacle of an industry which, although it was conducting its affairs in a manner that was in direct conflict with the interests of the community, remained almost completely free from effective public intervention. The community's interest in any particular industry seems to be primarily concerned with obtaining an uninterrupted flow of the industry's product or services

---

* In 1951, the membership of the local authorized Di Brizzi to spend $500 when he attended the ILA convention at the Hotel Commodore in Manhattan. (Four other delegates from the local got like amounts.) Di Brizzi exceeded his allowance by $937, which the financial secretary obligingly paid without consulting the membership. *Fourth Report of Crime Commission,* p. 27.

at prices the public can afford to pay. When the industry is a link in the country's distribution system, any interruption in its services has a peculiarly immediate and far-reaching effect on the whole community. Society has a less immediate, but nonetheless important, interest in an industry's hiring practices, because the community benefits when the hiring system produces a balance between the number of workers who offer their services and those whose services are needed. The existence of a chronic surplus or a chronic shortage of workers in a labor market implies an inefficient use of a productive resource and constitutes an expense to society through loss of production. A hiring system also maximizes production when it places workers in jobs they are best able to perform. This implies freedom of choice for both employers and workers, modified only by those measures which society has agreed are necessary if workers are to enjoy economic security—such as recognition of the seniority principle in promotions, lay-offs and rehiring. The community also has a stake in the impact of industry practices on social institutions in general. If these practices undermine the proper functioning of governmental bodies or tend to break down the community's standards of acceptable behavior on the part of individuals, the community suffers. Since practices in the New York longshoring industry patently ran counter to the best interests of the community, why did the public tolerate the situation for so many years?

For one thing, many of these requirements of society are long-range in character, and the public in general was not consciously aware of them. During the depression, when about one-fourth of the workers in the nation seemed to be "surplus," the retention of a chronic excess of workers on the waterfront clearly involved no immediate cost in lost production either to the people of New York or to the country at large. Only during World War II was the excess of longshoremen an obvious waste of manpower and although this soft spot in the war effort was pointed out by Senate investigators, it seemed inappropriate in wartime to risk disrupting cargo movements in the country's largest port by forcing a new hiring system on unwilling employers and union officials. Similar factors explained the community's lack of immediate interest in seeing that the most highly skilled workers made up the longshore gangs, rather than those workers who paid the biggest kickback or who were fortunate enough to have acceptable ethnic backgrounds. The resultant loss of efficiency was not reflected in an over-all increase in the cost of shipping services to the community, because the chaotic nature of the hiring system resulted in a docile work force, unable to bargain effectively for all those provisions in a collective bargaining agreement which would have added appreciably to the industry's labor costs. Even the losses from theft—three to five million dollars a year—were relatively small in relation to the value of the total volume of cargo handled (about sixteen billion dollars in 1953) and thus had only an insignificant effect on the per-unit price of commodities moving through the port. Because the economic inefficiencies of the industry raised no immediate problems, they did not force themselves upon the awareness of the community.

The social costs of the shape-up were more immediately apparent, but here, too, powerful factors were working against any broadly based public protest. The demoralization of the workers and the flagrant disregard by many waterfront personalities of both the law of the land and even the most elementary standards of decent behavior were periodically decried. But the community evidently needed some specific issue which would arouse indignation before pressure for reform could become effective. Here the sagacity of the ILA's long-range program of close political liaison with various levels of government showed itself. Local police officers could not be counted on to initiate action, because many had a vested interest in protecting a system which enabled them to supplement their inadequate salaries both by working on the docks as longshoremen in their off-duty hours and by sharing in the proceeds from the various rackets. The city administration had an equal interest in preserving the elaborate system which had been built up to ensure political support and patronage. The determination of city officials not to disturb the status quo was demonstrated in 1949 by O'Dwyer's whitewash appointments to the committee which studied the reasons for the loss in port business, and even more clearly during the 1951 strike. The rank-and-file revolt against the ILA hierarchy was more than two weeks old when a delegation of New York businessmen, who had come to demand that the city take some action to end the strike, were refused an audience with the mayor and told they were acting "like a bunch of Communists."

Citizens interested in reform received little encouragement from federal agencies charged with enforcing the law on the waterfront. The U.S. Immigration Service was apparently prevented by lack of personnel from pursuing a vigilant policy toward ship jumpers, and the Bureau of Internal Revenue was evidently unable to trace income-tax violations because of the bizarre bookkeeping procedures used on the waterfront. The Federal Bureau of Investigation does not seem to have interested itself in waterfront irregularities until after the Crime Commission's hearings,*

* The *New York Times* reported on January 19, 1953: "Since the last public hearings on December 19, the FBI district office here, on orders from Attorney General James A. McGranery, has put all its available agents on a full-scale investigation of the waterfront."

and the Coast Guard screening program was of no help in eliminating key waterfront racketeers because the Coast Guard's conception of a security risk was confined to ideological considerations, rather than to the effect of racketeering and theft on military shipments.

Not until business in the port was periodically brought to a standstill by repeated strikes, and not until inland concerns became alarmed over the gradually increasing diversion of shipping to other ports in order to avoid the inconvenience and arbitrary charges of public loaders, did larger segments of the community have some immediate, concrete issues around which people could be rallied. Thus, it was only when the industry ceased to provide the community with uninterrupted services at prices people were willing to pay that demands for reform received wide support. Indeed, it was the 1951 strike that tipped the scales. When both city and federal officials refused to take responsibility for trying to bring about a settlement,* state officials were forced to step in. It was Governor Dewey who finally appointed the board of inquiry which persuaded the strikers to return to work; once the state had intervened, state officials were under pressure not to withdraw until every effort had been made to prevent future jeopardy of state interests.† The governor directed the State Crime Commission to turn its full attention to the waterfront, and the commission's subsequent public hearings became the focal point which had been needed for so long to crystallize public opinion. The about-face in the community's attitude toward the waterfront which resulted from these hearings was strikingly reflected in the treatment of waterfront practices

---

* The Federal Mediation and Conciliation Service entered the dispute but withdrew after three days, and President Truman, appealed to for help by the rank-and-file strike committee, did not respond.

† Previously, Governor Dewey had tacitly accepted the hands-off attitude of other levels of government. As recently as May 9, 1950, he had sent Ryan the following letter (which appeared in the *New York Times* on March 29, 1953):

Dear Joe:

I would surely be delighted to come to the annual affair of the Joseph R. Ryan Association, if possible. As it happens, Mrs. Dewey and I have accepted an invitation to the marriage of Lowell Thomas' only son that week-end and we just cannot possibly make it.

It is mighty nice of you to ask me and I wish you would give my best regards to all the fine people at the dinner.

On behalf of the people of the entire state, I congratulate you for what you have done to keep the Communists from getting control of the New York waterfront. Be assured that the entire machinery of the Government of New York State is behind you and your organization in this determination.

With warm regards,
Sincerely yours,
Thomas E. Dewey

by New York's most influential newspaper. At the close of the hearings, the *New York Times* commented editorially:

> The ILA is controlled by labor gangsters who direct the kickbacks, extortion, thievery, usury, and other rackets on the piers and intimidate the longshoremen.
>
> The mobsters could not run the waterfront without the consent of the stevedores and shipping companies. These companies cooperate with the ILA—hiring criminals, bribing union officials—because the thugs keep the dockers in line.
>
> Neither the ILA nor the companies could perpetuate the system without at least the tacit consent of officials in New York and New Jersey. Many of these officials accept campaign contributions from ILA racketeers and stevedore executives, give them political jobs, keep up social contacts with them.[22]

The indignation of this editorial was in sharp contrast with the fatalistic attitude adopted by the paper only a year earlier toward the possibility of reform. During the 1951 strike, the *New York Times* had drawn attention to the risks involved in disturbing the status quo:

> In fairness to the ILA leadership and to the shipping industry, which is in a sense partly responsible for waterfront conditions, it must be conceded that the average dock walloper is in a class by himself as far as organized labor is concerned. He can be maddeningly contrary and irrational and is often unpredictable.
>
> Leading shipping executives who have dealt with Joe Ryan and his ILA for many years shudder to think what would happen if the Ryan hierarchy were overthrown by men with less control of the hot-headed, opinionated and stubborn sea-lawyers and salt-water politicians who make up the Eastern seaboard's waterfront labor force.[23]

Once a solid basis was laid for forcing reforms on the reluctant employers and union officials, consideration of workable alternatives to the shape-up was in order. Both in the Crime Commission hearings and in the hearings held by Governor Dewey just before the special session of the legislature which outlawed the old hiring system, several alternative proposals were presented by the parties and by interested civic groups.* Numerous references were made to the hiring systems in operation in foreign ports, especially in England, but with the exception of a few digressive comments by one or two persons, the organization of the longshore industry on the West Coast was completely ignored. No testimony was obtained from West Coast employers, and although Harry Bridges, presi-

---

* These plans are discussed in chapter 7.

dent of the West Coast longshoremen's union, submitted a 32-page statement explaining the operation of the West Coast hiring-hall system, it was not included in the record. New York employers, of course, had placed themselves on record in 1951 as being unalterably opposed to the Pacific Coast system:

> There has been much criticism levelled at [the shape-up] but no other practical method of hiring except the so-called hiring hall has been suggested. The hiring hall has been held illegal and those who favor it do not appear to be fully aware of the impact it would have on this industry. We know too well what has happened on the Pacific Coast to advocate the adoption of the hiring hall system or any modification of it.[24]

Since West Coast employers and their employees were operating hiring halls in several ports as early as the 1920's, and halls administered jointly by the union and the employers have existed on a coast-wide basis for 20 years, the NYSA assertion raises some interesting questions. What *has* happened on the Pacific Coast? Might those concerned with finding a solution to the New York waterfront problem have benefited from the experience in West Coast ports?

A shape-up on the New York waterfront

Anthony Anastasia

Joseph P. Ryan

Photo: *The Dispatcher*

Harry Bridges

Photo: *The Dispatcher*

Photo: *The Dispatcher*

Dave Beck

Harry Lundeberg

Photo: *Seattle Times*

Seattle longshore pickets being tear-gassed at Smith
Cove during the 1934 strike

Photo: Pacific Maritime Association

A meeting of the Seattle Joint Labor Relations
Committee—the "new look" in action

Clockwise: Martin Juggum, business agent, ILWU Local 19; Ralph Johnson, Labor
Relations Committee representative (partly hidden); Frank Jenkins, Labor Relations
Committee representative; L. C. Appel, president, ILWU Local 19; T. J. Green,
Rothschild-International Stevedoring Company; J. E. Ritchie, Pacific Maritime Asso-
ciation; Ward Settersten, Griffiths & Sprague Stevedoring Company.

Seattle longshoremen in their hiring hall waiting
to be dispatched to the docks

The peg board in the Seattle hiring hall, seen
from inside the dispatcher's office

4

The Seattle Waterfront

You can't scare me, I'm sticking to the union.[1]
—Union song.

Longshoring on the two coasts presents so many contrasts that one might almost be looking at two completely different industries. In West Coast ports, the industry has been administered with the conscious aim of keeping the waterfront free of the chaos and abuses usually found where men are hired on a casual basis. Longshoremen in each West Coast port are registered in a central hiring hall; they are picked for jobs in rotation so that their earnings can be kept equal; and the halls are closely policed by the employers and the union to prevent violations of the elaborate rules laid down for assigning men to jobs. Thus longshoremen on the West Coast work with as much regularity as workers in other industries.

For many years, neither the employers nor the union was willing to accept the other as an equal partner in managing the hiring system, and their mistrust of each other resulted in formal settlements on innumerable questions about how the halls should operate. This produced a system of industrial jurisprudence which codified industry practices down to the most minute detail. Careful records are kept on all aspects of the industry's operation. Since misconceptions about the hiring halls are so widespread, both the employers and the union are most willing to make this mountain of information available. This is in sharp contrast with the Port of New York, where many facts about the industry were unobtainable, partly because the waterfront was so chaotic that no one knew all the facts, and partly because the union and employers were (understandably) close-mouthed about their practices.

Pacific Coast ports are not infested with the gangsters and thugs who have added drama to the New York story, but the West Coast longshore industry is no less dramatic. The history of collective bargaining on the West Coast has been a history of a determined and cohesive group of employers battling for control of hiring with one of the most aggressive groups of workers in the country. Bitter, prolonged strikes over this issue have given the industry a widespread reputation for turbulence. And while individual personalities have been much less dramatized on the Pacific Coast than in New York, one of the most colorful figures in American labor history is the man who personifies West Coast longshoring in the public mind—Harry Bridges, president of the West Coast union.

An especially striking contrast is presented by the basic character of the two unions. In New York, the ILA has been attacked as a classic example of labor racketeering. On the West Coast, the union has also been under attack—but for different reasons. The International Longshoremen's and Warehousemen's Union has been held up for years as a classic example of political unionism, and it was expelled from the CIO in 1950 on the charge of "following the Communist Party line." It is only by two decisions of the U.S. Supreme Court that the federal government has been prevented from deporting or imprisoning Harry Bridges on the charge that he belonged to the Communist Party before becoming a naturalized citizen. A study of the political behavior and utterances of Harry Bridges, and of the union he represents, would be fascinating but is beyond the compass of this book. This discussion will be confined to the "business union" aspects of the ILWU as they relate to the hiring system, and the union's political actions will be touched on only when their relevance to the history or operation of that system is immediate. In their efforts to gain control of hiring, West Coast longshoremen and their union leaders have behaved no differently than the most politically conservative unions in the country when those unions have operated in industries where employment is irregular, such as in the printing, building, and maritime trades.

For purposes of comparison with the port of New York, the entire Pacific Coast would be the comparable unit since the number of regular longshoremen—15,000—is roughly comparable to the number of men who would be considered regular longshoremen in New York under a similar system. Hiring halls and working conditions are virtually identical in all West Coast ports, because rules governing the halls have been negotiated on a coast-wide basis since 1934 by the union and employers' association. Three relatively small ports, all in Washington state, are excluded from this agreement. They are known as "the exception ports" and their status is discussed below. After the ILWU and the Pacific Maritime Association have negotiated the master agreement covering longshore work, supplementary agreements covering dock work are negotiated in each port. (Unlike New York, where the term longshoreman covers men who work on the docks as well as those on the ship, a distinction is made on the West Coast between longshoremen and dockworkers. Longshore work is defined as handling cargo from the hold of the ship to the dock or to a railroad car or barge, or *vice versa,* when ship's slings and gear are used. Dock work is defined as cargo handling on the dock, railroad car, or barge, not in conjunction with ship's slings and gear. There is no fundamental difference in the qualifications for longshore and dock work but, in general, dock work is less arduous.)

The supplementary agreements differ only to the extent that the nature of the port differs—the type of cargo handled, the construction of the piers, and the equipment in use.

The system of industrial jurisprudence which has evolved for the administration of the agreement is also coast-wide and is designed to achieve uniformity in contract observance. The lowest level in the system is the Joint Labor Relations Committee in each port, composed of three representatives each of the employers and the union. If the members of the committee are unable to reach agreement, or if they feel that a basic question of contract interpretation is involved, the matter is referred to a similar committee which has jurisdiction over one of the four regional areas into which the Coast has been divided. The parties jointly retain impartial arbitrators in each area to whom disputes are referred from the Area Labor Relations Committees. Appeals from the decisions of area arbitrators are taken to a coast-wide committee of employers and union representatives, and final review rests with a coast arbitrator.

Since industry practices in West Coast ports are basically the same, it is possible to see how the system operates by examining a representative hiring hall. Seattle was chosen because it enjoys the unique distinction among United States ports of having been the first to abandon the shape-up in favor of a central hiring hall as a device to minimize the irregularity of longshore employment.

The Port of Seattle is a more compact unit than New York harbor and employs about one-tenth as many longshoremen. The map on page 147 shows the section of the port assigned to commercial shipping—an area approximately 10 miles long and including 95 piers and docks. Facilities for loading and discharging cargo are vastly more efficient than in New York. Railroad tracks running out on all piers in this section connect with the four major railroad systems which have terminals in Seattle. A through truck route is also adjacent to the piers and, unlike New York, Seattle pier warehouses provide ample storage space. The source of longshore employment which fluctuates most widely—foreign trade—is less important in Seattle than in New York, accounting for only about 20 per cent of waterborne commerce, but as in ports anywhere longshore employment is inevitably irregular.

Employers in the Port of Seattle are, for the most part, contracting stevedoring companies and terminal operators although, as in New York, some shipping companies operate their own stevedoring subsidiaries. Seattle employers are represented by the Washington area branch of the Pacific Maritime Association. The Washington area has 71 members, 19 of whom employ longshoremen directly; the rest are shipping companies or their Pacific Coast agents. Some longshoremen are employed by Seattle firms which are not members of the PMA; these are mainly inland firms such as flour-milling concerns which operate their own docks but are not engaged in the maritime industry.

Regular longshoremen and dockworkers in Seattle are members of Local 19, ILWU, which has had continuous contractual relations with Seattle employers since 1934. More precisely, the longshoremen were represented by Local 38-12, International Longshoremen's Association (AFL), from 1934 to 1937. When the majority of the West Coast longshoremen withdrew from the ILA and affiliated with the CIO, the Seattle local became Local 19, ILWU. In 1953, the membership of Local 19 was approximately 1,500. Marked differences between the ports of New York and Seattle can be seen in the internal administration of the longshoremen's unions. Unlike ILA locals, Local 19 has a very active membership. Regular meetings are held every two weeks with 200 members constituting a quorum; elections are conducted each year, customarily by using voting machines rented from the city hall; the initiation fee is $10 and dues are $4 a month; salaries of local officers are kept roughly commensurate with the earnings of longshoremen, and there is a tradition in the local that officers go off the payroll during strikes.

To supervise the hiring system, the Seattle Joint Labor Relations Committee, consisting of representatives of the union and the employers, meets every two weeks alternately in the office of the employers' association and the union, with the two parties taking turns in the chairmanships; special meetings are held when necessary. Two of the committee's primary duties are to adjust the number of men registered in the hall in response to the over-all needs of the port, and to serve as the second level in the grievance procedure—after the foreman and gang steward or business agent have dealt with the grievance on the job. As in other Pacific Coast ports, expenses of maintaining the hiring hall, including the salaries of the dispatching staff, are shared by the parties.

Here, in contrast to the shape-up or government-operated hiring halls, the problems of a casual-labor market are met by a hiring hall administered by the parties themselves. How well does the hiring hall work, and how did it evolve?

86

Labor unionism in Seattle was born in the atmosphere of a frontier, and labor relations on the Seattle waterfront have always had a flavor different from those in New York. First attempts to organize on the docks came at a time when Seattleites were still carving a city from the wilderness of Northwest forests, and while the original pioneers were still in the process of making their fortunes. The first longshoremen were predominantly rootless, undisciplined men—many were soon to join with fellow philosophical anarchists in the lumber camps to form the backbone of the Industrial Workers of the World (IWW). In contrast to the New York waterfront, which was flooded by waves of immigrants landing with their families in New York during the nineteenth century, labor was scarce on the frontier. As in any frontier area, in early Seattle longshoremen were highly mobile—they could always move on to Alaska or to another coast port if conditions on the docks were not to their liking. The freedom of movement enjoyed by workers in all frontier ports enhanced their bargaining power with the employers, who were busily engaged in establishing the West Coast shipping industry. Consequently the longshoremen influenced the structure of the collective-bargaining relationship to a much greater extent than workers in more settled parts of the country. One of the most striking features of West Coast bargaining history has been the constant pressure on employers to unify and coördinate their actions as a group in order to keep up with the ever-increasing cohesiveness of the longshoremen up and down the 1,200 miles of coastline. The drive of the workers to gain undisputed control of hiring forced first the union and then the employers to widen their range of effectiveness. Since both sides soon became about evenly matched, the battles for dominance on the docks were destined to be some of the most bitter in recent labor history. Only when the employers and the union finally agreed to accept the other as a partner in the hiring hall did the West Coast waterfront settle down to stability.

Early History

The first attempt of the dockworkers to corner waterfront jobs came in 1889, when Washington was still a territory, and Seattle, which had been incorporated as a city for only ten years, had a population of about 35,000. The men's first organization was a coöperative operated by the Stevedores, Longshoremen and Riggers' Union of Seattle. According to its articles of incorporation, the coöperative had a laudable purpose:

> . . . to improve the condition of its membership morally,

socially, and materially, by timely counsel and instructive lessons, and by assistance to obtain employment when in need.*

Men owning stock in the coöperative enjoyed preference in employment on the docks; new union members could not obtain shares until some original stockholder was ready to sell. This method of controlling jobs worked satisfactorily for a few years, but its inflexibility was unsuited to the rapidly expanding industry in the port. Around the turn of the century, the coöperative lost its monopoly position when new union members, seeing the best jobs always going to the original stockholders, refused to support the organization.

By 1902, a new union with some 300 members was operating in Seattle. This organization, the Longshoremen's Mutual Benefit Association, was originally affiliated with the ILA, but for reasons which are not clear its charter was revoked in 1903.[2] For a brief period, Seattle longshoremen switched their allegiance to Local 1, Pacific Coast Federation of Longshoremen, which appears to have been a dual organization (to the ILA) set up by the International Seamen's Union.† When the union secretary decamped with the funds, those Seattle longshoremen who were still interested in unionism returned to the ILA. The local in Seattle was weak, but there were enough union members scattered among the various coast ports to send a strong delegation to the ILA convention in 1904. The West Coast delegates persuaded the convention to establish the Pacific Coast District Council, No. 38, and to give district officers authority to grant local charters and pass on all agreements negotiated by its component locals.[3] The creation of an almost completely autonomous unit on the West Coast had far-reaching implications. First, district officials saw the entire coast as their responsibility and this led them to strive continuously to make the coast one single bargaining unit. Second, this decentralization of authority within the ILA permitted officers of the international union, most of whom were Easterners, to focus their attention on East Coast problems, and they lost touch with Western developments.

---

* The articles of incorporation are included in a collection of miscellaneous material donated to the Tacoma Public Library by a nameless, old-time Tacoma longshoreman. Also included in the material is his personal history of the many early attempts to organize longshoremen in the Northwest, hereafter cited as *Tacoma History*.

† Washington (State) Bureau of Labor, *Fifth Biennial Report . . . 1905–1906* (Olympia: 1906), p. 97. This raid by Andrew Furuseth, leader of the West Coast sailors' union, was apparently in retaliation against the ILA's move, a year earlier, to extend its jurisdiction to cover sea-going personnel. Although Furuseth succeeded, in 1907, in securing an order from the AFL restricting the ILA's jurisdiction to shoreside workers, the rivalry between sailors and longshoremen has persisted to this day on the Pacific Coast.

With the help of Pacific Coast District officials, the Seattle local gradually gained strength, and its recovery resulted in the formation of a strong employers' association.[4] Known originally as the Waterfront Employers' Union of Seattle, its effectiveness was demonstrated when it drove the ILA off the docks in the winter of 1907–1908, and it was not until 1911 that the Tacoma historian could report that "progress in organizing Seattle is being made." Again in 1912, the Waterfront Employers Union defeated the longshoremen after a long strike. But by 1915, Local 38-12, as the Seattle local was then designated, had revived sufficiently to enable the Pacific Coast District to secure a signed agreement and a wage increase from all employers in Puget Sound and British Columbia.[5]

Encouraged by this success, longshoremen up and down the coast opened their first attack on the shape-up which was then in use but which, as the Washington State Bureau of Labor noted in 1916, was strongly disliked: "The men . . . do not take kindly to the 'line-up' system of selecting crews which is in vogue. This method is called the 'shape' in New York."[6] When negotiations opened that year, the Pacific Coast District demanded a closed shop, presumably intending to insist that all men be hired through union halls. The employers refused, and 2,000 longshoremen in Seattle and 8,700 in other ports began a coast-wide walk-out. The strikers were met with determined resistance all along the coast and particularly in Seattle, where strikebreakers imported from the East were used extensively. In the third week of the strike, the U.S. Department of Labor succeeded in arranging a truce and appointing a mediator, but just as the men began returning to work a strikebreaker murdered one of the longshoremen. Seattle union members immediately posted a notice that unless all strikebreakers were discharged by 5 P.M. the next day, the back-to-work movement would halt. The employers ignored the ultimatum and the coast was again shut down.* The strike dragged on for more than two months with neither side willing to retreat on the issue of control of hiring but finally, on the 74th day, the men admitted defeat and returned to work on the employers' terms.

The unity displayed by the men during the 1916 strike convinced employers that drastic measures would be necessary to suppress the union. In Seattle, employers established their own hiring halls (they were euphemistically called "employment offices") and introduced the use of "rustling cards."[7] For a man to be hired, he had to report to one of these halls and

---

* A practice adopted soon after the creation of the Pacific Coast District contributed to the coast-wide solidarity of the union. Union members were permitted to transfer from one port to another, and many roving longshoremen had come to feel as much identity with fellow members in, say, San Francisco, as with those in Seattle.

present his card, which contained a history of his union activity. Despite this effective device for weeding out union men (rustling cards had been used earlier to blacklist IWW members in the Northwest lumber industry), the locals in Seattle and Tacoma were able, in 1917, to muster enough power to force the employers to participate with them in a regional panel of the National Adjustment Commission.[8] In December of that year, the commission handed down an award which forbade the use of rustling cards, prohibited employers from discriminating against ILA members, and placed the employers' halls under the jurisdiction of the U.S. Shipping Board. After July 1, 1918, the halls were to be closed and the men hired on the docks. This decision was accepted reluctantly by the employers, but was carried out as ordered. On its face, this award makes it appear that the union and the impartial member of the commission preferred the shape-up to a hiring hall, but this inference is unwarranted. The men considered the employers' halls as little more than "shape-ups with a roof over them" and were willing to forgo the protection these structures afforded against inclement weather because of their belief that decentralizing the hiring process would make blacklisting more difficult.[9]

The award provided a great stimulus to union organization. In 1919 the ILA was again able to negotiate a signed agreement covering all ports in Oregon, as well as those in Washington and British Columbia, with the Northwest Waterfront Employers' Union—an enlarged association designed to parallel and offset the bargaining strength of the union's regional structure. The employers agreed to a 10-cent wage increase, and to give preference in employment to union men. In return, the union agreed to take in all men then working regularly on the waterfront.[10] This meant accepting as union members men who had scabbed during the 1916 strike, and even several strikebreakers who had stayed on in Seattle and Tacoma; but the reluctance of the unionists to make this concession was mitigated by the fact that in 1919 longshore work was plentiful in these ports.

If Seattle employers interpreted the union's acceptance of this condition as a sign that Local 38-12 was losing its militancy, they were immediately disabused of that notion. The signatures on the contract were hardly dry when the local voted to participate in the nation's first general strike. The unions planning the general strike elected a committee of fifteen to run the strike and decide what work would be performed. In the words of the strike historian who recorded the requests received by the committee: "Longshoremen asked permission to handle government mails, customs, and baggage. Permit given for mails and customs but not for baggage."[11] When the ships' whistles sounded at 10 o'clock on the morning of February 6 announcing the start of the strike, longshoremen joined with the 68,000 other workers who brought Seattle industry to an almost complete halt for five days. Although the aims of Seattle workers in the general strike were never completely clear, it is not inappropriate to call this the longshoremen's first experience with using a strike as a means of political protest.*

The local's second political protest came the same year. Earlier, when American, Japanese, British, and French forces were gathering in Siberia for the Allied intervention in the Russian Revolution, Local 38-12 had sent President Wilson a resolution stating that Seattle longshoremen "will not handle munitions destined for Russia over the docks of Seattle." Their resolution was tested in October, 1919, when the SS *Delight* put in at Seattle to load Winchester rifles for shipment to American forces in Russia. The longshoremen, supported by the State Federation of Labor, refused to handle the cargo. At first, the employers threatened to cancel the preference-of-employment clause if the rifles were not loaded, but enough supervisory personnel were recruited to permit the SS *Delight* to collect its cargo and depart, and the threat was forgotten.[12]

Economic events in 1920 drastically changed the relationship of the longshoremen and the employers. As war-induced shipments fell off and business declined, activity in the port dwindled. By the end of World War I, Seattle was no longer a frontier town. The longshoremen, who had lost their mobility of earlier days, were hit hard by the shortage of work. Local 38-12 urged employers to share available jobs among its members by hiring them in rotation. The employers rejected the plan and, in an ill-timed move, the union struck. The local was completely defeated and its charter revoked for not having cleared the strike action through the Pacific Coast District. The 1920 strike marked the end of effective unionism on Seattle docks for the next 13 years.†

In both New York and Seattle, the ILA was ineffective during the 1920's but there the parallel ends. In New York, the union lapsed into docility after the rank and file unsuccessfully rebelled against their officials'

---

* The general strike was called to support the shipyard workers in their efforts to force a government agency, the Shipbuilding Adjustment Commission, to permit Seattle employers to pay a previously existing wage differential over the East Coast scale. The strike was touched off when a telegram sent by the commission to the Seattle Metal Trades Association (the employers) was delivered by accident to the Seattle Metal Trades Council (the unions). The telegraph message indicated that although employers were willing to pay the differential, they were being threatened with loss of government contracts if they broke the scale set up by the commission.

† During the postwar depression, the Seattle experience was duplicated in other Pacific Coast ports with the exception of the Tacoma local which maintained its
(Note continued on following page.)

acceptance of the "Woolworth Five-and-Ten Cent Award." In Seattle, the union was smashed on the issue of rotation in hiring.

The Employers' Hiring Hall

The disappearance of the union did not eliminate the problem of hiring practices on the waterfront. Control of hiring now rested exclusively with the employers, but dissatisfaction with the shape-up was widespread. It was evident that some acceptable alternative had to be found, and in 1921 Seattle employers embarked on the first effort made in any American port to "decasualize" the casual-labor market. The Seattle system was devised by Frank P. Foisie, then a young and recent addition to the staff of the Waterfront Employers Union. It was adopted, according to Foisie

> . . . as an outgrowth of realization by employers that they must voluntarily improve the conditions of the men as far as the resources of the industry made possible, if they were to have peace in the port and economy in cargo handling; and a feeling by the men that any new deal would be worth trying. The industry had suffered for years from recurring strikes, with striking on the job in between, much pilferage, high accident frequency, arbitrary load limits and minimum gang requirements. The men bore the burdens of a beach flooded with a great surplus, seeking uncertain work from dock to dock, under continuous labor excitement.[13]

The first steps in setting up the system were to establish one central hiring hall to serve the entire port and to limit the labor supply by registering in the hall only the number of men needed to serve the normal requirements of the port. The job of deciding which men should be registered and who should be eliminated from the labor force was carried out by a committee composed of four employers and four longshoremen. This committee began by making a careful survey of the work experience and qualifications of all men then working on the waterfront.

The status of about 800 men who had been working for the larger companies as steady employees ("company gangs") remained undisturbed, but the number of men who had formerly been hired as they were needed in the shape-up, and who were now to be hired from the hall, was cut from about 1,400 to 612. The first group weeded out were the "floaters"— those men who did not intend to make longshoring their primary occupa-

---

identity during the 1920's. The Tacoma historian (mentioned in footnote 1) recorded attempts of Tacoma officials to reëstablish locals in other coast ports in 1921, 1922, and 1923. Finally in 1923 he wrote, "Finis San Francisco, Portland, Vancouver [B.C.], and Seattle, under the old slogan 'We'll go it alone'."

tion. The total was then further reduced by a process of elimination based on such factors as a man's length of service, skill, family responsibilities, and permanency of residence.

The remaining 612 men were then listed on the roster in the hiring hall according to their skills. Some of them were organized into "hall gangs" in which men always worked together as a unit, and others were listed on an extra board from which they were dispatched as replacements in the hall gangs or as members of make-up gangs. A small group of men were registered as apprentices; they were dispatched from a try-out board after all regular men had been sent out. Casual workers were hired when, due to unusually heavy calls for longshoremen, the regular and try-out boards were exhausted.

A basic aim of the system, as explained by Foisie, was to improve the welfare of the men by equalizing their earnings. A conscious effort was made to divide work equally among members of company gangs and hall gangs—no company gang was permitted to earn more than a certain maximum per week if the earnings of hall gangs fell below a certain level. All men listed on the extra board were hired in rotation, and their earnings were roughly equal from month to month. A central paying office was installed in order to save the longshoremen much time formerly spent in collecting their pay from each employer.

The system embodied employee representation (company unionism)— a phenomenon typical of the 1920's. Joint committees were set up to administer the hall, supervise safety procedures, and negotiate wages and hours.[14] A manual was published assuring the men, among other things, that elections of worker representatives to the various committees would be free and by secret ballot, that committee members would enjoy freedom of speech, and that there would be no discrimination against union men. According to the hiring hall's founder, the employee-representation plan was taken bodily from the recommendations of President Wilson's Second Industrial Conference, and the procedures used in setting up the hiring system from the experience in British ports.[15]

Foisie's system operated almost without incident all during the 1920's. When port business fell off during the depression of the 1930's, the Joint Employment Committee did not replace names in the registered list when longshoremen dropped out of the industry. Only three men, all sons of disabled longshoremen, were newly registered during the depression years. In 1929, there were 664 names on the roster; only 525 men were listed when unionism again began stirring on the waterfront in 1933.

It is a tribute to the ingenuity and foresight of Frank Foisie and the other Seattle employers that the basic features of their hiring hall are still in use in Seattle, although a strong union now participates as a full partner in administering the system.*

Resurgence of Unionism

Several times during the period when the employers enjoyed undisputed control of the waterfront the nucleus of men who had maintained their interest in the ILA—most of whom worked in Tacoma—had attempted without success to revive the locals in Seattle and other Northwest ports.† When the National Industrial Recovery Act was passed in 1933, including section 7a (encouraging workers to organize), ILA members made another try at reëstablishing the Pacific Coast District organization. This time they were remarkably successful. Longshoremen up and down the coast responded enthusiastically to the appeals of ILA organizers,‡ and the Seattle local gathered enough support to force the resignation of the worker representatives on the employer-sponsored committee in November and to demand that delegates elected by Local 38-12 be substituted.

The men's receptiveness to *bona fide* unionism was based on several common complaints against the employers' hiring system. For one thing, the company union had been ineffectual in bargaining for higher wages. Although earnings of all men registered in the hall were equalized, the basic wage rate was low (despite a 10-cent increase given the men during the organizing campaign) and the men were bitter about their incomes. An even more frequently voiced complaint against the system was that men were forced to submit to a speed-up to keep their positions in company gangs, where earnings were higher than those of hall men. The men saw in the union a means of abolishing the use of company gangs and

---

* Foisie later became head of the Seattle employers' association, then head of the coast-wide employers group. He could never reconcile himself to accepting union participation in the hiring system he had created. The personal hatred which developed in later years between Foisie and the union's spokesman, Harry Bridges, played an important part in the savage industrial warfare which was sustained on West Coast docks for the next 14 years. When the employers' association was reorganized after the famous 1948 strike—which resulted in what many observers believe to be a permanent armistice between the parties—Foisie resigned as president of the Waterfront Employers' Association and became administrator of the Sailors' Union of the Pacific pension program.

† Pacific Coast District officers attempted to reëstablish the locals in the late 1920's, and had especially high hopes for their organizing drive in 1927, when an organizing meeting held in Olympia was attended by several international union officers from the East. The Tacoma historian wrote of the meeting, "Brother Joseph Ryan, first vice-president of the international, was present and made a great impression on the delegates, one and all."

‡ By 1933, Portland and Los Angeles employers had established hiring halls similar to the one in Seattle, but the shape-up still existed in San Francisco.

extending the rotation principle to all longshoremen in the port. Further-more, many longshoremen had a deep-rooted aversion against the pater-nalism of Foisie's system. A study made by the U.S. Department of Labor in the early 1930's emphasized this factor:

> The principal difficulty with the existing schemes . . . is not in the schemes *per se*. It is due primarily to the fact that the plan was promulgated and carried out by the employers against the strong opposition of organized labor.[16]

Union members were convinced that they were discriminated against in the halls and, even today, Seattle longshoremen refer to the old system as "working out of the fink hall." The Department of Labor's survey indi-rectly supported charges of discrimination by cautioning that in any new system which might be put into operation

> new registration of longshoremen and a new alignment of gangs shall be made compulsory in order to include the workers who hitherto for one reason or another have been excluded, or who voluntarily abstained from participation in the decasu-alization scheme.[17]

Seattle employers vigorously denied any anti-union bias in the halls, and Foisie defended their reluctance to recognize the ILA:

> The unwillingness of the employers in the past to enter into an agreement with the men is not based on opposition to union-ism, as evidenced by the fact that there has not been a single case of discrimination against the ILA men in all the years.[18]

Seattle employers originally refused to open negotiations with Local 38-12 on the grounds that the entire shipping industry would soon be reorganized under an NRA code then being debated in Washington. One section of the proposed shipping code, which had been drawn up by the American Steamship Owners' Association, provided that a National Ship-ping Labor Board be established to study methods by which longshore em-ployment could be made less irregular and to formulate national rules for hiring longshoremen. The history of longshoring on both coasts might have been far more tranquil had this code been adopted but, although it was approved by General Hugh S. Johnson, NRA administrator, it was rejected by President Roosevelt.[19] When abandonment of the code was announced, the Pacific Coast District immediately demanded that employ-ers open negotiations. Out of the employers' determination not to give ground on the union's demands in these negotiations, and the union's equally firm insistence on achieving its objectives, came the bloody 1934 strike and the nation's second "general strike."

The Great Strike of 1934

Members of the Pacific Coast District held two conventions in the winter of 1933 to coördinate their line of attack. Delegates from all major ports agreed to concentrate their efforts on two basic goals, a coast-wide agreement and union-controlled hiring halls in each port. A central negotiating committee was elected and early in 1934 discussions with the employers began in San Francisco. The longshoremen were willing to bargain on questions of wages and hours, but when the employers flatly rejected their demands for union hiring halls and a coast-wide agreement, the men voted in a coast-wide referendum to strike on March 23.[20]

The strike deadline was postponed when President Roosevelt requested the longshoremen to wait until a federal body, the Fact-Finding and Mediation Board, had investigated the dispute. The members of the board were immediately confronted with the confused question of who was represented in the negotiations. After several weeks of investigating, the board announced that the ILA negotiators had not demonstrated that they spoke for all longshoremen on the coast, and recommended that representation elections be held in the various ports. The board further pointed out that the employers involved in the discussions represented only San Francisco firms, and recommended that employers from all ports be called in on the negotiations. On the two key demands of the men, the board suggested a compromise, proposing that jointly operated halls be established in each port under a coast-wide agreement.[21] San Francisco employers accepted the idea of joint halls but balked at negotiating a coast-wide agreement. Employers in Seattle and the other ports refused even to recognize the ILA as the longshoremen's bargaining agent, and on May 9 a strike which was to last 83 days began in all Pacific Coast ports.

To most people, the 1934 waterfront strike is synonymous with the famous general strike in San Francisco,[22] but Seattle, too, was a battleground. On the first day of the strike, the 1,400 longshoremen in Seattle threw out a strong picket line all along the waterfront, and the employers, who had expressed confidence in the loyalty of their men the day before the strike deadline (the head of the waterfront employers had told reporters, "We do not think the walkout will affect Seattle"), immediately began recruiting strikebreakers.[23] It was evident that strikebreakers could not be taken through the picket lines in front of the docks without violence, so the employers loaded them in boats elsewhere in the harbor, sailed them in behind the picket lines, and housed them on unused ships. Among the first strikebreakers hired were athletes from the University of Washington, but when the recruitment program on the campus began to assume major proportions, University President Dr. Hugo Winkenwerder urged students to stay off the waterfront. When a group of students who had signed up as strikebreakers gathered at the university dock (located on an inland lake which is connected with the commercial harbor by a set of locks), they were prevented from boarding a ferryboat sent to pick them up by the university's dean of men, who refused to let the ferry tie up at the wharf.

The effectiveness of the coast tie-up was strengthened when five other maritime unions[24] stopped work, first in support of the ILA, but soon announcing demands of their own. Eight locals of the Teamsters in various ports announced they would not haul cargo from struck piers, but on the third day of the strike this support showed signs of weakening when Dave Beck, president of the Seattle Teamsters, announced that his truck drivers were returning to work in response to an appeal from the government. The teamsters ignored Beck's order and continued to support the strike, but the rift between the longshoremen and Dave Beck constantly widened from this time on.

The first open threat of violence in Seattle came on the ninth day, when Mayor John Dore called the strike "a soviet of longshoremen who are dictating what can be done on the waterfront," and threatened to open the port through use of his "official power." He was prevailed upon to postpone this action only by an urgent appeal from Assistant Secretary of Labor Edward F. McGrady, who hurried up from San Francisco and persuaded the mayor that the use of force in Seattle would upset negotiations then going on in the Bay area under the auspices of the President's mediation board. When the employers had seen how effectively the union was able to tie up the whole coast, they had reconciled themselves to bargaining with the ILA, and the four regional employers' groups—in Seattle, Portland, San Francisco, and Los Angeles—had sent representatives to meet with the union's negotiating committee in San Francisco. The mediation board proposed to the parties that the U.S. Employment Service be asked to operate hiring halls in each port, but this was unacceptable to either side. The employers took the position that accepting government halls would be tantamount to "indirectly favoring the closed shop," and the union refused on the grounds that government halls would be controlled by the shipping interests.[25]

Uncertainty about the union's position on the issues in the strike was created when Joseph P. Ryan flew to San Francisco in mid-May and, shortly after his arrival, announced that he had reached a settlement with the employers.[26] His settlement provided for separate contracts for each port and jointly operated halls in which employers would be free to select their men.* Ryan's appearance on the scene produced the first split in the ranks of the ILA. He had been able to persuade three of the old-time Pacific Coast District officials to go along with him and sign the agreement, but the rank and file received his efforts without enthusiasm. The San Francisco local overwhelmingly voted down the agreement. The newly elected leader of the San Francisco strike committee, a winch operator named Harry Bridges, announced the vote to the press,† characterizing Ryan's agreement as an "attempt by the employers to sound out the weak spots in the ILA organization."[27]

When it was learned in Seattle that San Francisco had rejected the settlement, Dave Beck urged local longshoremen to make a "separate peace." Learning of this unexpected support, Ryan set out for Seattle. While en route, he demonstrated his lack of understanding of the West Coast longshoremen's sentiments when he stated at Portland, "It is up to the locals in the Northwest to vote down San Francisco and save that local from itself,"[28] but after he met with delegates of the Northwest locals and found they shared the attitude of the San Francisco men, Ryan announced, "I have a different slant on it now . . . I don't blame the strikers if they reject the peace offer."[29]

The government's next move came in a statement by Assistant Secretary of Labor McGrady that the President might be asked to impose a shipping code limited to labor provisions. He said he recognized that Pacific Coast shipping companies would oppose such a code, but he drew attention to a strong inducement in the form of government loans and subsidies amounting to more than $300,000,000. Shortly therafter, the employers reversed

---

* The ILA would have been permitted to keep representatives in the halls to see that union members were not discriminated against, but it was also stipulated in the agreement that nonunion men were to be accorded equal treatment. Such a hall was aptly described by the men as "a shape-up with a roof over it."

† This was the first time Harry Bridges came to public attention, but his name was to be in the headlines for the next twenty years. Bridges was born in Melbourne, Australia, in 1901. Educated in Catholic schools, he became a sailor, coming to the United States when he was 19. For years, he worked as a longshoreman in San Francisco. From 1934 to the present, he has been almost continuously engaged in defending himself against the efforts of various government agencies to deport him for alleged Communist Party membership. In the late 1930's, two such actions were brought against him by the U.S. Immigration Service. In 1940, a bill to deport him was passed by the House of Representatives, but was dropped in the Senate when the U.S. Attorney general advised that it was a bill of attainder and could not stand a constitutional test. During the 1940's, the Justice Department brought two separate indictments against him which Bridges carried to the U.S. Supreme Court. Both were decided in his favor—one in 1945 and the other in 1953. In June, 1954, the Justice Department began a new proceeding against him on the same grounds as the earlier actions.

their earlier stand, announcing that they would accept government-operated halls, but the union continued its opposition.

Tension on the Seattle waterfront increased when it was learned that the union was holding out for control of the halls, and several shipping companies and fish-packing houses announced plans to move their operations to Los Angeles where the port was not so completely shut down. These announcements caused Dore's successor, Mayor Charles Smith, to threaten that he would "take action" to open the port of Seattle if a solution to the tie-up were not found. In response to this threat, Ryan and Beck called a hasty conference with Seattle employers in which a plan —again providing for joint operation of the hiring hall—was drawn up. Without waiting to see how the Northwest locals received their plan, Ryan and Beck flew to San Francisco to offer it there. While they were in transit, Seattle longshoremen voted it down.*

Two days later, Mayor Smith again appeared on the scene with an olive branch in one hand and a club in the other. First he offered a solution to the strike—the city would operate hiring halls for all types of maritime workers. The employers immediately accepted the offer, but the men turned it down. On the same day, the mayor announced that public officials in Seattle, Tacoma, Portland, and three small Washington ports had agreed on plans to "open" their ports simultaneously. Later that day, Seattle police appeared on the waterfront with a tear gas spraying device resembling a fire hose, and Mayor Smith, taking personal charge of a police detail, raided union headquarters and seized a cache of baseball bats.†

The next day brought news from San Francisco that Ryan's peace plan had been accepted by Thomas G. Plant (acting for the coast employers), that a new agreement had been signed, and that the strike was over.‡ But, again, the negotiators had neglected to consult the striking longshoremen, and the Ryan-Plant settlement—which failed to give the union control of the hiring halls—was overwhelmingly rejected in Seattle, Tacoma,

---

* While the men were voting, 25 strikebreaking seamen armed with clubs broke through the longshoremen's picket lines and sailed a tanker out of the harbor. Four shots were fired—by the strikebreakers, according to the chief of police—but they went wild. One picket was treated for injuries received from a club-wielding strikebreaker.

† The sheriff had sworn in 500 special deputies and placed an order for the bats with a Seattle factory. The union had sent pickets to the factory and seized the bats.

‡ Ryan and J. E. Finnegan of the Pacific Coast District had signed for the ILA. Observance of the agreement "by the ILA membership" was guaranteed by Dave Beck, by two officials of the San Francisco Teamsters' Union, by two members of the mediation board, and by Mayor Rossi of San Francisco. John F. Forbes of the Industrial Association of San Francisco guaranteed observance by the employers. Beck immediately announced, "The teamsters underwrite this agreement and will begin hauling material from the docks at once."

Bellingham, Olympia, Aberdeen, Longview, Astoria, Portland, San Francisco, and San Diego. Los Angeles longshoremen approved the agreement by a vote of 638 to 584, but remained on strike after learning how the vote had gone in other ports.

Ryan attributed the negative vote to the work of "Communists and strike agitators." He threatened to revoke the charters of recalcitrant locals and issue new ones to "men who want to work," but he grossly misjudged the determination of the Pacific Coast longshoremen.* As a result of Ryan's mediation efforts, the longshoremen entered into a formal alliance with the other striking maritime unions (now nine in number) setting up the Joint Maritime Strike Committee.[30] Harry Bridges, who had been recently moved up from the San Francisco strike committee to head the ILA coast-wide strike committee, was elected chairman of the new organization. He immediately announced that none of the striking unions would return to work until the demands of all were met.

Throughout America during the 1930's, the emergence of militant unionism in previously unorganized industries was often accompanied by charges that the unions were led by Communists. The vigor with which these charges were directed against the resurgent longshoremen's union, beginning in mid-May when Ryan's original settlement was rejected by the men and reaching a crescendo as the strike continued into its second month, was perhaps unparalleled elsewhere in the country. After Bridges was catapulted from the ranks into leadership of the strike, he became the focal point of these charges, but Seattle longshoremen were also to become the target of a similar attack.

When news of the formation of the new strike committee reached Seattle, the violence which had long been building up on the Seattle waterfront erupted. Pickets and police engaged in their first pitched battle at Pier 40, and a few days later city officials decided to open Pier 41 under police protection. The police force had been substantially enlarged, in addition to the 500 men who had been deputized by the sheriff, and a mounted unit had been formed. Before moving his men down to Pier 41 in a mile-long caravan on June 30, the chief of police gave them these instructions:

We are not looking for trouble but we are prepared for it.

---

* Ryan's presumption that he could arrogate authority to himself on the West Coast as freely as was his custom in New York was disclosed in subsequent testimony on how the agreement had been reached. ILA negotiators had been expressly instructed by the membership early in the strike that any settlement would be valid only after a coast-wide vote. However, T. G. Plant later testified that Ryan had assured him that he had authority to make a binding agreement and that it had been clearly understood between them that the agreement "was not to be submitted to a referendum vote of the men." Waterfront Employers Union of San Francisco, *Statement of Thomas G. Plant . . .* , pp. 18–19.

Some of you are armed with tear gas, some with guns. See that your guns are in good shape. But use them only as a last extremity, for the protection of life and property.

A strike council was appointed in this city weeks ago. The man at the head of it is one of the most prominent Communists on the Pacific Coast. That's all.

As policemen changed shifts in the assembly room that day, they were told, "Today's the day."*

Earlier, Seattle businessmen had formed a citizens' emergency committee, and when a special deputy was shot and killed in downtown Seattle by an unidentified group of assailants, the head of the citizens' committee —he was also president of the chamber of commerce—immediately called on the police to "run about 200 reds and aliens, who are responsible for a reign of terror, out of town." Later, the citizens' committee appealed to the governor to use the State Patrol to "run the reds and alien agitators out." Various other civic leaders added their voices to this appeal and when some urged the governor to call out the National Guard, Dave Beck became alarmed and cautioned the governor:

> . . . the use of the National Guard would mean the danger of organized labor getting away from its leaders in a movement of unrest. The San Francisco Teamsters voted for a strike because some of our men who were delivering freight across the Embarcadero, not intended for ships, were caught in the troubled area and gassed. Teamsters then voted for a strike despite anything their leaders could do.†

The governor wisely refrained from intervening, but city officials had by this time succumbed to the general hysteria. Police rushed 1,200 pickets again at Pier 41, dispersing them with tear-gas grenades, and reported to the press that "Communists were in the forefront of the crowd."‡ That

---

* Surprisingly, the first fatality in the Northwest occurred not at Pier 41 but at Point Wells, a Standard Oil dock about ten miles north of Seattle. During a brush between plant guards and pickets, a guard fired on the strikers, and Shelby Daffron, an ILA member, fell fatally wounded.

† *Seattle Times,* July 9, 1934. Other evidence indicates that the San Francisco general strike, which had started four days earlier, was touched off when San Francisco Teamsters tried to stop nonunion truck drivers from moving goods from one of the struck piers to an inland warehouse. In Seattle, the ILA had already appealed to the Central Labor Council to call a general strike in protest against police violence on the docks.

‡ Not all Seattle police were hostile to the longshoremen. Two members of the force were discharged and two others suspended for failing to go to the aid of a special pier guard who was pulled from a taxi and beaten by pickets as he arrived for work at Pier 41. The 25-year-old victim was the son-in-law of a vice-president of the American Mail Line.

evening, a police squad referred to as the "Red Raiders" descended on a meeting at Communist Party headquarters and arrested 28 persons. When the offenders were brought before the police court, the *Seattle Times,* the least sensational of Seattle's three newspapers, editorialized:

> Police Judge William R. Bell is fair and fearless. He started out yesterday by giving heavy sentences to Communist leaders in police raids. Immigration authorities will cooperate in cases involving aliens.

Two days later, Mayor Smith led 300 police (the chief of police had resigned) in a charge against some 2,000 pickets at Pier 40, precipitating a pitched battle in which the mayor himself was one of the tear-gas victims.*

In this explosive atmosphere, the Waterfront Employers Union mailed ballots to the 1,400 longshoremen, asking them to vote on these two questions:

> Do you want to return to work under the terms of the agreement of June 16?
> After the past 14 years of peace, don't you believe we should be able to settle our own affairs without the aid of Tacoma, San Francisco, Portland, or Washington, D.C.?

Most men turned their ballots in at union headquarters, but the employers later announced that 260 ballots had been received at their office and the men had voted "yes" by four to one.

Several equally unsuccessful attempts to get the men back to work had, meanwhile, been made by a new board appointed by President Roosevelt to make a thorough investigation of the dispute and to arbitrate if requested to do so. This was the National Longshoremen's Board whose recommendations finally brought the strike to an end.[31] When the new board first tried to persuade the parties to arbitrate the dispute, the longshoremen rejected arbitration on two grounds.† J. C. Bjorklund, secretary of the

---

* Jittery Seattleites were provided a few *opéra bouffe* incidents during this tense period. One morning, they read in their newspapers that Big Mike Maher, "Seattle's strongest policeman," had been beaten by pickets at Pier 41. The next day, however, the story of Maher's mishap was corrected in an official announcement that he and a fellow policeman had been relieving the boredom of patrolling the pier by "fencing" with their riot clubs in a friendly scuffle. Big Mike's partner had lost his footing on the oily dock and accidentally inflicted a deep gash over Maher's eye as he fell.

† A few days after the board's appointment, Ryan left for the East. He denounced Bridges as the major obstacle to a settlement and commented, "I've done all I can. If they want to carry on this strike forever, I can't do anything about it."

Pacific Coast District (and later elected sheriff in Tacoma), stated the union's position on control of hiring:

> Control of the hiring halls is the main thing longshoremen are striking for. The attitude of the longshoremen here in the Northwest is that we won't consent to arbitration of something we **know we are dead right on.**

A further reason for the longshoremen's refusal was their insistence that the employers deal simultaneously with the other maritime unions who were striking for similar objectives. Finally, on July 21, the 73rd day of the strike, the employers agreed to recognize the ILA and arbitrate all outstanding issues with the other maritime unions if the longshoremen would accept arbitration. A coast-wide vote was taken among ILA members on the question, "Will the ILA agree to submit to arbitration by the President's Board the issues in dispute in the Longshoremen's strike, and be bound by the decision of the Board?" Longshoremen in 17 coast ports voted 6,378 to 1,471 in favor of arbitration. In Seattle, where the vote was restricted to men who had been in regular company gangs or registered in the employer's hiring hall for at least six months before the strike, the vote was 762 to end the strike, against 102 to continue it.[32]

In an atmosphere of bitterness and mistrust inevitably produced by the violence and extreme charges and recriminations which had marked the strike, the men began returning to work on July 29. Arbitration proceedings were begun early in August and the National Longshoremen's Board handed down the decision on October 12. The award gave the longshoremen a coast-wide agreement but provided for joint operation of the hiring halls. The board ordered that longshoremen were to be dispatched from the halls "without favoritism or discrimination regardless of union or non-union membership," but they must have done so with tongue in cheek since they also provided that the dispatchers were to be selected by the ILA. The parties were further instructed to establish labor-relations committees in each port, composed of three representatives of the employers and three from the union, to supervise the halls, and process grievances. In the event of a dispute, either party could request the secretary of labor to appoint an arbitrator.[33]

The board's decision was received without enthusiasm by many ILA members because the halls were not to be exclusively controlled by the union. Viewed broadly, however, the longshoremen had real cause for rejoicing. Not only had their union survived an 83-day strike after lying dormant for 14 years, but the coveted coast-wide bargaining unit had been established. Certainly, from the men's point of view, joint control of the halls, with dispatchers elected by the union, was a great step forward over unilateral control by the employers.* It is true that the basis on which the long, bloody strike was ended differed little from the recommendations made by the original Fact-Finding and Mediation Board before the strike began but, in view of the employers' intransigent attitude toward unionism at the beginning of the strike, it is doubtful if the employers could have been persuaded to accept the board's recommendations without a clear demonstration of solidarity by the men.

A Breathing Space

During 1935, both sides fell back to regroup their forces. The employers laid the foundation for a permanent coast-wide association when Frank Foisie left Seattle to become coast coördinator of the four regional employers' associations in San Francisco. In an attempt to strengthen its position, the union made the first of a series of attempts to form a permanent organization among the maritime unions who had coöperated so effectively in the 1934 strike. In April, Harry Bridges, then president of the San Francisco ILA local, called a convention of interested unions at Seattle. Out of these meetings came the Maritime Federation of the Pacific.[34] Harry Lundeberg, at that time an official of the Seattle local of the Sailors' Union of the Pacific, was elected president of the new organization. The immediate objective of the federation was to coördinate the actions of all member unions during negotiations with the employers, and to secure a pledge from each union to support the demands of the others. This objective was achieved at the Seattle meetings.

Harry Bridges and some other young longshoremen who had emerged as leaders during the 1934 strike had more ambitious hopes for the federation. In 1935 John L. Lewis and his supporters founded the CIO on the principle of industrial unionism, and the labor movement throughout the country split up over the issue of craft unions versus industrial unions. Bridges and his group viewed the federation as the first step toward establishing the industrial concept in the maritime industry—an industry where craft divisions have been as deeply entrenched as in the building trades. Older ILA leaders, like Paddy Morris and William Lewis in Tacoma, who had kept the ILA alive on the West Coast during the 1920's when unionism was virtually dead in the other ports, vigorously opposed industrial unionism and deeply resented the newcomers. The fundamental

---

* The only exception to the joint-control award was the port of Tacoma, where the prevailing practice had been for hiring foremen to come to the union hall and pick their men. The award left the Tacoma system undisturbed.

104

disagreement within the ILA itself was one obstacle to the creation of one big maritime union.

An equally serious obstacle was the uneasy relationship between the longshoremen and the SUP. The traditional animosity between longshoremen and sailors, dating from the days of Dan Keefe of the longshoremen and Andrew Furuseth of the sailors' union, had been abandoned during the 1934 strike, but old antagonisms had been revived at the end of the strike when the sailors charged the longshoremen with deserting them.* From the founding of the federation, the ILA tried to secure agreement that whenever member unions planned to take strike action which would "put another member on the bricks," the affected union should be consulted. The SUP was never willing to surrender that much sovereignty, a factor which was to contribute to the growing rift between the sailors and the longshoremen.†

The ILA and the employers agreed to extend the contract without change in 1935 (in Seattle, only 23 ballots out of a total of 997 were cast against this action) but relations between the parties were far from harmonious. The ILA was new and aggressive, and the employers were still deeply reluctant to accept unionism.[35] The violence of the 1934 strike had left a heritage of mutual resentment and suspicion, making it difficult for the parties to work out compromises of the day-to-day disagreements that came up in interpreting the many new clauses in the contract and in setting up the new hiring halls. The Pacific Coast maritime industry was in constant turmoil during 1935 and 1936 with "quickie strikes" and "job action" the order of the day. "There was hardly a week in which there was not trouble at one of the four major and nearly 30 minor ports of the

---

* At the time the employers made their offer to arbitrate with all striking unions if the longshoremen would agree to arbitration, the employers' association had not formally recognized the other unions. Their offer was to arbitrate with only those unions who won representation elections to be held after the strike. Lundeberg expressed the SUP's bitterness at being left without recognition:

> When the longshoremen decided to arbitrate, and the Teamsters voted to call off their strike, the sailors agreed to do likewise in order to all go back together and maintain unity, although they went back with nothing in the way of gains for themselves. Instead, they were forced to fight inch by inch through job action up and down the Coast in order to establish conditions.

Actually, representation elections were held immediately after the longshoremen's arbitration award was handed down and the SUP was granted full recognition. In January, February, and March of 1935, awards similar to the longshoremen's were handed down for coastwise, off-shore, and Alaska shipping. Robert J. Lampman, "Collective Bargaining of West Coast Sailors, 1885–1947," p. 159.

† At the 1936 convention of the Maritime Federation, a resolution endorsing consultation was passed over the SUP's opposition. Harry Lundeberg was reported to have declared, "The hell with you guys. When the SUP wants to strike, it'll strike." Bridges had by then replaced Lundeberg as president of the federation.

Coast."[36] When the longshoremen were not losing pay because of their own disputes with employers, they were frequently stopped from working by the picket lines of other maritime unions. It is ironic that much of the time lost by longshoremen in 1935–1936 was spent in supporting their present-day enemies, the Sailors' Union of the Pacific.

The 1936 Strike

As the date for renewal of the contract approached (September 30), both parties were well prepared for the negotiations. Earlier in the year, the employers had created the Coast Committee for the Shipowners, headed by T. G. Plant, to coördinate their negotiations with the maritime unions, and the Maritime Federation of the Pacific had established a coördinating committee to represent them. As negotiations on the longshore agreement began, the battle for control of hiring was again joined. It soon became clear that the differences between the parties was so great that a strike was almost inevitable. The employers first announced that when the agreement expired they would hire only at the docks, but this was soon changed to insistence on joint control with "neutral persons responsible to the Joint Labor Relations Committees" substituted for dispatchers elected by the union.[37] The ILA renewed their demand for full control of dispatching and also insisted upon retention of the six-hour day, which meant, in practice, payment of overtime for work in excess of six hours. The employers contended that the six-hour day had been instituted in 1934 merely as a temporary spread-the-work measure, and demanded a change of shift at the end of six hours to reduce overtime payments.*

When negotiations became deadlocked, the employers offered to arbitrate these and peripheral issues but in a coast-wide referendum the longshoremen voted 9,938 to 489 against arbitration and set a strike deadline for October 28. Officials of the maritime federation explained this overwhelming rejection of arbitration on the grounds that the employers "will not arbitrate any points unless all of the 1934 agreements are scrapped and we agree to blanket arbitration."[38]

The shipowners then indicated a willingness to extend negotiations indefinitely with the various unions in the maritime federation under the auspices of the U.S. Maritime Commission, which had just been created by Congress and was to have jurisdiction over all sea-going workers after October 26. The sea-going members of the federation—whose principal

---

* According to the employers, these were substantial. They asserted that in 1936 longshoremen received overtime pay for approximately 45 per cent of the time worked.

demands were for union hiring halls and cash payments for overtime rather than time off—were receptive to the employers' suggestion. The ILA accepted the Maritime Commission's authority to investigate the dispute but urged the other unions not to abandon the strike deadline of October 28. When the new Maritime Commission made the mistake of telling the sea-going unions that their strike deadline was "unacceptable," Bridges pointed out, "The way to make the Commission say the unions have a right to run hiring halls is to put on a little pressure," and the unions reaffirmed their original decision to strike on schedule.

T. G. Plant, speaking for the Shipowners' Committee, summarized the employers' position on the united demands of the maritime federation as follows:

> These union demands would have permanently taken from employers the right to select, from among union members eligible, the men to man their ships and to fill shoreside jobs. The question of union recognition is not involved. We do not seek to abolish hiring halls. . . . Employers believe that the owners should have this right. Employers believe owners are entitled to select, from among union men eligible, their own crews and reject men, in their opinion, who are unfit and unsatisfactory. The union leaders seek to deny employers this fundamental right. Union leaders insist that they shall be the ones to determine in whose hands owners must entrust their ships. They have called a strike in an attempt to seize this and other means of completely controlling the maritime industry. To resume negotiations under current circumstances would be useless.[39]

Negotiations were broken off, and the employers announced that their hands were tied by their commitment to await the outcome of the Maritime Commission's investigation, which was to take some six months according to Commission Chairman Rear Admiral Harry G. Hamlet.

Just before the strike deadline, the unity of the maritime federation was put to a severe test when 27 eastern and foreign steamship companies (none of which were members of the Shipowners' Committee) offered the longshoremen, but not the other unions, a settlement on the ILA's terms. Harry Bridges, speaking for the maritime federation, replied that the longshoremen viewed the offer favorably but as members of the federation were forced to reject it. "It is useless unless the sea-going unions are granted what they ask—the hiring halls and cash overtime pay."

Members of the federation began their scheduled strike on October 29, and the 1,400 Seattle longshoremen set up the picket lines they were to walk for 98 days. While prestrike negotiations had been proceeding in

San Francisco, preparations for the strike had been carried out in Seattle in a vastly different atmosphere from that which had prevailed in 1934. Mayor John Dore, who had called the 1934 strike a "soviet of longshoremen" and had threatened to open the port by force, was again heading the city government but the mayor had undergone a fundamental change of attitude. Dore, one of Seattle's more bizarre contributions to municipal government, delivered an address to a group of Young Democrats on the University of Washington campus one afternoon two weeks before the strike deadline, in which he praised Bridges highly and declared "days more interesting than the French Revolution are coming to this country." In a speech that evening in the Everett Labor Temple, he announced that if the shipowners used what Dore referred to as "gorilla guard tactics" against the unions, he would give the operators "a touch of hell." Going a step farther, Dore threatened to take control of the police department to prevent use of policemen as strikebreakers.*

Even after the strike started, the community maintained a coöperative attitude toward the strikers. The maritime unions were permitted to use public halls for their meetings, and the local press and radio were generous in allotting space to the federation's public statements. The employers themselves adopted a far less hostile attitude toward the strikers than they had in 1934. No attempt was made to use strikebreakers, and the employers confined their public statements to explanations of their position on the issues of the strike, rather than making personal attacks on union leaders.†

When the strike had been in progress for almost a month, Seattle maritime unions and the shipowners attempted to negotiate an interim agreement—allowing relief ships to sail to Alaska where residents were protesting hardship, complaining that they were cut off from food shipments by the strike. In mid-November, the parties were given an additional incentive to arrange for ships to sail to Alaska when President Roosevelt announced that the government-owned Alaska Railroad was considering the purchase of ships to serve the territory. Eleven days later Alaska shippers signed an agreement in Seattle which met the unions' strike demands. The local strike committee also permitted several special cargoes to be moved—some vital to Washington farmers and one consigned to the Salvation Army.

The determination of the parties to prevent a repetition of the violence

---

* During the strike, two unsuccessful efforts were made to recall the mayor.

† This more responsible attitude existed in other ports, as well. In some cities, public debates between the parties were held before large audiences and the strikers appointed guards to help the police maintain order on the picket line. *Monthly Labor Review*, XLIV (April, 1937), 813.

of 1934 did not signify that either side was willing to abandon its original position. Neither employer nor union negotiators in San Francisco seemed to feel any urgency about reopening discussions, and they ignored several offers by government mediators to break the deadlock by setting up a system of government-supervised hiring halls for the maritime industry.*

The first break in the strike came on the 52nd day, when T. G. Plant and Harry Lundeberg announced that a separate agreement had been signed covering the SUP. As Lundeberg put it, "The sailors want to show the other unions the way home." Further strain was put on the rest of the unions in the federation by Plant's simultaneous announcement that the shipowners hoped to settle next with the marine firemen. This put the longshoremen under pressure to make a separate agreement, and at that time they were confident they could secure their demands.[40] But Bridges repeated the ILA's refusal to reopen negotiations until demands of the other unions were met. Another two weeks passed before the major issues outstanding betwen the shipowners and the remaining five unions were resolved. On January 6, ILA negotiators met with the Shipowners' Committee for the first time since the strike began. With the longshoremen's position weakened by the possibility of other major defections from federation unity, it took the ILA and the employers almost a month to reach any settlement the ILA negotiating committee was willing to submit to the membership. Finally, on February 4, an agreement was approved by the membership in a coast-wide vote (1,096 Seattle longshoremen voted in favor, 104 against) and the strike ended.

The 1936 strike was the second major struggle for control of hiring between West Coast longshoremen and their employers. The ILA emerged from the 98-day strike without obtaining union control of the hiring hall —their major objective. Nor did the union get the 5-cent hourly raise they had demanded in later stages of the strike. On the other hand, they did obtain preference of employment, and the six-hour day which was retained in the contract meant that longshoremen would continue to receive overtime pay for two or three hours a day on most jobs. The employers on their side successfully fought off the union's drive for control of the halls and obtained assurance that the Joint Labor Relations Committees and provisions for arbitration would be more fully utilized in the settlement of grievances. But they did not win neutral dispatchers. By the time the 1936 strike had gone into its 98th day, it was obvious that a compromise

---

* Admiral Hamlet, chairman of the Maritime Commission, had been recalled to Washington, D. C., shortly before the strike began, after he had succeeded in thoroughly enraging both employer and union representatives. He was replaced as the government's representative by Edward F. McGrady, who, as an assistant secretary of labor, had attempted to mediate the 1934 strike.

on the issue of hiring was a necessary condition of their mutual survival, and the parties reconciled themselves to temporarily accepting the status quo.[41]

New Affiliations

As soon as the waterfront settled down to normal the employers reorganized and strengthened their association as they had after the 1934 strike. T. G. Plant resigned as chairman of the Coast Committee for the Shipowners, and a permanent coast-wide organization, the Waterfront Employers Association of the Pacific Coast, was formed in June, 1937. Almon E. Roth, a former comptroller of Stanford University, was named president.[42] Creation of the new association reflected the growing strength of the maritime unions and a recognition among employers of their own need to secure unity of action. Discussing industry-wide bargaining at a meeting of the American Management Association two years later, Roth explained the advantages of a strong employer association:

> . . . operation under a master contract makes it possible for employers to adopt and practice one of Labor's own slogans, which reads—"An Injury to One is an Injury to All."[43]

The wisdom of the employers' action was to be demonstrated soon after it was taken. West Coast maritime employers did not have to meet the threat of another coast-wide strike for ten years, but their unity was frequently put to the test during the next few years by the jurisdictional warfare which broke out recurrently among the many craft unions in the industry.

Almost simultaneously with the formation of the new employers' association, the longshoremen also established a new organization. Ever since Ryan's behavior in the 1934 strike, West Coast longshoremen had been skeptical of his leadership. His actions during the 1936 strike made a break with him inevitable. Ryan had first agreed to support the Pacific Coast District but had later reneged, and when Bridges protested, Ryan removed him from the union's international executive board.* A few days before the district held its 1937 convention, Ryan stopped Bridges' salary as a district officer "for attempting to disrupt the ILA form of organization on the East and Gulf coasts."[44] When Bridges suggested to the convention that a referendum be conducted on the question of accepting John L. Lewis' invitation to join the CIO, delegates received his recommenda-

---

* After Ryan withdrew his support during the strike, Bridges had called him a strikebreaker. When news of this criticism reached Ryan in New York, he responded, "Every knock from Bridges is a boost." *Seattle Times,* Dec. 2 and 16, 1936.

tion with enthusiasm, and in July the membership voted overwhelmingly for CIO affiliation. By August, the Pacific Coast District of the ILA had become District 1 of the International Longshoremen's and Warehousemen's Union, CIO, and Harry Bridges had been appointed CIO western regional director. The Seattle local became Local 1-19.[45]

There were, however, exceptions to this change in affiliation. In the coast-wide referendum, four ports in the State of Washington—Tacoma, Port Angeles, Anacortes, and Olympia — had voted overwhelmingly against the CIO. Olympia later reversed this decision and joined the ILWU, but the other three locals insisted on retaining their affiliation with the ILA and thus with the AFL. These came to be known as the "exception ports," and this relatively small group of AFL longshoremen* were destined to disrupt the entire shipping industry on the West Coast.

The longshoremen's agreement had been renewed without modification on July 30, 1937—less than two weeks before the union received its CIO charter and changed its name—but early in 1938 the employers raised the question of whether the ILWU was the same group with whom they had a contract. The union's response was to ask the National Labor Relations Board to certify it as the bargaining representative of all Pacific Coast longshoremen. The employers, who in this period were still only reluctantly accepting coast-wide bargaining, argued that the appropriate unit for bargaining purposes should be restricted to longshoremen in the employ of a particular employer at a particular port, but the board rejected this principle. In a precedent-making decision in June, 1938, the board established the multiple-employer association covering the entire coast as the appropriate unit, and designated the ILWU as the sole bargaining representative.†

The ILWU held its first convention in April, 1938, and commemorated their new status by staging an elaborate mock burial ceremony for their former international president. To the accompaniment of a funeral dirge, a coffin draped in black crepe was slowly carried into the convention hall by eight pallbearers and set down in the center of the stage. One of the delegates delivered the oration, which went in part:

---

* Tacoma had about 500 registered longshoremen, Anacortes about 35, and Port Angeles about 90. U.S. National Labor Relations Board, *Decisions and Orders,* Vol. 32, p. 677; hereafter cited as 32 NLRB 677.

† 7 NLRB 1041–42. In support of their contention that they represented the majority of the longshoremen, the ILWU had presented evidence that 9,557 of the 12,860 Pacific Coast longshoremen had signed cards designating District 1, ILWU, as their bargaining representative. Conveniently ignoring this evidence, Joseph Ryan told a Senate committee later in the year, "We are going to ask this committee or some other committee to stop the National Labor Relations Board from breaking up our organization." U.S. Congress, Senate Committee on Commerce . . . , *Amending the Merchant Marine Act of 1936,* p. 1075.

We have assembled here today to pay the last tribute of disgust and disrespect which the ILWU renders to all phoney labor leaders. . . . Here lies Joseph P. Ryan, who was both phoney and finky, knowing that he believed in the eternal principle of the shipowners. He valued the almighty dollar, never spoke the truth, and was unjust in his dealing with all union men. . . .

As delegates filed past the coffin they were led in song:

> Yes, we'll bury old J. P.,
> The biggest phoney of the ILA!
> His days are done—he's gone to hell,
> So what do we care what he had to sell![46]

But all was not levity at the first convention. Delegates were concerned about the effect on coast-wide unity of the negative vote in the "exception ports," and about the widening breach with the SUP. Not only did the longshoremen resent Lundeberg's break with the other unions in the maritime federation by negotiating a separate settlement in the 1936 strike, but in bargaining sessions toward the end of the strike the traditional controversy over which union would supply workers to load steam schooners* had again broken out between the ILA and SUP.

Convention delegates were faced with the immediate problem of what to do about the emergence on the East Coast of a new CIO seamen's union. Directly paralleling the SUP, the National Maritime Union had just been certified by the NLRB as the bargaining representative for certain shipping lines which had been hiring SUP members on the West Coast. West Coast sailors were planning strike action to force the shipowners to continue bargaining with them, and the first convention of the ILWU had to decide whether longshoremen would support the claims of the NMU or the SUP. The convention's vote to back their fellow CIO members meant, inevitably, open conflict with the West Coast sailors.

The first clash came at Seattle in 1938. The SS *Timber Rush* came into port in April, and the SUP immediately picketed the ship. Seattle longshoremen at first refused to cross the picket lines of the sailors but finally agreed to abide by the ILWU convention ruling and work the cargo. Thus came the open break which had long been brewing and which divided the waterfront unions into two hostile camps. In one camp were the ILWU and the NMU; in the other, the SUP, the AFL longshoremen in the "exception ports," and Dave Beck of the Teamsters Union. This also meant the end of the Maritime Federation of the Pacific. From 1938 until it

_____

* On the West Coast the term "steam schooner" refers to those dry-cargo vessels which ply coastal waters, primarily serving the smaller lumber ports.

was dissolved in 1941, the federation was little more than an arm of the ILWU.[47]

The open break between the Teamsters and the ILWU had occurred shortly after the 1936 strike, while the longshoremen were still in the AFL. During the strike, Bridges had given a speech before a large crowd in Seattle—Beck's home territory—in which he made his famous threat, "The ILA is not going to stay on the waterfront, but is going inland."[48] This move was the product of the ILWU's experience in their two major strikes:

> Harry Bridges discovered during the 1934 strike that cargoes could be moved by rail if the waterfront was tied up. His next move, therefore, was to try to achieve control of freight movements by enrolling the warehousemen . . .[49]

After ILA organizers appeared at uptown warehouses in major coast ports, Beck started an organizing campaign of his own among warehousemen,* and through the powerful influence of the Teamsters on the AFL executive board, he obtained a jurisdictional award covering "those employed in warehouses located back from the marine docks or the waterfront."[50]

When the West Coast longshoremen left the AFL, they no longer were bound by this award. They continued organizing inland warehousemen, with greater success in other coast ports than in Seattle. There the Teamsters had a decided edge over the ILWU. The mercurial Mayor Dore had undergone another change of heart toward the longshoremen after the 1936 strike. Beck had been instrumental in Dore's reëlection as mayor, and Dore was ready to pay his political debts. The lengths to which he was prepared to go in supporting Beck in the battle over warehousemen was indicated by his remarks before the 1937 AFL convention:

> When the CIO–AFL fight got hot in the city of Seattle, I announced as Mayor of that city and as a private individual that I was going to do everything humanly possible to make that an AFL city. . . . The Mayor of Seattle has great executive powers . . . [and] I have laid down a rule and have enforced it relentlessly that there will be no picketing in that city by anybody unless that picketing is approved in writing by the Seattle Labor Council."[51]

The strength of the coalition among the ILA, SUP, and Teamsters was

---

* In Seattle, when ILA warehousemen struck in 1936, they were told by their employers that they could return to work only if they changed their affiliation to the Teamsters Union. Selig Perlman in Marquand, *Organized Labor in Four Continents,* pp. 374–375.

demonstrated when the crucial *Timber Rush* left Seattle and put in at Tacoma, where AFL longshoremen respected the SUP picket lines and refused to work the cargo. The employers, acting on their new philosophy, "an injury to one is an injury to all," immediately served notice that they were closing the entire port until the *Timber Rush* was serviced. As ships diverted from Tacoma arrived at other ports, the tie-up spread down the coast. ILWU longshoremen were willing to work the ships, but as soon as the sailors posted pickets, teamsters refused to haul the "hot" cargo.*

The coast had hardly quieted down after the SUP won its battle for recognition when it was disrupted by the five hundred longshoremen in Tacoma. They had never been reconciled to the NLRB certification of the ILWU as their bargaining representative, and in August, 1940, Tacoma longshoremen took a leaf from the SUP's book and struck to force the employers to recognize and bargain with the old ILA locals. The employers protested that they could not do so, because they were bound by the NLRB certification, and asked the coast arbitrator, Wayne Morse, to hear the dispute. Morse held for the employers but the Tacoma men ignored his decision and continued their strike.[52] This tie-up, like the sailors', spread down the coast as Teamsters and SUP members refused to handle ships or cargo diverted from Tacoma.

Work was finally resumed when the NLRB agreed to rehear the ILA's case on September 12. In a disputed decision, the NLRB upheld the ILA by ordering that new representation elections be conducted in the three "exception ports."† The new elections were held in July, 1941, and the ILA was certified.[53] Since that date, the three locals have bargained separately with Washington employers. To deal with the "exception ports," the Washington branch of the coast-wide employers' association maintains a separate legal entity called the Waterfront Employers of Washington, which has the same staff and uses the same offices as the coast-wide group in Seattle.

---

* The coöperation between Dave Beck and Harry Lundeberg, forged during this period, still exists. At the 1951 AFL convention, the two labor leaders announced a "mutual assistance pact to drive 'Communist influences' from the Pacific Coast waterfront." *Portland Oregonian,* Sept. 22, 1951. It will be recalled that in 1953 and 1954, the Teamsters and the Seafarers' International Union, of which Lundeberg is president, played a prominent role in the AFL campaign to oust the old ILA in New York—a development which gave the ILWU an intimate concern about the outcome of that contest.

† 32 NLRB 668–691. Board member Edwin S. Smith vigorously dissented, arguing that the history of bargaining and the nature of the industry pointed to a coast-wide unit as the only practical solution. He drew attention to the absurdity of the 33 Anacortes longshoremen bargaining on equal terms with the Waterfront Employers Association of the Pacific Coast, and the irony of Tacoma—historically the leader in the fight for coast-wide bargaining—now championing the cause of bargaining on a port-to-port basis.

It is ironic that although Harry Bridges and the ILWU have the reputation of being the disruptive force in West Coast waterfront history, it was the AFL faction who initiated and perpetuated most of the work stoppages during this period. It is significant that in the first negotiations between the new ILWU and the employers, in November, 1940, the traditional struggle for control of hiring was suspended while the parties gave first priority to improving procedures in the agreement for compromising differences and avoiding work stoppages.

In the past, tie-ups had frequently resulted from conflicting interpretations of needlessly vague contract provisions. The new contract carefully redefined those provisions and clearly specified the meaning of such terms as "refusal to work cargo according to the agreement," "work stoppage," and so on. Also, the machinery for arbitrating disputes was substantially revamped. The old arrangement had been cumbersome and slow, and had produced disparities in contract interpretations in the various ports. To provide an agency which could reconcile any discrepancies growing out of the decisions of local arbitrators, the present Coast Labor Relations Committee was set up. To speed up the arbitration process, the local arbitrator in each port was required to be available day or night to be called to the scene of any "beef," which he was to decide on the spot. If the parties were dissatisfied with his decision, work was to continue while they carried the dispute to the Coast Labor Relations Committee and, if necessary, to the coast arbitrator as the final step in the judicial process.

The execution of this agreement reflected the growing willingness of the employers and the union to accept each other on equal terms. It came at a time when the intricate jurisdictional lines between the competing maritime unions had finally been fairly well drawn, and 1940 seemed to foreshadow a new era. As a close observer of the industry predicted:

> . . . The evidence of improved performance, chiefly in the form of practical cessation of all job stoppages . . . give every assurance of continued peace on the Pacific Coast waterfronts during the life of the agreement.[54]

World War II

When the United States entered World War II in December, 1941, the experience of the parties with more than a year of peace proved a useful foundation for meeting wartime problems. They were able to work together successfully on recruitment, allocation of manpower, and productivity. Frank Foisie, who had become president of the Waterfront Employers Association, publicly praised Bridges and the ILWU for their coöperation. In Seattle, the representatives of Local 19 on the Pacific Maritime Industry Board wrestled with the difficult problem of recruiting enough men to load the ships carrying supplies to Pacific battlefronts, and when the need to find more workers in the tight Seattle labor market was especially acute, Local 19 even suggested the possibility of using prisoners of war on the waterfront.[55] Members of the Joint Labor Relations Committee worked together to prevent bottlenecks and, after one of their inspection tours of the docks, they reported in the committee minutes a finding which, viewed against the background of their prewar relations, is especially interesting:

> Employer members stated they believed work was being performed in a very good manner on all docks visited, except the Army Dock—and this might be the fault of management.[56]

Like the parties to collective bargaining in other industries during the war, the ILWU and the employers each sought, through decisions of government agencies, to secure advantages they had not been able to get through collective bargaining.* The union pushed for an extension of job control, while the employers tried equally hard to recapture control of hiring in a case carried to the National War Labor Board in 1944.[57]

The ILWU urged the board to award them what amounted to a closed shop by proposing that preference in registration, as well as in employment, be given to union members. The employers objected, arguing that the union was already adequately protected, because registration was largely based on seniority, so that union members who had preference in employment automatically were given priority in registration. The board denied the union's demand, asserting the union really intended "to abridge the right of employers to offer an objection when a name comes up for registration."

The ILWU also asked that the employers agree not to discriminate "because of union membership and activities, race, creed, color, sex, religious or political beliefs, or national origin." Pointing out that they were actually formalizing existing practices, because the employers did not dis-

---

* On the other hand, unions sometimes found themselves fighting off wartime orders which took away gains they had negotiated. The ILWU achieved a substantial victory in 1942, when it helped persuade President Roosevelt to amend an executive order prohibiting payment of overtime except after eight hours a day or forty hours a week. The ILWU joined other unions in a vigorous protest to Washington, pointing out that observance of the order would mean abandonment of the prized six-hour day won in the 1934 strike. The order was amended a few days later to allow the secretary of labor to exempt any industries where an existing arrangement "was operating successfully . . . [or was] advisable for the successful prosecution of the war." (These policies were embodied in Executive Orders 9240, 9248, and 9340.)

116

criminate against men for any of these reasons, the board granted the union's request with the exception of "sex." The union's inclusion of sex in the proposed clause apparently caused some consternation among board members who were unable to visualize women doing longshore work, but the union pointed out that women were already driving lift jitneys in inland warehouses and could do this on the waterfront.

On their part, the employers demanded the right to have steady gangs and men assigned to them but the board denied the request, noting that this practice had ceased in Seattle, Portland, and Los Angeles in 1935, and in San Francisco in 1939, and that it would conflict with the principle of equalization of job opportunities and earnings. Arguing that the sharp distinction made between longshoremen and dockworkers sometimes forced them to keep idle men standing by, the employers further proposed that they be given the right "to shift longshoremen between ship and dock and *vice versa.*" After hearing testimony that older men liked to be classi-fied as dockworkers rather than as longshoremen—who are dispatched to the more arduous and dangerous work in the ship's hold—the board denied the employers' demands, pointing out that they were permitted under the contract to lay off unattached men, or gangs as a unit, if they were not needed.

The employers also urged the board to strengthen their ability to disci-pline workers, declaring that a longshoreman discharged for cause on one day could be, and was in some cases, redispatched to the same employer the next day. They proposed that a discharged man should not be redis-patched to any other job until his case was disposed of by the Joint Labor Relations Committee. The board noted that employees did not customarily lose their right to employment in an entire industry merely because they had been discharged by one employer, and ordered that the employers' request be limited to the prevention of redispatching to the employer who had discharged the man until the case had been disposed of.

Finally, the employers urged that dispatchers, instead of being elected by the longshoremen in each port, should be selected from among the membership of the union, but by the Joint Labor Relations Committee. They also demanded the right to maintain a representative in the hiring hall at all times. Pointing to a high turnover of dispatchers, they argued that these proposals were made in the interest of increasing efficiency in dispatching. The ILWU was silent on the request for an employers' rep-resentative in the hiring halls, but insisted that if the dispatchers were to enjoy the confidence of the men, the longshoremen themselves must be able to exercise control over them through the processes of election and recall. The board held that the Joint Labor Relations Committee should establish standards which must be met by candidates for the dispatching job, and that the dispatchers should continue to be elected by the union. It also decided that both the employers and the union should be free to maintain representatives in each hiring hall at all times.

The decision of the National War Labor Board added a few minor refinements to the contract but, in the main, the hiring halls remained virtually unchanged. Until the passage of the Taft-Hartley Act, the question of who was to control hiring remained in abeyance.

The 1946 Strike

The end of the war in the fall of 1945 brought an end to wartime coöperation in West Coast longshoring. As curbs on wage increases loosened and labor's wartime no-strike pledge ran out, longshoremen grew as restless as other workers throughout the country. In 1946, they joined other maritime workers and those in the auto, steel, coal, and railroad industries in strikes of a magnitude unknown in the country since the period just after World War I.

With another coast-wide strike looming in the offing, West Coast longshoremen again took the initiative in trying to secure united action by the craft unions in the maritime industry. In February, the ILWU and six other maritime unions met to make joint plans. In May they formed the Committee for Maritime Unity and set a strike deadline for June 15.*

The longshore agreement had expired on October 1, 1945, and longshoremen were working without a contract while their negotiators tried unsuccessfully to reach an agreement early in 1946. The touchy question of control of hiring was not at issue but the parties could not agree on a wage increase—the issue then uppermost in the longshoremen's minds. The tempers of ILWU negotiators became understandably frayed as the longshoremen grew increasingly restive, seeing wage increases in other industries were reported in the press almost daily. The employers' spokesmen grew increasingly irritated too, because they were fighting on two fronts: trying to hold back the pressure for increased wages on one hand, and on the other to defeat the ILWU's campaign of that year to bring walking bosses and checkers into the union—a story too long and complicated to tell here.[58] A walkout by the longshoremen was narrowly averted in

---

* The members were the ILWU, NMU, MC&S, Inlandboatmen's Union, American Communications Association, and Marine Firemen. All but the Firemen were CIO affiliates. AFL maritime unions rejected an invitation to join, instead establishing an AFL Maritime Trades Department with Harry Lundeberg and Joseph Ryan as officers. On the other hand, the Brotherhood of Railroad Trainmen assured the Committee for Maritime Unity of their support. *Seattle Times,* June 7, 1946, and Lampman, *op. cit.,* p. 295.

April, when President Truman appointed a federal fact-finding board[59] and the temper of the men was not improved when the June strike deadline of the Committee for Maritime Unity arrived and the employers refused to concede any more than the board's recommendation of a 22-cent an hour increase. Substantial as it was, this wage offer was one cent less than the employers had given the ILA "exception ports" a few days before the ILWU original strike deadline in April. Consequently, it was with reluctance that the longshoremen agreed with the other CMU members to call off the scheduled strike and accept the fact-finding board's recommendation. The ILWU's failure to obtain parity with their ILA rivals was made more palatable, however, by the knowledge that the increase would be retroactive to the expiration date of the old contract—more than eight months earlier—which meant back payments of several hundred dollars for some longshoremen.

The longshoremen and the other CMU unions had hardly reached these settlements in June than they began negotiating new agreements which would take effect September 30. Control of hiring was again by-passed in the longshore negotiations, with the union demanding another wage increase and inclusion of a safety code in the contract. Whether the parties might have been able to reach a peaceful settlement on these issues in less troubled times is uncertain. The rest of the summer was so hectic that the parties hardly had an opportunity to consider their negotiations calmly —the SUP and NMU kept the employers' harassed negotiators junketing back and forth across the country;* a series of strike deadlines were announced and then postponed by the maritime unions; and the dying Wage Stabilization Board's attempts to establish parity between the two factions were overridden by higher authority in the person of John R. Steelman, the President's stabilization director. As members of the CMU, the longshoremen became enmeshed in all the sudden walk-outs and back-to-work movements of the various unions, and on October 1 they "hit the bricks" for their own demands. The employers announced their acceptance of the safety code[60] and a 15-cent increase for the ILWU on October 18, but negotiations were stalemated over the perennial ILWU-SUP conflict about loading work on steam schooners. The parties finally agreed to send that issue to arbitration but picket lines of other striking unions kept the longshoremen from getting back to work for another month. On November 17, the last pickets were withdrawn from the waterfront and the 48-day strike was over.

---

* Lundeberg had called an SUP strike on June 6 despite President Truman's threat to break the strike with military personnel, explaining that the sailors had lost patience with the shipowners "who are detained in Washington, D.C., negotiating with the CIO unions."

The Committee for Maritime Unity had enjoyed brief success as an integrating force among the maritime crafts but this organization—like the Maritime Federation of the Pacific before it—was dissolved when relations between the two strongest members, the ILWU and the NMU, broke down after the strike. Waterfront employers, after seeing the havoc wrought by the battles between the competing crafts in the maritime labor movement, might well have watched with some regret the death of this second attempt to introduce the industrial-union concept in the shipping industry.

The 1948 Strike

The year 1947 was quiet on the Pacific Coast waterfront. When the contract came up for renewal in June, both parties agreed to extend it without modification while they waited to see whether Congress was going to pass the Taft-Hartley bill then being debated in Washington. But in 1948, when negotiations on a new agreement got under way, the old battle over control of hiring was reopened in an atmosphere of hostility unequaled since 1934. Frank Foisie, spokesman for the employers, now armed with the Taft-Hartley Act, was obviously convinced that the act was a perfect weapon with which to resurrect his system of employer-controlled hiring halls—and to remove his old adversary, Harry Bridges, from the bargaining table. The longshoremen, fearing that a strict application of the new law could mean the emasculation of their union, as well as the end of their hiring system, were determined to fight both the employers and the law.

Passage of the Taft-Hartley Act posed peculiar difficulties for the longshoring industry. Under section 8a (3), it is an unfair labor practice for an employer to discriminate in hiring, tenure, or any term or condition of employment for the purpose of encouraging or discouraging union membership—he cannot agree with a union that he will hire only union men. The concession of the Taft-Hartley Act to union security arrangements comes in the form of a proviso to this general prohibition. Under the proviso, an employer is permitted to sign an agreement requiring his workers to join the union after working 30 days. If there were no more to the section, it would allow what is in common parlance a "union shop" agreement, although it clearly forbids either a closed shop or a preferential hiring agreement (such as the ILWU's) since men must be given 30 days to join the union after they are hired. But there is more to section 8a (3). It further provides that an employer is guilty of an unfair labor practice if he discriminates against an employee under the type of agreement permitted by the act when "he has reasonable grounds for believing that membership [in the union] was denied or terminated for reasons other than failure of the employee to tender dues and initiation fees uniformly required as a condition of acquiring or retaining membership." Thus, what the act really permits is a maintenance-of-dues contract effective 30 days after employment.[61] Moreover, as originally enacted, the law forbade even such a maintenance-of-dues contract unless a majority of the employees "eligible to vote" (rather than a majority of those voting) had voted in an NLRB-conducted election to authorize the union to make such an agreement, and the union had filed certain information with the board, including non-Communist affidavits signed by the union officers.[62]

Section 8a (3) raised serious problems for the ILWU. Satisfying the election requirement raised no significant problems, but the kind of union security agreement the union would then have been able to obtain was not conceived for a casual-labor market like the waterfront. An agreement permitting the union to insist only that a longshoreman join the union and maintain his dues payments after 30 days of employment obviously was of no value to the ILWU, where typically a job lasts only a few days. The union would hardly have been induced to abandon its job rotation policy in order to acquire a union security arrangement which confined the union's disciplinary powers over its members to insisting that they pay dues. As a Senate committee observed after examining the potential impact of the Taft-Hartley Act on the ILWU's hiring hall and those of other maritime unions:

> . . . over most of this industry there really is no intermediate position between the complete open shop and some form of closed shop. The casual nature of the employment renders a union shop, for instance, impractical.[63]

As negotiations opened in 1948, the employers seemed to have an airtight case when they contended that the old contract provisions granting preference of employment to ILWU members, the union's participation in the registration process, and the hiring hall system itself, conflicted with the Taft-Hartley Act. Declaring that the hiring hall was "The Number One issue—one that will have to be settled before any contract can be signed," the employers went over the heads of union officials and began mailing copies of a kind of house organ called *Shoreside Reports* to the longshoremen at their homes.[64]

The evolution of the positions taken by the parties was substantially this: The employers were willing to continue the hiring halls but insisted on exclusive control. In addition to the contract provisions already mentioned which they viewed as contrary to the Taft-Hartley Act, they held that the selection of dispatchers by the union was also violative of the act. The union conceded that preference of employment based on union membership might conflict with the new law, but maintained that union selection of dispatchers did not, asserting that the dispatchers merely performed routine duties in dispatching men according to the agreement and were under the control of the labor relations committees.

In an effort to resolve the conflict over this last issue the ILWU proposed that authority to select dispatchers be vested in the coast arbitrator or, alternatively, that the existing method be continued in effect until a legal determination (court decision on the legality of traditional hiring hall practices) was made. Rejecting this suggestion, the employers countered with a proposal that dispatchers be selected by the director of the Federal Mediation and Conciliation Service, his appointee, or some other neutral person. This, in turn, was rejected by the union.

The employers then proposed adopting the "Taft-Lundeberg formula" which they had worked out with the SUP the previous year,* but the suggestion was dropped after the employers admitted it would result, in effect, in an open shop in longshoring.[65] Unlike the SUP, which had not found it necessary to hire casuals (nonunion men) during peak periods, ILWU dispatchers would have had to dispatch anyone, whether a registered longshoreman or not, if he had ever worked even as a casual on the waterfront. Certainly the formula was incompatible with hiring longshoremen in rotation. The union then offered as a counterproposal a clause giving preference in employment to longshoremen on the basis of seniority, and basing new registrations also on seniority.

The parties failed to come to any agreement and, on June 3, a fact-finding board was appointed by the President under the national-emergency provisions of the Taft-Hartley Act. The board found the preference-of-employment clause and the method of dispatching to be the issues of overriding importance and predicted that agreement would not be reached.[66] The board's report was made on June 11, and was followed a few days later by a temporary order restraining strike action, not only by the ILWU, but also by the NMU, Marine Cooks and Stewards, the Marine Firemen, the Marine Engineers, and the Radio Operators, all of whom were negotiating new contracts.

---

* This formula gives preference in employment to men previously employed by one or more of the companies signatory to the agreement, thus in practice it gives preference to SUP members because the union had had a closed shop for years. Sailors continued to be dispatched from the union hiring hall. Senator Taft consulted with Lundeberg and Gregory Harrison, the shipowners' representative, in working out the formula, which Taft believed complied with the act bearing his name. U.S. Congress, Senate Joint Committee . . . , *Labor-Management Relations, West Coast Maritime Industry*, pp. 25–26.

With the two basic issues unresolved, the parties took up the ILWU's other demands for an 18-cent wage increase and reduction of the work shift from nine to eight hours. The employers countered with an offer of 5 cents and no change in the work shift. On June 21, they antagonized the union by filing unfair labor practice charges against them on three counts: that the ILWU was "refusing to bargain until the other five unions had signed agreements" under section 8b (3);* "refusing to bargain for a new hiring hall" under section 8b (3); and "demanding a contract continuing the present illegal hiring-hall-union-dispatcher setup" under section 8b (3).[67]

On July 2, the U.S. attorney general obtained an 80-day injunction which prohibited a strike or lockout until September. Within a few days after the "cooling-off" period began, the employers charged Seattle longshoremen with "deliberately flouting the 80-day injunction by causing a slowdown which has reduced cargo handling operations by about a third." Not long after, they announced that 460 Seattle longshoremen had been discharged for engaging in slowdowns, and on July 19 the Waterfront Employers Association announced in San Francisco that banana shipments to San Francisco and Seattle had been discontinued. Explaining that "it is impractical for the banana shipper to send a ship north of Los Angeles unless it calls at two substantial ports," the WEA continued, "San Francisco lost the banana business because of the Seattle slowdown."[68]

Seattle employers were further annoyed by a heritage of the Wobbly era. Just as IWW stickers, "Join the One Big Union," used to be pasted on railroad cars and bunkhouses in Western mines and lumber camps, small stickers began appearing on lift trucks, bulkheads, pieces of cargo, and on the walls of longshoremen's lunchrooms, reading:

"Keep Cool for Eighty Days"

"Don't Get All Heated Up"

"Safety Slogan:
In watching safety, don't forget
You'll Get Phew monia if you sweat."

"There's Ways and Ways
Of Cooling Off for 80 Days"

A union official commented later about the injunction period, "The em-

---

* In 1948, no formal organization such as the Maritime Federation of the Pacific or the Committee for Maritime Unity existed, but the ILWU was supporting the demands of the other unions named in the injunction.

ployers were damned glad when the 80 days ended. The status quo was maintained but it cost them plenty."

As the injunction period drew to a close, the employers mailed a seven-page issue of *Shoreside Reports* to ILWU members containing the employers' final offer on which the men were supposed to vote before they were free to strike. The offer consisted of ten proposals—the 5-cent increase and the following which are pertinent to the hiring hall issue: that dispatchers be selected by the Federal Mediation and Conciliation Service; that registered men be given preference in employment, rather than extending the "preference shall be given to union members" language of the existing contract; and that in adding new men to the registered list, preference would be given to men previously employed in the industry. The port labor relations committees would decide how many should be registered; the employers, who would be registered.

In a curious revelation of how little they understood the rank-and-file support for their union officers, the employers had issued a statement to the press the day before mailing their final offer to the men, charging that the ILWU was "guided strictly by the Communist Party Line."* When the National Labor Relations Board polled the men in the secret election required by the Taft-Hartley Act on the question, "Do you accept the Employers' last offer?" the 26,000 longshoremen and affiliated maritime workers showed their reaction to the employers' tactics, and their opinion of the Taft-Hartley Act, by boycotting the election. The board reported the results as follows:[69]

Number of eligible employees	26,695
Ballots marked "yes"	0
Ballots marked "no"	0
Ballots challenged	0
Total ballots cast	0

The ILWU conducted its own coast-wide referendum in their customary manner of taking strike votes, and the membership voted 97 per cent against accepting the employers' last offer.

Even in this hostile atmosphere, it seemed possible that the negotiators in San Francisco might reach a settlement before the 80-day injunction expired. The ostensible hurdle to agreement was overcome when Bridges and Gregory Harrison, WEA general counsel, orally agreed to compromise on the crucial hiring-hall issue by continuing the existing system and

---

* WEA news release, August 10, 1948. Before the date of the vote on the final offer, another irritant was added. On August 22, ILA longshoremen in the "exception ports" were given an increase of eight cents an hour—three cents more than the employers were offering the ILWU.

124

inserting a clause in the agreement committing them to renegotiate any offending provisions in the event of an adverse court decision. But on the last afternoon, disagreement arose early in the negotiating session when Bridges reminded the employers of the ILWU tradition that a new contract would not become effective until the membership voted upon it. Harrison contended that it should become effective immediatly upon execution.[70] Then, just before adjourning for dinner, Bridges reminded Harrison of the ILWU's commitment not to sign an agreement until settlements had been reached with the other maritime unions. Harrison replied that he understood that to be so, and the session was adjourned. When the parties met again at 8 P.M., Harrison raised the question of the actual hour of the strike deadline, saying he understood it to be midnight. Bridges insisted that it was not until 10:30 the next morning, when the 80-day injunction expired. Bridges then pointed out that the wording of the "saving clause" had not yet been worked out, and that the language of this clause, the wage increase, the 9-hour shift, and two other minor points were the issues yet to be settled. Harrison responded that since the other maritime unions were not meeting in bargaining conferences that evening, there was no likelihood that agreements could be reached with them before midnight. The employers left the room briefly to caucus and, when they returned, announced that their last offer made in negotiations would remain open until midnight. Bridges replied that the offer was rejected. Harrison left the meeting with the other employers, remarking, "We'll see you later." Bridges retorted, "We'll see you on the picket line." Thus began the work stoppage which was to last 95 days, a stoppage which some people called a strike and others called a lockout.

From the outset, the employers seem to have been seriously divided on the question of their strike strategy. The dominant group in the association —led by President Frank Foisie and Gregory Harrison—were determined to seize what appeared to be a highly favorable opportunity to unseat Harry Bridges as ILWU president. On the first day of the strike, the atmosphere on the waterfront was electrified when the employers announced they were withdrawing all offers and would not bargain further with a labor organization which had failed to comply with the non-Communist affidavit provision of the Taft-Hartley Act. In a coast-wide referendum on whether ILWU officials should file such affidavits, the membership overwhelmingly rejected the idea.*

---

* The total vote was 10,740 against to 376 in favor. Members of Local 19 cast 1,468 ballots against filing the affidavits to 19 in favor. *Seattle Times,* Sept. 10 and 11, 1948. The vote in Seattle on this question is of particular interest because the membership of Local 19 has always been the most politically conservative group in the ILWU.

Waterfront employers then began referring to the dispute as a "political strike," contending that it was the "irresponsibility of the union leadership" which prevented a settlement. To prove the irresponsibility of Bridges, the WEA called attention to "1,399 recorded work stoppages since 1934." Seattle led the list with 413; Los Angeles had had 365; San Francisco, 347; and Portland, 274.[71]

The intransigent attitude of the employers' spokesmen cost their association much of the support from firms outside the association which they had enjoyed in Seattle in other strikes. On the first day of the strike, three Seattle stevedoring firms, none of whom were members of the WEA at the time, signed an agreement with Local 19 accepting the existing hiring-hall provisions and granting a 15-cent wage increase. These firms continued to operate during the strike. A few days later, Local 19 offered to handle Army cargo in Seattle if the 15-cent increase were paid and if the Army agreed not to hire men through a member of the Waterfront Employers Association. The Army's port of embarkation, however, undertook to "go it alone" by hiring longshoremen in a shape-up at their pier rather than through the hiring hall because, as port officials stated, "The Army doesn't want to take sides." The Army's success in hiring was limited by the presence of 1,200 pickets at the Army docks, and a short time later port of embarkation officials awarded a contract to one of the stevedoring companies which had settled with the union. Subsequently, Local 19 members were regularly dispatched from the hiring hall to the Army docks.*

The Seattle Port Commission signed a similar agreement with the local a month later, and when the Alaska Steamship Company refused an offer from Local 19 to work "under *status quo* conditions" if the company would agree to make any gains growing out of the strike settlements retroactive, the government-owned Alaska Railroad organized an ocean-going barge company to carry cargo to the territory. This concern signed an agreement with the ILWU and operated during the strike, subsequently dropping out of the industry.

Cargo was diverted from Seattle to Tacoma early in October on the

---

* An incident occurred during this period which must have impressed Army officials. A reserve Army captain told his superiors he was reluctant to cross the picket lines because he was a member of Local 19 and intended to go back to longshoring when his tour of duty was over. He was handed the ultimatum, "Either cross the picket lines and report for work in the POE or you'll be wearing civilian clothes." He appeared the next morning at the port of embarkation pier—but on the picket line, wearing civilian clothes. *Seattle Times,* Sept. 17, 1948. As a former Army enlisted man, I was mystified by the captain's ability to make this decision with impunity, but I was unable to find any mention of disciplinary action by the Army in the Seattle press.

assumption that ILA longshoremen would handle it. Local 19 sent a token picket line to the Tacoma docks and, at first, longshoremen there refused to work diverted ships. This policy was abandoned after Harry Lundeberg and other AFL officials met in Tacoma to persuade the ILA local not to support the striking CIO unions, and Local 19's pickets were run off Tacoma docks by AFL seamen and longshoremen.* This development challenged the ILWU's tactical ability. Their first move was to hire a speedboat, which, covered with signs urging AFL longshoremen to stop working the "hot" cargo, weaved about Tacoma docks. This proved unsuccessful, so an airplane fitted out with a loud-speaker system was hired to swoop down over the ships, broadcasting appeals to the longshoremen to stop work, in the manner used by the Army to urge enemy troops to surrender during World War II. After a few days of addressing their captive audience in this fashion, Local 19 abandoned its efforts, and Tacoma longshoremen continued to work the cargo unmolested. The significance to the employers of having an open port during a coast-wide strike was indicated by the presence on October 26 of twenty-one ships diverted from Seattle waiting in the open harbor at Tacoma to load and discharge their cargoes.

National CIO officials entered the strike on October 14 when Allen S. Haywood, director of organization, informed the employers that the CIO would underwrite any contracts leading to a settlement if the employers would drop their insistence on the non-Communist affidavit.† Two days later the ILWU, attempting to reopen negotiations which had been broken off 44 days earlier when the strike began, made a proposal for the election by secret ballot of a rank-and-file negotiating committee. The employers rejected this proposal, giving their reasons in a letter to Bridges:

> . . . the composition of any negotiating committee which
> may be selected is not the key to our present impasse. The prob-
> lem, as you well know, is the future administration and observ-
> ances of any contract between ourselves and the ILWU, under
> its present leadership. Your 14-year party line record of irre-
> sponsibility and double dealing proves that any contract which
> you and your leadership are ultimately to administer, no matter
> how or by whom negotiated, is worthless.[72]

---

* The president of the State Federation of Labor justified this action by saying that the AFL had an obligation "to rescue the rank and file of the CIO unions from a leadership working day and night to mislead them and deliver the future welfare of the State of Washington to out-of-state or foreign control." *Seattle Times,* Oct. 9, 1948.

† At the time of this proposal, CIO president Philip Murray was, like John L. Lewis and many other union officials, still refusing to sign the non-Communist affidavit.

The coast-wide strike picture began to brighten two weeks later. In a major political upset, Harry Truman was reëlected President after campaigning vigorously against the Taft-Hartley Act. A few days after the election, Almon E. Roth, who had left the WEA to become president of the San Francisco Employers Council, contacted the WEA, the ILWU, and the CIO offering to join with the latter in underwriting a settlement. The employers were persuaded to withdraw their insistence on non-Communist affidavits and, along with the union, agreed to this proposal on November 8. A few days later, the WEA announced that a new 18-man negotiating committee had been chosen, and negotiations were resumed. On November 18, the end of the strike came in sight when Bridges told reporters, "The employers are showing evidence of very good faith."* The longshore strike actually ended on November 25—the 84th day—but longshoremen did not get back to work until December 6. They were delayed by the traditional "steam schooner beef" when the sailors refused to work until shipowners assured the SUP that the new longshore agreement did not take work on steam schooners away from them.

The new contract was to run for two and one-half years. Observance of the contract was "underwritten" by the CIO and the San Francisco Employers Council, both of whom agreed to withhold their support of any strike or lockout unless they were notified in advance and unless they approved the action taken. Three provisions in the new agreement were major victories for the ILWU: retention of the clause giving preference of employment to union members; the provision that the hiring hall would continue to operate without change; and a 15-cent wage increase (which brought the straight-time rate to $1.82). The employers won continuation of the nine-hour shift. The statement announcing the end of the strike was made by Harry Bridges for the ILWU; R. J. Thomas for the CIO; and Dwight C. Steele and Colonel John Kilpatrick for the WEA.[73]

Anyone following the strike closely might well have wondered where Foisie and Harrison were. Speculation concerning their status was increased when, the day after the strike ended, the WEA repudiated rumors of a reorganization as "malicious, untrue, and unfounded."[74] But skeptics were inclined to take the rumors seriously and a leading shipping industry trade journal commented ". . . a spokesman for an anti-Foisie group in the WEA said the strike could have been prevented by good judgment—

---

* *Seattle Times,* Nov. 19, 1948. Perhaps the most significant change in the employers' negotiating team was the addition of Dwight Steele, president of the Hawaiian Employers Council. A few years earlier, Steele had established good relations with the ILWU while an official of a California employers' group which bargained with the warehouse branch of the union. Kerr and Fisher, "Conflict on the Waterfront," *Atlantic Monthly* (Sept., 1949), p. 19.

it's time for a new team."[75] To those members of the WEA who, from the outset, had been unconvinced of the necessity of a strike, Foisie's and Harrison's policies had seemed less than rational. The strike had pushed marginal companies to the point of going under and when larger companies such as Matson and the government-owned American President Lines sided with the group who wanted to end the stoppage, it meant a major shift in alignments within the association, which made a reorganization inevitable.[76]

The suspense was ended early in 1949, when the Waterfront Employers Association merged with the Pacific American Shipowners Association to form the present employer group, the Pacific Maritime Association, with O. W. Pearson, whose background included experience as a sailor and as a longshoreman, as its first president. The new association immediately announced that a basic principle of its operation would be an emphasis upon "more direct employer participation in all phases of labor relations." The new agreement had also provided that lawyers would no longer serve as negotiators; they would handle only those matters in which legal questions were clearly involved, thus eliminating much of the adversary attitudes which had characterized earlier negotiations. The policy shift in the employers' group had been foreshadowed in the final issue of *Shoreside Reports,* which employers mailed to the longshoremen on December 21, after the end of the strike:

> Longshoremen, the public, and the employers have some-
> thing very special to celebrate. There's something new under
> every Christmas tree on the Pacific Coast . . . It's a promise—
> a very real one—of peace and goodwill on the waterfronts of the
> Pacific Coast. We can and we must make this Christmas spirit
> last throughout the year and on into the years to come.

What was the significance of the 1948 strike? When negotiations for the agreement began, it seemed clear that passage of the Taft-Hartley Act had finally put the employers in a position to recapture unilateral control of hiring. But even with the new law on the books, they were forced to compromise on the hiring-hall issue and, instead, directed their efforts to driving a wedge between the rank-and-file and the union leadership. Rather than being disaffected by the continued attacks on their leaders, ILWU members interpreted the employers' action as an attempt to dominate their union, and they closed ranks. The ILWU emerged from the 95-day strike in a stronger position than they had ever held in the industry. In 1949, the ILWU found itself dealing with an employers' group more fully prepared than any of its predecessors to accept the union as an integral part of the industry and as a partner in running the hiring hall.

129

The New Look

With the end of the 1948 strike and the change of leadership in the employers' association, the armed-truce atmosphere which had existed on the waterfront for fourteen years disappeared. Labor relations on the Pacific Coast assumed what has been popularly known in the industry as the "new look"—one of genuine willingness of the parties to coöperate for their mutual benefit. Early in 1949, an employer spokesman said of the new attitude toward collective bargaining, "We have a new spirit and we know that if we supplement it with the right kind of action, we can turn it into new jobs for all hands." An ILWU official echoed these sentiments:

> We're not trying to kid anybody that the man who writes the check and the man who gets it aren't two different people, but we know equally well that they have a wide field of mutual interest . . . We should concentrate on our areas of agreement, not our areas of disagreement, in order to obtain a fair share of world cargo.[77]

Indeed, economic considerations had made the "new look" much overdue. Truck and rail competition had made serious inroads in the volume of cargo shipped through West Coast ports during the protracted waterfront tie-ups, and this trade had not been recovered. "In 1947 there were only 60 ships in inter-coastal trade—compared with about 160 in 1939."[78] The industry's difficulties were further complicated by the fact that efficiency of cargo handling had dropped significantly in the atmosphere of hostility, distrust, and open warfare of the last decade.* Faced with these critical conditions, the parties undertook—for the first time in their bargaining history—a series of joint conferences on ways to increase port activity, improve safety conditions, and institute technological improvements. To dispel the industry's reputation among shippers for unreliability, every effort was made to avoid work stoppages. This desire was reflected in a clause added to the section of the agreement entitled "No Strikes, Lockouts, and Work Stoppages" which said: "There will be no 'hip pocket' working, dispatching, or safety rules; or unilateral union membership or business agents' rules or rulings." The clause has succeeded in ending a practice which had been the cause of many on-the-job disputes and "quickie strikes." West Coast longshoremen have traditionally carried

---

* Productivity in the longshoring industry defies precise and reliable measurement, but the employers attempted to arrive at statistical comparisons in several surveys. U.S. National War Labor Board, *Termination Report* . . . , vol. 26, pp. 534–566. And, as Kerr and Fisher have noted (see preceding note), "The pace of work in San Francisco prior to 1934 was reputed to be as fast as in any port in the world." The coming of unionism had undoubtedly affected productivity.

well-thumbed copies of the contract, always prepared to cite section and clause when they felt they were being ordered to do something "illegal." Summoned to the ship when the foreman stood his ground, the business agent invariably supported the men, and a work stoppage ensued. Under the "hip pocket" clause, the parties agreed that work would continue during such disputes while the Joint Labor Relations Committee in the port interpreted the contract.

As an employer representative in Seattle described the new relationship, "The point seems to have been reached where both parties are making an effort to understand each other's problems." The new sense of coöperation has been reflected at all levels of contact, not just at the top. The writer expected to witness an example of "job action" when touring the waterfront with the business agent of Local 19 in 1951. The business agent noticed that the gangplank of a ship discharging cargo lacked a safety net—no small matter in longshoring.* He reminded a ship's officer standing near-by of the ship's responsibility to put down a net, and when the officer said he was busy and would look after it in a minute, the business agent said, "OK, be sure you do," and walked away.

Since the advent of the "new look," the parties have had to resort to arbitration far less often than during the hostile era,† and "quickie strikes" have been almost completely eliminated. The success of the parties in avoiding work stoppages is shown in the following comparisons:

	1946–1948	1949–1951
Number of strikes	15	3
Workers involved	115,000	6,600
Duration of strikes (in days) .	259	9
Man-day losses	4,200,000	30,000‡

* In a Joint Labor Relations Committee meeting a few days earlier, an accident was discussed which occurred when longshoremen jumped from the dock to a ship a few feet from the pier without a safety net. One man had been badly injured when he slipped and fell between the ship and the dock. An employer member of the committee asked, "What the hell's the matter with those men? Won't they ever learn safety?" An old-timer on the union side of the table responded, "Do you remember how many beefs we've had over waiting on the dock until a net was put down?"

† Kerr and Fisher report that there were 250 arbitrations between 1934 and 1948. The first coast arbitrator was Judge M. C. Sloss, who served from 1934 to 1936. During the troubled period after the 1936 strike, no arbitrator was appointed until Wayne Morse, then dean of the University of Oregon Law School, was chosen in October, 1938. He served until arbitration machinery was suspended during the war while the Pacific Coast Maritime Industry Board and the War Labor Board were functioning. Stuart Daggett served in 1945, Harry Rathbun in 1946, Clark Kerr in 1947, and Arthur Miller in 1948. Sam Kagel has served from 1948 to the present time. During the first three years of the "new look" in Seattle, Washington Area Arbitrator David M. Roderick had only seven proceedings.

‡ Pacific Maritime Association, *Strikes and Work Stoppages*. These figures cover
(*Note continued on following page.*)

An incident which before the "new look" would surely have destroyed the favorable comparison in these work-stoppage figures occurred in September, 1949. Since the previous May, the ILWU Honolulu local had been on strike, primarily against the Matson Navigation Company. Since Matson is responsible for roughly 20 per cent of longshore work in San Francisco, and is a member of the Pacific Maritime Association, it was feared that the Hawaiian strike would spread to the mainland, but employers assured the public that Matson had made no demands on the PMA which might involve the West Coast in the strike. In Seattle, PMA officials expressed optimism, "We are confident that all the unions and all the employers will make every effort to preserve the record established to date."[79]

Matson kept its word to the coast shippers, but repercussions of the Hawaiian strike nevertheless reached Seattle in September, when a Hawaiian Pineapple Company barge was loaded by strikebreakers in Hawaii and towed to Seattle, stacked high with cartons of canned pineapple. Fred Kamahoahoa, a member of the Honolulu local, arrived by plane one jump ahead of the barge, prepared to picket any dock where the barge might attempt to unload.* Given the cold shoulder by Seattle employers, who even refused to sell fuel to its tug, the barge remained in Elliott Bay— Seattle's open harbor—for a few days, then moved forlornly on to Tacoma where ILA longshoremen refused to unload the cargo.

Moving out to sea, the barge proceeded southward, turned into the mouth of the Columbia River, heading toward Portland. But the "longest picket line in the world" beat the barge into port and the pineapple moved on again, this time up-river, through the locks at Bonneville Dam, coming to rest finally at the small, nonunion river port at The Dalles, Oregon. Here, on September 28, AFL Teamsters were found who were willing to unload "hot" pineapple.†

---

not just the longshoremen, but all West Coast maritime workers. The main causes of the time lost in the "new look" period were a brief dispute which involved the ILWU in a jurisdictional battle among Alaska fish cannery workers; a dispute between the SUP and Marine Engineers; and between the SUP and the ILWU over steam-schooner work.

* Depicted in West Coast newspapers as "the longest picket line in the world," the aloha-shirted Hawaiian longshoreman was a publicity bonanza for the ILWU. Wherever Kamahoahoa went, his picture appeared in the newspapers with an accompanying story of the 125-day strike in Hawaii, including the fact that the barge was operated by a nonunion crew.

† Longshoremen from the Portland local were on hand in force to prevent unloading and, when the teamsters tried to drive through their ranks, a fight broke out. Twenty-two ILWU members were arrested for rioting and, in July, 1951, the Hawaiian Pineapple Company was awarded damages of $201,000 against the ILWU, and two truck drivers who were injured in the fracas, $77,000. *Dispatcher,* Aug. 31, 1951. Since the union's financial affairs are conducted on a "pay as you go" basis— unlike many unions, the ILWU does not maintain large cash reserves—the damages awarded the Hawaiian Pineapple Company have not been collected. The two truck drivers settled with the union out of court.

132

The pineapple-barge incident, while not without musical-comedy overtones, was a grim and impressive demonstration of the significance of the "new look." Where, in the past, local strikes had often spread up and down the coast, and where the employers—as well as the union—had adopted the philosophy "an injury to one is an injury to all," keeping an ILWU strike which lasted more than five months localized in Hawaii was a tribute to the firm determination of the parties to keep the peace in Pacific Coast ports.

A new and potentially serious threat to the "new look" was posed in the middle of 1950, when the National Labor Relations Board handed down its award on the unfair labor practice charges filed by WEA officials against the ILWU during the heat of the 1948 strike. Shortly after the strike ended, the employers had joined the ILWU in requesting that the charges be dropped. The employers had pointed out to the board:

> It would be extremely unfortunate from the standpoint of the industry and the public if the present harmonious employer-union relationships were to be upset by an order of the National Labor Relations Board requiring a change in hiring practices.[80]

Nevertheless, Robert Denham, the National Labor Relations Board's general counsel, declined to concur in the request. The board accordingly heard the original charges: that the ILWU had violated section 8b (3) by refusing to bargain until the other maritime unions reached settlements, and by refusing to bargain for a new hiring-hall arrangement; and that section 8b (2) had been violated by the union's insistence on retaining a union-elected dispatcher. Denham had added a further charge that section 8b (2) had been breached when the ILWU struck to maintain the prefential hiring clause in the contract, and this point was also considered by the board.

The board ruled in July, 1950, that the clause in the agreement negotiated *after* the strike giving preference of employment to union members clearly violated section 8b (2) and ordered the parties to cease giving effect to that clause. The other charges were dismissed on the reasoning that the union's strike action had not violated either section 8b (2) or section 8b (3), because the strike had not been called over any issues prohibited by the act. From the evidence presented on the history of negotiations before the strike, the board concluded that the employers had offered to continue the preferential hiring provision, subject to a saving clause providing that "in the event of a legally binding decision of any court on this issue, the whole subject shall be subject to re-negotiation," and that the union's acceptance of this offer—before the strike—made

133

"the subsequent conflict between the parties not related to the hiring provisions, but to the [union's] economic demands."[81]

The parties decided not to act immediately on the board's order to change the wording of the preferential hiring clause—a decision which was going to cost them some money a few years later—but when a new agreement was drafted the following year the language of the offending clause was changed to read:

> Preference of employment and dispatching shall be given to registered longshoremen who were registered and available for employment in any one of the occupations covered by Section 1 of this agreement as of June 1, 1951, including registered longshoremen absent from the industry or inactive because of leaves of absence granted by the Labor Relations Committee or because of illness or other reasons certified to by the Labor Relations Committee.

Thus, despite a law which to many observers spelled the doom of the hiring hall, in the atmosphere of the "new look" the parties were able to preserve their hiring system virtually unchanged.

Another incident occurred in 1950 which, at the time, appeared to jeopardize the newly developed coöperation between the parties. This was the CIO's expulsion of the ILWU in August on the charge that

> . . . the policies and activities of the International Longshoremen's and Warehousemen's Union (ILWU) are consistently directed toward the achievement of the policies of the Communist Party rather than the objectives set forth in the constitution of the CIO.[82]

Some observers thought that after the ILWU was expelled, the CIO would establish a dual longshoremen's union—as it has in the electrical industry, for example—and that the ILWU would be torn by factionalism, with the Pacific Coast waterfront returning to the jurisdictional battles of the 1930's.* Factionalism did not develop, although there always have been "right" and "left" wings in the union. The CIO did make an attempt to establish a dual union and sent organizers to San Francisco in 1951, but when they were rebuffed by ILWU members the CIO abandoned the campaign. To anyone familiar with West Coast longshore history, the failure of the CIO's attempt to "raid" the ILWU came as no surprise, and the relationship between the union and the employers remained undisturbed.

---

* Indeed, one labor newsletter told its readers "the majority of Bridges' membership is *now* supposed to be in revolt against him . . . He's through." *John Herling's Labor Letter* (Washington), July 29, 1950.

The political complexion of the ILWU was given attention by the federal government, as well as by the CIO, in 1950. That was the year the U.S. Coast Guard began its program of screening "security risks" from the maritime industry. Because of its reputation as a "left-wing" union, the ILWU was excluded from the list of maritime unions invited to attend the meetings in Washington, D.C., where the screening program was formulated and plans laid for implementing it. However, presidents of three ILWU locals considered to be in the "right wing" of the union were invited individually and shared in the deliberations. One of them was J. A. Hopkins, president of Local 19, who signed the agreement setting up the program; the others were from Longshore Local 10 and Ships' Clerks Local 34. (Both locals are in San Francisco.)

After the screening program was announced, ILWU delegates from all locals met several times to discuss it. When strong differences in opinion developed as to whether or not the union should coöperate with the Coast Guard in administering the program, the membership was polled in a coast-wide ballot. The vote was 6,750 to 1,935 (an unusually light vote) to coöperate with the program.[83] Two members of Local 19 subsequently served on the Seattle local board which processed appeals of persons denied security cards,* but the ILWU was denied representation on the national appeal board in Washington, D.C.

While coöperating with the program, the ILWU urged the Coast Guard to improve the procedures used in the screening process. The union particularly requested the Coast Guard to furnish the appellant with specific written charges against him and to give him the right to confront and cross-examine his accusers.† The union further demanded court review when a man was denied a card. They also set up a committee to assist members denied cards in processing their appeals before both the local and national boards.

By the summer of 1951, most Seattle longshoremen's applications had apparently been processed, although Coast Guard officials consider the number of men granted security cards, as well as the number denied them, to be "classified information."[84] The effect of the screening program showed up in the notation *No CG Pass* written alongside the names of

---

* ILWU representatives were William Laing, chief dispatcher, and J. A. Hopkins, who was reëlected president of Local 19 in 1951, and business agent in 1952. The PMA delegate was J. E. Ritchie. Public members were Rev. Jerome Toner of St. Martin's College, and Professor Joseph Kane of Seattle University (both are Catholic schools).

† In June, 1952, a Seattle federal judge ruled that maritime workers screened off the waterfront must be specifically informed of the charges against them before an adverse finding was made. This decision was upheld by the 9th Circuit Court of Appeals in September, 1953.

about a score of men on the dispatching board in the hiring hall. Some names on the board also carried the notation *No Navy Pass,* indicating that those men had been refused passes required to work at the Navy installation (Piers 90 and 91). In the summer of 1949, the Navy had reprocessed the records of all Seattle longshoremen, refusing to issue passes to 52 men "for security reasons." The Navy public-relations officer had issued a press release stating that the men had been rejected for various reasons, but that "none were denied passes because of communistic connection."[85] This inscrutable comment was the only explanation the Navy was willing to make in response to requests from both the ILWU and Seattle employers who asked for clarification or for a hearing.*

The screening program added one more complication to the job of the dispatchers. When a dispatcher is sending out a gang to fill employers' orders and finds it necessary to abandon strict rotation by skipping over a man's name because that gang will go to a restricted pier, he must dispatch the man in the first gang going to a commercial pier. In June, 1951, union members of the Joint Labor Relations Committee called the employers' attention to the fact that some men had been rejected for work in unrestricted areas because they did not have security cards. They requested the employers' concurrence in the following agreement:

> Until such time as the U.S. Coast Guard or other Governmental Agency restricts either the entire waterfront or certain areas on the waterfront, the Union and the Employers agree that longshoremen shall be dispatched to commercial cargo operations without prejudice.

The employers argued that such an agreement was unnecessary since the clause in the master contract giving preference in employment to registered men already assured these men adequate protection. The proposal was left in abeyance when the employers gave assurance that they would not discriminate against men without cards on commercial piers.[86]

Although the screening program had an incalculable impact on the individual longshoremen who were denied cards, and has complicated the dispatching system, it did not disturb the working arrangements between the employers and the union. No insuperable problems have arisen, because the Coast Guard has not declared the entire port a restricted area and there has been enough commercial cargo to provide all longshoremen with regular work. The implications of such a program for the ILWU, a

---

* Officers of Local 19 told me that some of these 52 men eventually received Navy passes, and that others had their initially granted passes later revoked. Some men received Navy passes but not Coast Guard cards; while others were cleared by the Coast Guard but not the Navy.

union with a reputation for militancy and radicalism, are uncertain. Although over 6,500 ILWU members demonstrated by their referendum votes that they approved of the screening program and presumably saw in it no threat to their union, almost 2,000 other union members opposed the program, presumably sharing the views of Harry Bridges and some other ILWU officials that

> . . . far from being a "security" program it is a blacklisting program. In other words, the ILWU is convinced that measures promulgated in the name of "national security" are, in effect, intended to smash not only this organization but any and all trade unions which fail to accept and carry out the present government's policy, whether foreign or domestic.[87]

Without any of the traditional preparations for siege which had characterized so many earlier negotiations, the employers and the union negotiated the 1951–1953 agreement containing the new preference-of-employment clause required by the Taft-Hartley Act, a 5-cent wage increase, and a pension plan wholly supported by employer contributions which provided payments of $100 a month—in addition to Social Security benefits—to all longshoremen aged 67 who had worked in the industry 25 years. Payments to the older men could not begin immediately because it took the National Wage Stabilization Board nine months to decide whether or not industry pensions were inflationary, but by 1953 more than 1,500 West Coast longshoremen had retired on their pension benefits.*

The 1951 negotiations also reflected the desire of the parties to remove the last vestige of their earlier need for calling on the government to compromise their differences. The old agreement still provided that the secretary of labor select arbitrators when the parties could not agree on a choice. During negotiations, the ILWU proposed that this responsibility be given to E. D. Conklin, the stenotypist who had recorded almost all bargaining sessions and arbitrations of the industry. At first, the employers were startled by the suggestion but, upon reflection, they agreed because they realized that Conklin understood the bargaining relationship far more intimately than any other "outsider."

One protracted work stoppage occurred on the Seattle waterfront dur-

---

* In Seattle, the first beneficiaries of the plan were listed in the minutes of the Joint Labor Relations Committee on June 6, 1951:

Reg. No.	Date of Birth	Age	Reg. No.	Date of Birth	Age
72	Dec. 5, 1874	77	571	Dec. 18, 1884	67
65	April 2, 1884	67	142	Sept. 14, 1871	80
657	Dec. 14, 1876	75	232	Aug. 17, 1882	69
1225	May 31, 1881	70	2031	April 21, 1883	68

ing the life of the new agreement, but on that occasion the longshoremen were innocent bystanders. They were prevented from working by a dispute among the AFL foremen in the port, a dispute directly attributable to a man whose name had virtually disappeared from West Coast longshoring fifteen years earlier—Joseph P. Ryan. When the sensational public hearings of the New York State Crime Commission disclosed the extent of corruption in the ILA, 90 of the 110 members of the Seattle ILA foreman's local disaffiliated, saying, "We refuse to pay any more dues to a gangster-dominated outfit." They immediately formed an independent union, the Ship and Dock Foremen's Union of Washington, and set up a hiring hall from which waterfront employers hired them for work. The few "loyal" ILA foremen, aided by the SUP, kept the port tied up for a month in an unsuccessful attempt to force the independents back into the ILA or prevent them from working. When the picketing was enjoined on December 10, the foremen resumed their duties and the longshoremen were able to get back to work.

Despite numerous threats to its existence, the "new look" has survived on the Pacific Coast for more than six years, and there are many indications that it will continue. In other industries, the typical experience has been that once the principle of coöperation in collective bargaining has been accepted by the parties, a spirit of mutual respect and willingness to accept joint responsibility has reinforced itself.[88] In West Coast longshoring, the bargaining relationship until 1948 was a continuing struggle over exclusive control of the hiring system, but once the parties reconciled themselves fully to joint participation they committed themselves to working closely together on a day-to-day basis—a commitment which should cement their coöperative relationship firmly with the passage of time. What *is* the West Coast hiring system, and why is control of it so crucial as to produce fourteen years of almost unremitting warfare?

5

The Hiring Hall

The hiring hall is *the ILWU.*—ILWU pamphlet.[1]

Three aspects of the hiring hall particularly strike the observer—the rational solution it provides to the complex problems of a casual-labor market, the foolproof system which has been devised to prevent abuses in the dispatching process, and, most important, the power vested in the hands of whoever runs the hall.[2]

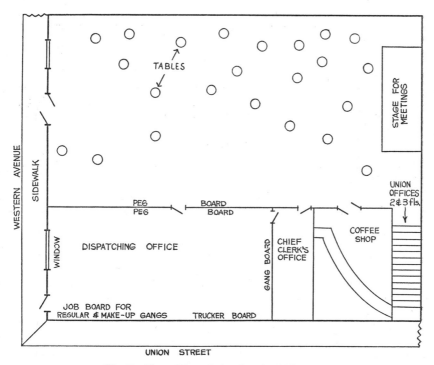

Fig. 2. Floor Plan of the Seattle Hiring Hall

The hiring hall, in the center of Seattle harbor, is primarily a dispatching center, but the large room shown in the sketch of the floor plan in figure 2 serves not only as an assembly area during dispatching periods, but as a recreation center for the men during the day, and as the hall for union meetings. Union officials have their offices on the second and third floors and are easily available to the members when the men come in to get their work assignments. The building is also provided with well-equipped club rooms for retired longshoremen. Reflecting the in-group attitude of the longshoremen, the coffee shop shown in the sketch is operated by a retired longshoreman and his wife, and janitor service in the hall is provided by two ILWU members elected annually by the local. The office next to the coffee shop is occupied by the chief clerk of the hiring hall, an ILWU member selected by the Joint Labor Relations Committee to keep records on the dispatching system. The dispatching office is staffed by five dis-

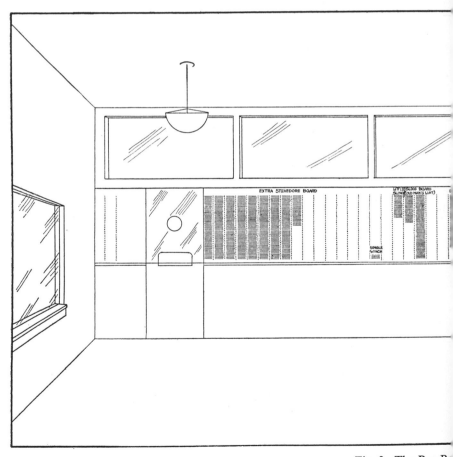

Fig. 3. The Peg Bo

patchers elected from among the membership of Local 19 for one-year terms.

The Peg Board

Perhaps the best way to understand the mechanics of the hall is to see, first, how the men are classified according to their skills and abilities, and then how the dispatchers assign them to jobs. The peg board shown in figure 3 separates the dispatching office from the main room. Except for a few minor differences, the side facing the main room is identical with the side shown in the sketch. The names of the longshoremen are listed on both sides of the board, and alongside each man's name is a hole in which he places a small peg if he is in the hall and wants to be dispatched. The pegs, which are about the size of a lead pencil about two inches long, are in a trough at the base of the peg board. When a man "pegs in," the

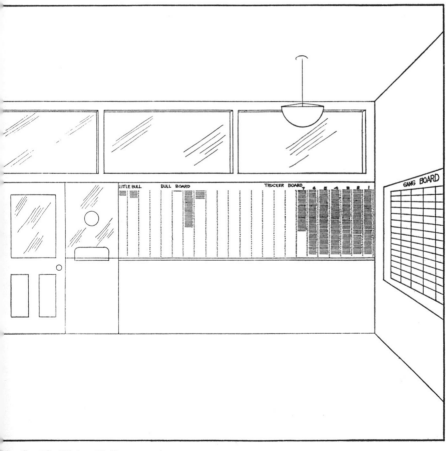

the Seattle Hiring Hall

peg shows both in the main room and inside the dispatching office.

The titles which appear along the top of the peg board show the breakdown of the labor force according to skill, experience, and personal qualifications of the men. The classifications reflect the ability of the system to protect the jobs of older and injured men, and the willingness of both the employers and the union to "take care of their own."

Extra Stevedore Board.—Most longshoremen are listed in this classification. These are the hold men—the least skilled of those who work on the ships.

Single Winch.—These men—all old-timers—confine themselves to the relatively easy (in the physical sense) job of operating the winches on those older ships equipped with two single winches on either side of the hatch. (Newer ships are equipped with double winches set close enough together to be operated by one man.)

Little Sling.—On this list are men who have been temporarily injured and who are dispatched to the easier jobs of handling the ship's slings while recuperating. Men are put on this list by the executive board of Local 19, usually for 60 to 90 days.

Sling Board (Old Man's List).—These are men who are too old for most jobs or men who have been permanently injured. Sling jobs, involving lighter work, are reserved for them.

Deck List.—These are the skilled men—the winch drivers and hatch tenders. They are the gang bosses of make-up gangs, and are comparable to leadmen in industry.

Little Bull.—These men work in pier warehouses and docks, rather than on the ships. Men on the Little Bull list, like those on the Sling and Little Sling lists, are the older men and those who have been temporarily or permanently injured. They are dispatched to the easiest jobs using mechanical equipment.

Bull Board.—These are the skilled dockworkers—the men who operate the motor vehicles used on the dock and in the warehouse, such as "push bulls," heavy vehicles equipped with a special bumper used to push railroad cars into position; jitneys which pull a string of small trucks; and fork lift trucks used to pick up and stack cargo loaded on skid boards in the warehouse and on the dock. In addition to the men who "work off the Bull Board," some men listed on the Extra Stevedore Board are qualified to operate these vehicles and can be so dispatched in emergencies.

Trucker Board.—Most dockworkers are listed in this classification. They are comparable to the men on the Extra Stevedore Board but are, in the main, older men who have chosen dock work (as against work in the hold) because it is less strenuous and requires less agility.

142

Approximately 1,400 men were registered in 1953 with the Joint Labor Relations Committee as regular longshoremen and dockworkers.* Most of these men are listed on the peg board, the two largest groups being the 650 extra stevedores and the 300 truckers. The other major group in the labor force consists of the members of regular gangs. About 250 in number, they are not listed on the peg board. The method of dispatching regular gangs is described below.

The Dispatching Process

In filling orders for men, the dispatchers are guided by a set of precise, detailed rules laid down in the supplementary agreement covering dispatching procedures in the port. When employers need men, they telephone the hiring hall, giving the number of gangs and extra men required, the name of the ship, the time when the men should report, and information about any special characteristics of the cargo, such as commodities which are dangerous or especially unpleasant to handle and which some men might not want to work or which require special clothing. Orders for regular day gangs† are placed with the dispatcher any time during the previous day up to 2:30 P.M.; for night gangs, any time during the same day up to 2:30 P.M. Orders for extra longshoremen and dockworkers are placed any time during the previous day up to 4 P.M.; and for men to work at night up to 4 P.M. the same day. Special provisions are made for dispatching men on weekends and as replacements for members of regular gangs who have not shown up for work.

Although the principle underlying the dispatching process—equalization of earnings—applies to all registered longshoremen and dockworkers, the methods of dispatching men in the different classifications necessarily vary. In Seattle, a standard longshore gang includes ten men: one hatch tender, who is the gang boss and who directs the work of the winch operator; one winch driver, who alternates every working hour with the hatch tender to relieve the strain of operating the dangerous machinery; six hold men, who stow the cargo; and two sling men, who manage the loading and unloading of cargo on the dock. When a gang is dispatched to a ship, it continues to work during its regular shift until the loading or discharging is completed or until the gang's hatch is idle for a complete shift. Thus, gangs may work for a week or ten days on a particular ship.

---

* The 120 walking bosses, 250 checkers, and 25 supervisors and supercargoes in the port are not considered in this description because they are not dispatched through this hiring hall.

† The day shift begins at 8 A.M.; night work at 7 P.M. When it is uncertain whether the ship will be ready to load or discharge cargo by 8 A.M. the following morning, employers call for gangs to be in the hall at 7 A.M. If they are not dispatched by 9:15, they are released and receive four hours "call-in pay."

To ensure that the rule of strict rotation is observed in dispatching men who "work off the peg board," a foolproof system has been devised. For each list, there is a "master peg." This is about twice as long as the men's pegs and is painted a bright color to distinguish it from theirs. During a regular dispatching period, the dispatcher selects men for make-up gangs following the rule that the next man on the list is the first man out. He removes the master peg from the hole where it stopped in the last dispatching period, and moves it down the list until he comes to a peg alongside the name of the first man who is pegged in. As he inserts the master peg in the board, it pushes out the man's peg which falls into the trough below. As the gangs are made up, the master peg travels down the lists one after another, pushing out the men's pegs in succession. If the dispatcher violated the rotation policy, the men in the hall could easily detect it, because the master peg would appear below some pegs still in place when a man was being dispatched ahead of his turn.

Exceptions to strict rotation are permitted only when notations appearing after men's names indicate special reasons why they cannot be dispatched to particular jobs. For example, the inscription "no wheat" after a man's name indicates that he should not be sent to a job trimming wheat because he is allergic to wheat dust. When the dispatchers are required to pass over a man for this reason, or because he has "No Navy" or "No CG" after his name, they send him out on the first job where such a disqualification is not applicable. On the other hand, notations next to some men's names on the Extra Stevedore Board indicate special skills, such as ability to operate a lift truck. In emergencies, these men can be dispatched ahead of their turn if their special skills are needed.

The goldfish-bowl character of this process is an important element in the successful operation of the system. Sometimes, when a dispatcher passes over a man's peg for some reason, the man rushes up to the window of the dispatching office demanding to know why he was passed over. Though the dispatcher is under pressure to complete the dispatching job quickly, it behooves him as an elected official to take time out to give a satisfactory explanation to the aggrieved longshoreman—and to the other men waiting in the hall. Such disputes do not occur often. The men know the order of dispatching being followed and they can see from the orders listed on a large blackboard in the dispatching office what job the dispatcher is currently filling. Thus they can easily check on the propriety of any exceptions to strict rotation.*

---

* The major cause of such misunderstandings is the screening program. When the Coast Guard declares a pier a "restricted area," the dispatchers are immediately notified, but sometimes the men learn of the Coast Guard's action only when they are passed over in the dispatch because they have no pass.

144

In making up gangs, dispatchers first select two men from the deck list. The first man picked is designated as the hatch tender—as long as the gang works together, this automatically makes him the gang boss—and the second man as the winch driver. To ships equipped with single winches, dispatchers send an additional winch driver from the Single Winch list. (Only five men are on this list—an indication of the decreasing number of such ships still in use.) Two men are then picked from the Sling Board, or Old Man's List. Finally, the six men who will work in the hold are picked from the Extra Stevedore Board. The dispatcher calls the names of the men in the gang over the public address system and gives the dispatching slip containing the names to the hatch tender, who presents it to the walking boss when the gang reaches the ship.

Make-up gangs are dispatched according to a definite pattern, so that the gangs with the greatest distance to go from the hall to the job will be dispatched first. This pattern can be discerned by checking table 4 against the map in figure 4. Gangs for special work, such as coal-pouring gangs, bulk-grain gangs, and oil-pumping gangs, whose compositions are set forth in the dispatching rules, are made up and dispatched in the same manner as standard gangs.

When the last man has been dispatched in any one period, the master peg remains next to his name, indicating that the next man on the list will be the first man dispatched in the next period. Sometimes it becomes necessary to send replacements from the hall between regular dispatching periods. When this is done, the master peg does not move from where it stopped at the end of the last period. Consequently, the men do not have to remain in the hall in order to prevent "losing their position" in the sense that the master peg might travel past their names between periods, which would, in effect, put them at the bottom of the list. Thus, a man working off the peg board can learn when he is likely to be sent out by coming to the hall and checking the position of the master peg on the board. Because there are so many men working off the peg board, they are requested not to telephone the harassed dispatchers to ask where the peg stopped.

Regular gangs are dispatched on a different and somewhat more complicated basis. These gangs are not "regular" in the sense that they work regularly for one employer, but are so designated because they are composed of men who work together as a team. When a regular gang does not have its full complement of members, it is filled by men listed on the peg board. They are dispatched according to the principle, "the low-earnings gang goes out first," rather than in rotation. A running account of each gang's earnings is kept by the dispatchers on the Gang Board shown in figure 3 on the right wall of the dispatching office. When a gang working a ship are told that their job will finish that day, the gang boss calls the hiring hall around 1:30 P.M. and reports the total earnings per gang member on the job they are just completing. The dispatcher taking the call adds this amount to the gang's cumulative earnings and records the new total alongside the gang's number on the Gang Board. To ensure that members of regular gangs will be as able as the men working off the peg board to keep the dispatching process under close scrutiny, several checks have been provided to maintain the accuracy of the figures on the Gang Board. When the gang boss comes back to the hall, he files a written form with the chief clerk on which he reports the total amount earned by his gang. Every few days the clerk checks the Gang Board against his records and corrects any errors in the totals which might have been made by the dispatchers on the basis of the phone conversations. Then at the end of each four-week period, the clerk prepares a report on the earnings

TABLE 4

ORDER IN WHICH GANGS ARE DISPATCHED FROM
THE SEATTLE LONGSHORE HIRING HALL

1. Everett[a]
2. Point Wells[b]
3. Blake Island[c]
4. Stimson Mill
   (#103 on map)
5. Nettleton Mill
   (#5 on map)
6. Ames Terminal
   (#6 on map)
7. Lilly Mill
   (#20 on map)
8. Fisher Flouring Co.
   Mill (#20 on map)
9. East Waterway
   (#23a, 23b, 23c
   on map)
10. Ford Plant
    (near #18 on map)

11. Pier 19
12. Pier 90
13. Pier 89
14. Pier 88
15. Pier 24
16. Pier 25
17. Pier 28
18. Pier 29
19. Pier 30
20. Pier 35
21. Pier 36
22. Pier 37
23. Pier 38
24. Pier 39
25. Pier 42S
26. Pier 42N

27. Pier 43
28. Pier 44
29. Pier 46
30. Pier 48
31. Pier 50
32. Pier 51
33. Pier 54
34. Pier 55
35. Pier 56
36. Pier 57
37. Pier 58[d]
38. Pier 65[e]
39. Pier 66[e]
40. Pier 69[e]
41. Lining gangs

a Everett is 26 miles north of Seattle. There is a longshore local in that port, and Seattle gangs are sent there only when the demand is extraordinary.

b Point Wells—an oil pumping station—is 14 miles north of Seattle.

c Blake Island Anchorage, 9 miles from the center of the Seattle waterfront, is a point at which dangerous cargo, such as explosives, is loaded. Men must go by launch to this anchorage.

d The hiring hall is approximately abreast of Pier 58.

e Piers 65, 66, and 69 are industrial piers and are served out of order because the urgency of completing jobs is less than for ships at the other piers.

Source: Chief dispatcher, Seattle, August, 1951.

146

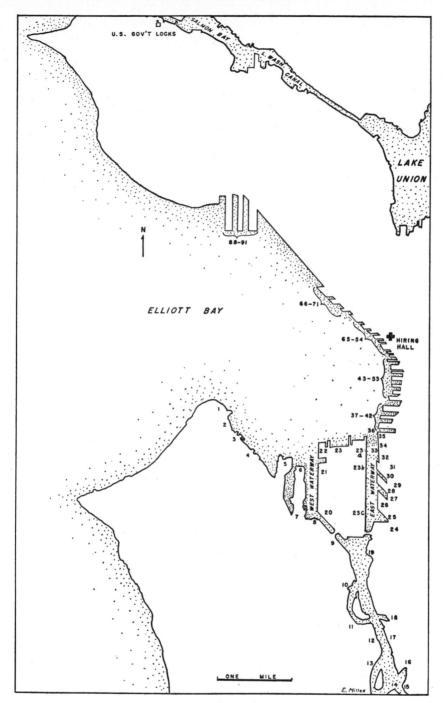

U.S. GOV'T LOCKS

SALMON BAY

L. WASH. CANAL

LAKE
UNION

N

88-91

66-71

ELLIOTT BAY

65-54

✚ HIRING
HALL

43-53

37-42

36
35
34
33
32
31
30
29
28
27
26
25
24

1
2
3
4
5
6
22 23
21
23
a
23b
23c

WEST WATERWAY

EAST WATERWAY

7
8
9
20

19

10

18

11

12
17

13
16

14 15

ONE   MILE

E. Miller

Fig. 4. The Port of Seattle

147

of all gangs, sends a copy to the Joint Labor Relations Committee and posts a copy in the hiring hall. At any time, members of regular gangs can see at a glance where their gang stands in relation to the others, since the Gang Board is easily visible from the hall.

The actual job of assigning regular gangs is carried out on a large blackboard, called the Order Board, shown in figure 5.* When employers call in and order gangs, the dispatcher finds the gang with the lowest earnings and then writes in next to that gang's number on the Order Board the name of the ship, the pier, and the starting time for work. When the port is busy, a gang calling in at 1:30 P.M. to report the end of their present job will call back at 3:30 P.M. and be assigned to another ship the next day. Individual members of regular gangs, being comparatively few in number, are permitted to call in to get the dispatching order of their gang if they do not want to bother coming to the hall. Figure 5 shows that when Gang No. 1 calls in they will be told to report to the SS *Planter* at Pier 44 at 8 A.M. on Monday. But there are not always enough jobs to keep all the regular gangs busy. When members of Gang No. 26 call in, the dispatcher will see by glancing at the Order Board that they have not been assigned new work and he will tell them to call in again at 3:30 P.M. on Monday, after new orders have been placed. The versatility of the system in keeping both the dispatchers and the men informed about all the special characteristics of the various jobs is indicated in the explanatory notes on figure 5.

---

* The board is on the back wall of the dispatching office, opposite the peg board. Its location is shown in figure 2, and the board is shown in detail in figure 5. The Order Board is on a slide, and can be pulled down for the purpose of making notations, and then raised to a position where it is easily seen through the windows above the peg board by the men in the hall.

1	Planter 44 8 am Mon	13	Jackson 91 w 7 pm Summit	25		37		49	
2	Planter 44 8 am Mon	14	Quick 51 8 am Mon	26	Call 3:30 Mon.	38		50	
3	Jackson 39 N 8 am Mon	15	vacation Call Aug. 10	27		39	Vac. Call 3:30 July 30 - Aug 12 Aug. 13	51	
4		16	Seafarer 48 8 am Mon	28	SW Pampas 48 8 am Mon.	40		52	
5		17		29		41		53	
6	Mormacland 88 8 am Mon.	18	Banana Parismina Term. 8 am Mon.	30	Vac. Call 3:30 July 30 to Aug 12 11th	42	Vac Call Aug 12 July 28 - Aug 11	54	
7	Patrick 39 S 1 PM Sun	19	Quick 51 8 am Mon.	31	SW Francisville 29 8 am Mon.	43	Vac Aug 2nd Call 16th	55	
8		20	Fogs into Water am Francisville 29 8 Mon.	32	Vac. to Aug. 11th	44	Vac Call 8-6 3:30	56	
9		21	Banana Parismina Term 8 am Mon.	33	Seafarer 48 8 am Mon.	45	Mormacland 88 8 am Sun	57	
10	Mormacland 88 8 am Mon	22	Seafarer 48 8 am Mon.	34		46	Planter 44 8 am Mon.	58	
11		23		35		47		59	
12		24		36	Planter 44 8 am Mon.	48	Patrick 39 S 1 PM Sun	60	

Fig. 5. The Order Board

148

After dispatchers have assigned all regular gangs and have made up the required number of additional gangs from the peg board, they start filling the orders for men needed for warehouse work. Dock workers are dispatched in rotation from the Trucker Board, shown in figure 3 on the right of the peg board. The jobs for which they are needed are listed on the Truckers' Order Board shown in figure 6. Men dispatched "to the ship"—who move cargo to and from the ship's side—are called first. These dock workers, like the longshoremen, continue to work the ship day after day until the job is completed. Men dispatched "to the floor"—who work in the pier warehouse—are assigned to the same job for only three days in succession, turning over on Monday and Thursday. This is done for two reasons: first, to equalize job opportunities for all truckers, and second, to preclude the possibility of men becoming regularly attached to a particular employer. The union insists on this arrangement because of its conviction that in earlier years men had to speed up to hold regular jobs in particular warehouses. Men working off the Trucker Board are dispatched to the docks and pier warehouses according to the same pattern as the make-up gangs.

One of the unique features of the dispatching system is that when there is plenty of work to go around, the men enjoy considerable freedom to choose their jobs. This can be shown by describing how a longshoreman who works off the peg board goes about pegging in. He comes into the hall at 7 A.M. and looks up at the Order Board to see where make-up gangs are needed and what the jobs are. Knowing the order in which gangs and men are dispatched, he is able to decide whether or not he should peg in immediately. Suppose he is in the hall on Sunday, August 6 (see figure 5).

•W sville 29 8 am/Mon.	61 Jackson 39 N 8 am/Sun			1– Make-up Pennsylvania 28 – 8 am/Sun
Call	62 Patrick 39 S 7 PM/Summite			1– Make-up Jackson 39 N – 8 am/Sun
aon 91 W 7 PM/Sun	63			4– Deck 2 sl.–16 liner 28 – 8 am/Sun
	64			6– Trimmers – P. 25 8 am Sun.
	65 Franciswille 29 SW 8 am/Mon.			1– Make up – Patrick 39 S 7 PM/Sun
3 30 Mon.	66			1– Barge gang– Sam. Dep. 8 am Mon
eafarer 48 8 am/Mon	67 Patrick 39 S 7 PM/Summite			1– Make up Pier 29 – 8 am Mon
lvania 28 8 am/Sun	68			1– Make up Pier 44 – 8 am Mon
	69 X X X X X X X X X			1– Make up Pier 48 – 8 am Mon.
	70			1– Make up Pier 51 – 8 am Mon.
	71 Pampas 48 SW 8 am/Mon.			

the Seattle Hiring Hall

He sees that the first make-up gang will be dispatched to Pier 25, and the job is trimming grain. If he particularly dislikes this work, he waits until the master peg has passed his name in the dispatch for this order and then pegs in. If he hasn't been dispatched when he sees that the gang is being made up to go to Pier 29, where they will have to work with logs in the water, he can "pull his peg" until the master peg is safely past, then peg in again. Dispatching is completed quickly and, even if he pulls his peg a number of times, he would not have to remain in the hall for more than about an hour in order to pick the job he wants to work on for the next few days.

Dock	Ship		Floor		Dock	Ship		Floor		Dock	Ship		Floor	
	B	T	B	T		B	T	B	T		B	T	B	T
Ames	1	1	3/2	9/5	P.30					P.58				
Fishers					P.35					P.66				
EWW			1	4	Wharf No.7					P.69				
Ford Plant					P.36	13/1 Grain Trucker	42/2 Trucker			P.88				
P.24			3 Jets	12	P.37			10	28	P.89				
P.25					P.39			5	12	P.90				
P.28					P.42 SOUTH			7	28	P.91				
P.29	5	3			P.42 NORTH			8	30		2 carps Ban. Term.				

63 Truckers – Banana Term. 9:00 AM   ← 8:00 a.m.

Figure 6

A dock worker who works off the Trucker Board can choose among jobs in the same way. Unloading bananas, for example, is heavy, unpleasant work, despite newly installed mechanical equipment, and some men pull their pegs when truckers are being dispatched to the banana terminal.

A member of a regular gang is less free to choose jobs. If he decides not to work a particular assignment, he must notify the dispatcher that a replacement is needed in his gang and the replacement stays with the gang until the job is completed. When the port is active, the gang member could be dispatched individually after all men on the peg board, but if work were slack he would probably have to wait until his gang completed its present job and was sent to a new one. Also, of course, a gang member who dodges disagreeable jobs eventually becomes unpopular with other members of his gang.

In addition to enjoying a remarkable freedom to choose a job that fits his physical capacities or his personal preferences, a longshoreman has

150

some control over the type of work group to which he belongs. He can decide, within limits, whether he wants to attach himself to a regular gang where he would work continuously with the same men, or whether he wants to work off the peg board where the gang will be composed of different men each time he is dispatched. Many longshoremen prefer the variety of working with new and different gang members and the freedom of not having to report for work every morning. On the other hand, a long-shoreman who wants to be in a regular gang has only to find one which does not have a full complement of men and which will accept him as a member—not a difficult task. Also, if a group of men who are friends want to work regularly together, they can form a new regular gang by going before the local's executive board and requesting the new classification. When so authorized, the man chosen as the gang boss informs the dispatchers, who strike an average between the highest and lowest earnings on the Gang Board and assign that earnings position to the new gang.

Extra Men

Since the number of men registered in the hall is consciously kept down to a point where the men are assured of working regularly, many occasions arise when there are not enough regular men to fill all the employers' orders. Traditionally, the parties have maintained a reserve to draw on during these peak periods by giving an additional group of men what might be described as "limited registration," thus assuring them of priority in hiring after all the registered men. Historically, the number of these "permit" men fluctuated as shipping activity picked up or declined. After World War II, the combination of a sharp drop in shipping activity and the influx of returning service men who claimed their right to return to their prewar registered status created a situation where for the first time there was an excess of registered men. After the war, the number of "permit" men gradually dwindled away as the men in this group found they were not getting enough work to justify staying in the industry. It was not until the Korean War emergency arose suddenly that a reserve was again found necessary. Since the beginning of the Korean War, some 400 to 600 men have been listed on the Temporary Labor Pool Board set up in a smaller hall on the second floor of the building. They are dispatched after the registered men according to the same principle of rotation. Whenever a pool man is dispatched to replace a member of a regular or make-up gang, he stays with that gang until the job is finished. While pool men are dispatched either as longshoremen or dock workers, depending on the need, some pool men are qualified to operate winches and to function as hatch tenders. Consequently, a few temporary gangs can be made up entirely from their board. The need for the pool was expected to disappear with the cessation of hostilities in Korea, so pool men were not given permanent registration, nor are they members of the union. To cover their *pro rata* share of the expense of maintaining the hall, they pay a monthly fee set by the Joint Labor Relations Committee.

When unusually heavy demands for men have exhausted the supply of both the registered men and the pool men, Seattle dispatchers draw on a number of sources for casual workers. Fishermen and other maritime workers, historically a source of longshoremen everywhere, have provided a dependable supply of men who know ships and rigging and who fit easily into longshoring. Three fishermen's unions have offices on the second floor of the building housing the hiring hall, and the dispatchers usually call there first to ask the locals to send down any unemployed fishermen. And when some union is on strike in the area, the dispatchers call that union office to see if some of the strikers would like a day's work on the waterfront.* The State Employment Service has a casual-labor office in Seattle which can provide men, and Army personnel from nearby Fort Lawton are sometimes dispatched from the hiring hall during their off-duty hours. If all other sources are exhausted, dispatchers call on a private employment agency which charges its clients 50 cents per referral. Casual workers, unlike men listed on the Temporary Labor Pool Board, pay no fee for the services rendered them by the hall. If a casual worker is dispatched as a replacement for a gang member, however, he has the right to remain with the gang until the job is finished.

Occasionally, there are so many ships in port that there are not enough gangs to go around even though enough casual workers are available, because of the shortage of skilled men to operate the winches. When this happens, the employers call together an allocations committee, which has the job of seeing that the available gangs are shared equitably among the various stevedoring firms. The employers' association has a staff member who daily determines the number of gangs needed for each 24-hour period, keeps track of which gangs are working on which ship, and attempts to forecast labor requirements as far ahead as possible. When he sees there will be a shortage which he cannot alleviate by telephoning the various

---

* The dispatchers told me that among the best workers who had been sent to the hall by other unions were ten members of the embalmers' union. One employer made the following comment on this judgment: "It may well be, under our present rate of production, that the ten members of the embalmers' union were among the best workers secured from the outside because the rapidity of movement evidenced on the ships might have been somewhat comparable to the movement evidenced by other bodies they had worked with in the past, and so they felt completely at home."

152

employers and asking them to cut down the size of their orders,* he calls the stevedores who make up the allocation committee, and they determine the number of gangs each employer shall have dispatched to him.

From this description of the hiring hall, it is obvious that the system is primarily oriented to satisfying the longshoremen's desire to enjoy job security and, at the same time, to enjoy the widest latitude in choosing jobs. It is also apparent that the influential role of the union in the operation of the hall makes for an unusually high degree of union security. But how well does the hall serve the interests of the other two groups which have a stake in its operation—the employers and the community?

---

* Sometimes certain employers—particularly the stevedoring firm at the Army's port of embarkation pier—are suspected of ordering more gangs than they need, a situation reminiscent of the labor hoarding by shipyards during World War II.

6

Who Wants the Hiring Hall?

An Injury to One Is an Injury to All.—Labor slogan.

In Seattle, the hiring hall is the heart of the longshoring industry. Because of its key position, the hall could not survive if it did not satisfy at least the minimum needs of the four groups who have an interest in the hiring system, and the mere fact that the present Seattle system has lasted for twenty years seems to indicate that it does meet these basic requirements. To answer the question of whether the hiring hall meets more than the bare minimum requirements of a workable system, we can use the check list of what a hiring system is supposed to do for each of the four groups.

The Employers

Where labor requirements fluctuate as widely as they do in longshoring, the most important objection raised by employers to regulating the supply of labor arises from a fear that an adequate labor force will not be available during periods of peak activity. The first question to consider, then, is how the hiring hall system has affected the supply of labor available to Seattle employers.

When, in 1934, union delegates began participating in meetings of the Joint Labor Relations Committee and sharing in decisions on the size of the labor force, the parties had the distinct advantage of being able to draw on the experience that both employers and workers had gained in watching the operation of the old employers' hall for more than a decade. With this experience to guide them on the number of regular men required, and with the depression bringing to the waterfront hordes of unemployed —both skilled and unskilled—who could be hired as casual workers, it is not surprising that the record contains no evidence of labor shortages before World War II.

154

Even then, the causes of the reported shortages were not attributable to the hiring system, but rather to the acute general shortage of manpower which typified Northwest industry during the war. World War II brought great expansion in shipbuilding and aircraft production to the Puget Sound area, and men were gradually attracted away from the waterfront to the safer and easier jobs in war plants which mushroomed almost overnight. The long work week in the war plants further cut down the number of men available on the waterfront, because war workers who spent six or seven days a week on their regular jobs were no longer interested in coming down to the hiring hall for a day's work as a casual worker. Under these unfavorable conditions, the value of the joint machinery for administering the hall was clearly demonstrated in the way the parties coöperated to recruit enough longshoremen to meet the greatly expanded needs of the port. This was accomplished on a coast-wide basis through the Maritime Industry Board, and locally through the Joint Labor Relations Committee.[1] During the war period, the committee was almost entirely engaged in desperate attempts of both employers and the union to secure more men.*

When the war ended in 1945, and port activity shrank back to a peace-time level, the wartime shortages were gradually replaced by an excess of registered men. Faced with low earnings, as too few jobs were being shared by too many men, almost 800 longshoremen left the industry in 1946. During this cutback, Local 19 proposed that some men who had been working in the industry during the war, and who had shown themselves to be good workers and potentially good union members, be added to the registered list. The employers' response to this proposal reflects their complete acceptance of the philosophy underlying the hiring hall— that the labor force must be limited. They opposed the motion, pointing out that returning service men were already swelling the labor force:

> . . . it would be very unwise to attach more men to the industry as this could only result in trying to spread the little work that there [is] among more people and there would be the result of unemployment claims, dissatisfaction, etc.[2]

The registration list was left relatively unchanged and no shortages were reported to the Joint Labor Relations Committee until the summer

---

* The minutes for July 12, 1944, contain a letter from the Maritime Industry Board defending themselves against criticisms from the Seattle JLRC that they were not attacking the labor shortage problem vigorously enough. "The Army, the Navy, the War Shipping Administration, the Office of Defense Transportation, the War Manpower Commission, the United States Employment Service, the Waterfront Employers Association and the ILWU are all working on the manpower shortage."

of 1950, when the Korean War began. The immediate response of the parties to another war emergency again demonstrated the hiring system's ability to adjust the labor supply to changing needs. A special meeting of the committee was called and the following motion was passed with the understanding that the union must refer the action to the union membership for final approval:

> The Labor Relations Committee shall immediately arrange for the recruiting of a temporary pool of men in the Port of Seattle in such a number as may be needed for use during the emergency. Such men shall not be placed on the registered list and shall only be dispatched when men on the registered list are not available. The temporary pool shall be terminated at the request of either the Union or the Employers.[3]

The union membership approved the action at a meeting that night, the pool board was set up the following day, and soon after some 650 new men were assigned numbers for the Temporary Labor Pool board. In setting up the pool, the parties agreed that the additional men would be recruited through recommendations of longshoremen on the registered list. This approach to the recruitment problem has been explained by the head of the employers' association as follows:

> It was our thinking that had we opened the door through newspaper advertisements, an approach to the State Employment Service, or elsewhere of a public nature, we would have received literally thousands of applicants as it is pretty generally known that the longshore hourly average is somewhere in the neighborhood of $2.50 overall. We believed that it would have taken a great deal of time to screen the group and as our objective was to immediately fill the needs of the Port with reasonably effective extra men, we felt that we would not be far off base in taking recommendations from the longshoremen themselves.*

Through the addition of these temporary-pool men, the port was able to keep supplies flowing steadily to the Korean battle front. The pool was so successful that no mention of a labor shortage appears in the minutes of the Joint Labor Relations Committee until a year later.†

---

* D. W. Cornell, Washington Area manager, PMA, letter to the writer, April 18, 1952. "Screening" in this instance refers to ensuring that the men were physically capable of performing longshore work, and were determined to make themselves regularly available. In September, 1950, at the request of the Army, 200 more men were added.

† There was one exception. One very brief shortage was reported in September, 1950, when the dispatchers were not able to make up enough gangs, because many skilled workers—winch drivers and hatch tenders—were working as hold men at the Army ammunition dump about 20 miles north of Seattle. Because of the penalty

(Note continued on following page.)

In July, 1951, the employers reported that they were having to resort to the services of the allocations committee far too often, and that even after a "fair sharing" of gangs among employers, there still appeared to be a constant shortage. The cause of the shortage, they pointed out, was that many registered longshoremen were not making themselves available regularly. Payroll records covering the first quarter of 1951 showed that out of 1,400 registered men, 179 had no earnings at all in that period, and another 126 had earned less than $500. The employers pointed to the inefficiency of permitting 20 per cent of the men to remain on the registered list when they were "guilty" of low earnings—a traditional ground for deregistration because it usually indicates that men are not reporting in regularly. The employers then moved that the committee check on how many of these low earners were ill or injured,* and that any man who could not offer a reasonable explanation for his absence be dropped from the list. The union members of the committee concurred, and also offered to recommend to the membership of Local 19 that no members be granted traveling cards authorizing them to visit other ports while the shortage lasted. The committee also decided that until enough new men were registered, no more than six regular gangs would be permitted to go on vacation at any one time. These temporary measures alleviated the shortage while new men were given permanent registration to replace the low earners.

Thus, a review of the 20 years of experience Seattle employers have had with the jointly operated hiring hall shows that the system provides an orderly adjustment of the labor force to meet changing needs in peace time, and has proved its adaptability to emergency conditions by operating to the advantage of both parties in two wars. An additional feature of the system which is designed to ensure that enough men will be available is the requirement that individual longshoremen assume the responsibility of having replacements sent to their jobs when they are unable to work. The dispatching rules, a copy of which is distributed to each longshoreman, provide:

> Being on the job is the responsibility of the man dispatched.
> If sickness prevents reporting on the job, the hiring hall must be called: Eliot 7844, for a replacement . . .

---

rate for handling explosives, they could draw $3.64 an hour as hold man, instead of the $2.02 rate for deck men on commercial cargo. The shortage was immediately solved by a JLRC ruling that dispatchers must fill the needs of Seattle employers before dispatching men to the Army dump.

* There is a large blackboard in the hiring hall on which the hospital or home addresses of sick or injured men are recorded for the information of their friends. It is not always kept up to date, but in August, 1951—a month after this proposal was made—I counted 81 names on the board.

> Failure to report on the job after being dispatched will result in your being cited on the blackboard in the hiring hall to appear before the Grievance Committee which meets in the Union office every Wednesday at 2:00 P.M. Failure to appear before the Grievance Committee will prevent dispatching until member does appear.

This rule not only has the advantage to employers of shifting the responsibility for minimizing the effects of absenteeism to someone else—an advantage for which stevedores might well be envied by many other employers—but it also shifts to the union the job of disciplining offenders. The union judges the cases and fines or suspends men who fail to "replace themselves"; the employers become involved only if they think the penalties are too light or when the union requests the Joint Labor Relations Committee to deregister men for repeated offenses.

Another feature of the system—the necessity of having to maintain an allocations committee—is a nuisance, but Seattle employers apparently do not regard this concomitant of limiting the labor force as a serious evil. They have shown by their own actions that they want to avoid the chronic labor surplus which could obviate the need to share gangs in peak periods. The costs of such a surplus—unemployment claims, dissatisfactions—would be greater than the cost of maintaining an allocations committee.

The hiring hall adequately passes the test of providing employers with a large enough labor force to fill their needs. The next question is, whether the hiring hall supplies employers with enough men who have the necessary skills to fill their particular job requirements. Under ordinary circumstances, the hiring hall provides an admirable answer, because men are listed on the peg board according to their skills and abilities, and are dispatched according to their job classifications as deck men, sling men, lift truck drivers, and so forth. Before men are assigned to these classifications, employers have ample opportunity to observe their performance while the men serve in an apprentice category, and a man's classification can be changed if he does not measure up to the job. Strong presumptive evidence exists that Seattle employers are reasonably well satisfied with the skills of men sent to them from the hall, because most registered longshoremen have worked on the waterfront for 10 to 15 years and the employers have never proposed setting up a training program in periods of normal activity. But when a sudden and sustained need for a much larger labor force arose during the two wars, employers found that not enough extra men were trained as winch operators and hatch tenders to enable the dispatchers to increase the number of make-up gangs as they were needed. In World War II, and again in the Korean War, the Joint Labor

158

Relations Committee had to set up training programs, and it became increasingly evident that the industry had to face the problem of improving skills if employers were to have an adequate reserve of skilled men for emergencies.[4]

With these two experiences behind them, the parties included a clause in the 1951 agreement providing that joint committees be created in each port to establish qualifications for promotions and to pass on such promotions. Perhaps out of this first step of offering workers clear-cut incentives to improve their skills will come a formal and permanent training program. Nevertheless, an inherent disadvantage of the hiring hall as it has operated is its failure to produce automatically enough skilled workers to cover continuing emergencies.

A more serious disadvantage of the system for the employers is their inability, under the strict rotation rule, to hire men on a permanent basis. Rotating the entire labor force, employers contend, results in a serious loss in efficiency. It will be recalled that in the old hiring system run by the employers before 1934, about 800 men were employed regularly by the larger companies as members of "steady" or company gangs, and that only about 600 men were registered in the hall and dispatched in rotation. In 1935, the union insisted that company gangs be eliminated and, since then, both longshoremen and dock workers have worked for one employer only long enough to complete the particular job for which they are dispatched.[5]

The employers vigorously opposed the elimination of steady gangs and, after several unsuccessful attempts to reverse the policy in negotiations with the union, they raised the issue again in the 1944 War Labor Board case. Holding that restoration of steady gangs was their most important demand, they asserted:

> . . . familiarity promotes efficiency and sound industrial relations, and the cessation of continuous employment of the same group by the same employer has caused a heavy loss in productive capacity. . . . Such continuity of employment decreases the burden of dispatching, relieves the need for reporting to the hiring hall, and lessens travel time.[6]

The union conceded that steady gangs would increase efficiency for certain employers and eliminate hiring problems for certain longshoremen, but argued that these very virtues emphasized the countervailing vices of favoritism and inequality of work opportunities:

> Equalization is the fundamental objective of the union, and equalization includes equal requirements of reporting, equal

division of the desirable jobs, equal acceptance of unpleasant tasks, equal regularity as well as quantity of employment, and equal sharing of the work when times are bad.[7]

The War Labor Board decided that in the face of the ten-year history of operation without steady gangs, the employers' arguments did not outweigh the union's position to an extent which warranted destroying the existing system, and ruled that the status quo be respected. It might be said that the board "decided" the issue but did not settle it. It was raised again in the negotiations that preceded the 1948 strike, and even during the "new look" period employers have spoken of their inability to use steady gangs as their main criticism of the hiring system.

The concern of the employers seems to be two-fold. First, they want to have enough control over their working force to obtain satisfactory work performance, and they hold that steady gangs are necessary to do this. Second, they feel that any system which involves rotating the entire working force is less efficient and, therefore, more costly than one permitting a core of regularly employed men. Obviously, an employer has less control over men who work for him only a few days at a time than over steady employees, but it should be recognized that in the Seattle system the employers are not without some means of control. Their ability to hire willing workers is lessened, but not wholly destroyed, by delegating to the Joint Labor Relations Committee the decision of whether or not to add certain new men to the registered list. Also, the concomitant of selection, the right of discharge, is provided for the employers in the collective bargaining agreement:

> The employer shall have the right to discharge any man for incompetence, insubordination or failure to perform the work as required in conformance with the provisions of the Agreement.
> Such longshoremen shall not be dispatched to such employer until his case shall have been heard and disposed of before the Port Labor Relations Committee, and no other employer shall refuse employment to such longshoreman on the basis of such discharge.

That this clause does, in fact, give employers a meaningful right to discharge men for cause is borne out in the minutes of the Joint Labor Relations Committee, which contain numerous instances of men and gangs submitting grievances claiming unfair discharge. In some cases the men's claims were upheld and they were awarded back pay for the time they had lost; in others, the claim of the discharging employer was upheld by the committee. Occasionally, where men were repeated offenders, they were deregistered. If the union members of the Joint Labor Relations Committee had refused to concur in any of these decisions, the employers could have carried the case up through various levels of the grievance procedure; but the minutes covering the "new look" period contained no instances where the committee found it necessary to resort even to the next level. The evidence is inconclusive, but it suggests that the Seattle disciplinary system resembles that of other unionized industries and that Seattle employers enjoy as much freedom to discipline men as any employers who deal with a strong union.

Furthermore, the nature of longshoring makes it possible for an employer who is dissatisfied with the pace of work to locate and remedy the cause even though he does not have steady employees. According to a tradition in West Coast longshoring, men "meet the hook"—they move cargo as fast as the ship's gear brings it or takes it away. If the cargo is not moving fast enough, presumptive evidence exists that the winch operator or the lift truck operator is the bottleneck. As far as hold men are concerned, it is unlikely that individual men will consistently loaf on the job because, as Foisie, Stern,[8] and others have indicated, there is heavy group pressure on each member of a hold gang to do his share of the work, since work not performed by him must be absorbed by the other gang members. If the entire gang were slowing down, their low productivity would be evident and they could be discharged within the terms of the contract for "incompetence, insubordination, or failure to perform the work."*

The employers' contention that rotation of the entire labor force increases costs could be evaluated by examining the record of productivity before and after steady gangs were abolished. In various arbitration and fact-finding cases before 1948, the employers charged that efficiency had declined. The arbitrators and fact-finders conceded the plausibility of the charge but judged the evidence unreliable.[9] Even if the productivity figures of the employers were accepted, the record is inconclusive as far as isolating the cause of a decline in productivity is concerned. According to the only survey covering Seattle—a study made in 1939 by the accounting firm of Price, Waterhouse and Company—the volume of tons handled per man-hour in the port fell 10.5 per cent between 1933 and 1938.[10] But the reëstablishment of a strong union and the hostile relationship between the parties during those years would probably have caused a drop in productivity of this magnitude whether or not steady gangs had been abolished.

The union's unwillingness to compromise on this issue stems from two

---

* It is true that the employers were unable to counteract the slowdown in Seattle during the 1948 80-day injunction by wholesale discharges, but conditions during that period can hardly be considered to have been normal.

factors. The longshoremen have traditionally associated steady gangs with a speed-up, and the promise of union organizers to eliminate steady gangs was one of the principal reasons for the immediate success of the union's first organizing campaign in 1933. A Seattle delegate reported to the second ILWU convention that Seattle longshoremen considered the elimination of steady gangs as their most valuable gain through unionism. This change, he said,

> . . . has proved very satisfactory in Seattle as all gangs have become familiar with the working of all types of cargo and it has also helped considerably in stopping the speed-up in order to be preferred on a good dock or job.[11]

The continued existence of the "new look" should reduce the men's fear of a speed-up, but their other objection to steady gangs is probably more permanent. This is a deep reluctance to divide the union into what would amount to first- and second-class membership. Having learned in the old employers' system that steady gangs consistently made higher earnings than hall gangs, in spite of the employers' conscious effort to keep earnings equal, union members are afraid that dividing the membership into steady and casual workers would, in periods of declining employment, generate serious internal conflicts and weaken the cohesiveness of the union. It is unlikely that the union will retreat from its adamant position on this issue, and the employers will probably remain dissatisfied with their inability to secure steady employees.*

One feature which was of great importance to New York employers under the shape-up requires only passing comment in a discussion of the hiring hall. Seattle employers have never based their case for reinstituting steady gangs on the ground that the hall sent them undependable or dishonest workers. Indeed, the operation of the hiring hall removes the very aspects of a casual-labor market which attracted criminals to the New York waterfront. As the head of the West Coast employers' association has stated:

> . . . the hiring hall in our opinion has the effect of improving the character of the men themselves; because it gives them greater stability of employment and earnings, it gives them dignity.[12]

Theft on the New York scale is unheard of on the Seattle waterfront

---

* Another feature of the system which conceivably results in some loss in efficiency is the acceptance by the employers of the philosophy that the industry should "take care of its own." However, there has been no suggestion that the older and injured men should be jettisoned. In fact, Seattle employers take pride in the industry's record of protecting the jobs of disabled men.

162

and, while pilferage exists—as it does wherever longshore, trucking, or warehouse work is performed—losses through pilferage constitute a minor problem to Seattle employers.* The willingness of the employers to rely on the recommendations of registered longshoremen as the best method of recruiting new workers reveals their respect for the judgment and integrity of their employees.

A final consideration of importance in evaluating the hiring system is its impact on the employers' desire to obtain workers under conditions not unilaterally imposed by the union. The fourteen-year struggle between the employers and the ILWU to get control of the hiring hall shows how acutely both perceived the importance of the union's participation in the operation of the hall as a basic element in the strength of the union. Through the union's strength, the longshoremen were able to demand from the employers wages and other conditions which made the men the envy of many other industrial workers. As long as the employers remained basically opposed to accepting the union on equal terms, they viewed the union's part in the hiring hall, as well as the union's contract demands, as being unilaterally imposed on them. Even under the "new look" some employers still feel they are at the mercy of the ILWU, but there are clear indications that the majority see benefits in dealing with a strong and responsible union.

When hearings were held in April, 1953, on proposed revisions of the Taft-Hartley Act, West Coast waterfront employers had an excellent opportunity, had they so desired, to offer amendments which would have excluded the ILWU from participating in the hiring hall, as well as proposals which would have crippled strong unionism in general. Instead, the testimony of J. Paul St. Sure, president of the Pacific Maritime Association, before the Senate Labor Committee was, on the whole, an effort to persuade the Congress to leave the maritime industry alone. He assured the senators several times that all West Coast maritime hiring halls were operating well and in complete compliance with the act: "Insofar as the so-called Lundeberg formula is concerned, or so far as the joint operation of hiring halls with the ILWU is concerned, we believe each formula works satisfactorily."[13] St. Sure dwelt at length, with justifiable pride, on the many advantages the hiring hall gives the men. He pointed to the

---

* The employers have questioned this evaluation of the importance of pilferage, but in my interviews with employers, union officials, and longshoremen, and in the minutes of the JLRC, pilferage was rarely mentioned. The contention of the employers was that the lack of notations of pilferage in the minutes is not indicative of a lack of pilferage or whole package loss. In the first place, employers say, many other groups of workers get a crack at the cargo other than the longshoremen, and secondly, the great majority of pilferage and loss of whole package cargo can never be pinned down to an individual or group. In any event, the employers do not attribute pilferage to the hiring system.

high earnings and good working conditions enjoyed by the longshoremen and concluded: "The longshoreman has dignity and respect. The west-coast longshoreman has a good home and lives there; he is not a wanderer on the waterfront." (During this part of his testimony, Senator Taft, who was present, might well have wondered if the speaker were not a representative of the ILWU.) St. Sure summarized the employers' position on the halls as follows:

> The employers I represent must treat the hiring hall as an institution highly desired by employees because of economic advantages to them which are separate from the matter of union security. Any attempt to do away with the hiring hall would result in prolonged strife and economic chaos in the industry. The operation of hiring halls on the west coast clearly demonstrates that they can operate lawfully and provide the inherent advantages that I have indicated the longshoremen find in their halls.[14]

Taken alone, this statement does not indicate unqualified enthusiasm among employers for the halls, but merely a recognition that the longshoremen insist on having them. But St. Sure's other recommendations show a positive approval both of the hiring hall and of strong unionism.* Commenting on proposals to outlaw industry-wide bargaining, St. Sure stressed the absolute necessity of permitting coast-wide bargaining in the West Coast maritime industry, and addressing himself to a suggestion that government-operated halls might be a proper answer to the maritime hiring problem, he stated the West Coast employers' strong opposition.[15] Even more significantly, he urged that the Taft-Hartley Act be amended to protect the union from harassment under the law's union-shop provisions. He offered the Pacific Maritime Association's proposal that the ILWU be permitted to enter into an agreement which would give them a union shop covering men on the registered list:

> We are simply suggesting that the hiring hall procedure in effect take the place of the direct employer in an ordinary indus-

---

* Interestingly enough, the ILWU shares St. Sure's approval of dealing with a powerful, well-organized opponent. Harry Bridges said:
> We find it important, in making the machinery [of the hall] work, that there be a strong employers' association . . . Joint policing of the Agreement is essential to its successful operation. Moreover, the Association disciplines its members, just as the union does its members. The result is a substantial uniformity in policy and program among the employers which makes for a minimum of disputes, and for harmonious labor relations.

International Longshoremen's and Warehousemen's Union, *Statement by Harry Bridges . . . before New York State Crime Commission* (1953), mimeographed.

try and therefore the hiring hall be used as the basis for the establishment of a union shop. . . . Otherwise, actually we feel that these unions—perhaps I should not argue so strenuously from their point of view, but we have to live with them—these unions are denied the right by reason of the character of the industry in which they work of ever getting a union shop.

Thus, on the whole, the hiring hall operates satisfactorily for the employers. It meets the test of giving them an adequate supply of longshoremen, both in the quantitative and qualitative sense. The prohibition against steady gangs is disadvantageous to some employers to some indeterminate degree, but even in the absence of steady gangs the employers are generally able to obtain satisfactory work performance from the men sent out from the hall in as high a degree as most employers who deal with a strong union. The presence of a strong union in the industry has undoubtedly raised labor costs by bringing constant pressure on employers to raise wages and improve other working conditions, but the employers' ultimate acceptance of unionism and their willingness to argue the case for strengthening the union's authority indicate that they no longer consider the union to be unilaterally imposng the conditions under which they operate.

The Longshoremen

It was suggested in chapter 3 that, if a hiring system is to serve the interests of workers, it should provide them with enough information about alternative jobs to permit an informed choice among all possibilities open to them. This implies an ability to make reasonably reliable estimates of the earnings and other conditions which are important to workers. These other conditions include the chance to achieve economic security; to control their own affairs; to receive fair treatment by management; to work with compatible fellow workers; to preserve their self-respect and to enjoy satisfactory social status; and to use their abilities in ways that seem most appropriate to them.

A mere description of the Seattle hiring hall shows clearly how well it satisfies the first test. Since the hall constitutes the "labor market" for the stevedoring industry, concentrating all the information about jobs in one place puts the worker in the enviable position of being able to make a truly informed decision whether he should sell his labor as a longshoreman. He can find out about all available jobs on the waterfront from the various boards in the hall, he knows that working conditions on all jobs are those itemized in the agreement, and he knows how much he can expect to earn (current earnings are posted in the hall). The only major variable he must estimate in order to decide whether he wants to make his living as a longshoreman is the volume of future activity in the industry—an estimate facing a worker choosing a job in any industry.

Furthermore, a worker knows that if he decides to remain in the industry he will have an equal chance at all jobs, and that he will enjoy both basic elements of economic security—protection against losing his job and relatively high income. Using the same criterion that was applied to the earnings of New York longshoremen, earnings in Seattle are more than "adequate." According to the City Worker's Family Budget, a Seattle longshoreman with a wife and two children would have had to earn about $4,000 in 1951 to sustain "a decent and healthful level of living." In 1951, more than 70 per cent of Seattle longshoremen earned more than $4,000.

TABLE 5

ANNUAL EARNINGS OF REGISTERED LONGSHOREMEN*

SEATTLE, 1951

Annual earnings in dollars	Number of men	Per cent of total
5,000 and over	756	50.6
4,000 to 4,999	336	22.4
3,000 to 3,999	189	12.7
2,000 to 2,999	95	6.3
1,000 to 1,999	75	5.0
0 to 999	44	3.0
Total	1,495	100.0

The high earnings possible in longshoring make especially important the ability of a longshoreman to hold his job. In Seattle, the two ways in which a man's claim to his job can be adversely affected are first, being discharged by a particular employer, and second, and far more important, by being deregistered. If a man discharged by a particular employer "for cause" feels that he has been unjustly treated, he has the protection of a clearly defined grievance procedure and the backing of a strong union in processing his grievance. A Seattle longshoreman is in a better position than workers in other industries as far as discipline is concerned, because he can be dispatched to other longshore jobs while his grievance is being

* I am indebted to the Washington Area branch of the Pacific Maritime Association for running off these wage data in intervals which could be compared with the earnings of New York's longshoremen made available through the New York State board of inquiry's investigations. In 1951, of 72 occupations for which the U.S. Department of Commerce published average annual earnings, only one (security and commodity brokers, dealers and exchanges) showed earnings above $5,000. *Survey of Current Business,* 32 (July, 1952), 22.

processed by the Joint Labor Relations Committee, rather than being removed from the payroll.*

The same rules hold for deregistration. Because removal from the registered list is of such vital importance, special attention was paid in examining the minutes of the Joint Labor Relations Committee (for 1944–1951) to any clues that men had been dropped from the registered list for arbitrary reasons. During those years, eleven longshoremen appealed the action of the committee in deregistering them.

Anthony Able† was dropped from the roster "at the union's request" on September 17, 1947. The reason was not given. One month later, Able appeared before the committee asking reinstatement. At this meeting, he alleged that he had had a disagreement with a union membr while loading ammunition at Mukilteo during the war and had been denied membership in the union for no other reason. The union members of the committee, on the other hand, charged that Able was a "trouble-maker, both on the job and in the office," and stated that his deregistration had been recommended by the executive board of Local 19 and confirmed by the membership for that reason. The employers moved to hold the matter over pending an investigation and at the committee's next meeting:

> Employers stated they were still considering this individual case but wished to call the Union's attention to the necessity for a full explanation in those cases where the Union recommended that a man be dropped from the roster for other [reasons] than lack of earnings.[16]

At a special meeting which concerned other matters a few days later, the employers moved to reinstate Able "on the grounds that he had been dropped without sufficient cause." At this and the following meeting, the parties failed to agree, and the case was held over again. One month after Able had first requested reinstatement, the employers moved to take the dispute to the Area Labor Relations Committee, but the minutes of subsequent meetings contain no reference to the case until two years later. In January, 1951, Able again wrote the committee asking reinstatement. He appeared at the meeting an January 31 and before the executive board of Local 19 in April. In June, the membership voted to reinstate him, and on June 6, 1951, he was given full registration status and accepted as a member of the union.

---

* The current agreement extends the protection of the same grievance procedure to nonunion men who claim unjust treatment by the dispatchers.

† The names used in these cases are fictitious. Except for Jones and King, all were permit men, that is, they were not members of the union but were in a kind of apprentice classification, working under a permit from the union.

H. B. Baker was dropped on April 7, 1948, for nonpayment of dues.*
The committee heard his explanation on May 12, and he was reinstated
at that meeting.

Nicholas Charles wrote the Waterfront Employers Association in May,
1948, alleging that he had been dropped from the list after inequitable
treatment by the union in his application for membership. He was invited
to appear before the committee at its meeting on May 12, but when he
failed to appear his case was dropped.

Steve Douglas appeared before the committee on May 26, 1948, to
appeal deregistration. Payroll records and his own statement showed
excessively low earnings in 1945, 1946, and 1947. In 1945, he had left
the industry for a long period without getting a leave of absence from the
committee, and two complaints of "failure to replace himself" were in the
record. It was also alleged that several times he had caused a disturbance
in the dispatching hall and in the union office when intoxicated. The committee unanimously confirmed the previous action by canceling his registration.

Ronald Evans had been dropped because of low earnings. When he
submitted evidence on May 9, 1948, of sickness in his family which had
prevented him from working, he was reinstated.

James Fox and *Grant Green* were dropped from the register on July 7,
1948. They appeared before the committee and requested reconsideration
on August 11, but the committee held that according to their own statement they had voluntarily left the industry for other work, and the original
action would stand.

J. J. Hull was dropped on December 8, 1948, for nonpayment of dues.
His dues paid up, he was reinstated December 15.

R. C. Ingersoll had been dropped from the list because of having left
the industry but showed that this absence was "involuntary" and was reinstated on December 22, 1948.

Howard Jones had been deregistered because of low earnings, but presented evidence of illness and was restored to his original registration.

Ramsey King, whose registration number indicated that he had joined
the industry in 1936 or 1937, requested reinstatement in June, 1950. The
minutes show that the union presented "a statement and earnings records
demonstrating reasons for Mr. King's cancellation from the list of registered longshoremen." The employers moved to restore his registration but
the matter seems to have been dropped after the next meeting (June 28,
1950) when the union took the position that "Mr. King is not a member

---

* Dues of permit men, like the fee later charged temporary pool men, were equal
to a *pro rata* share of the cost of maintaining the hiring hall.

of the union and has not performed work in the industry for over two years."

The fact that in more than eight years only eleven men out of about 800 who were deregistered considered the action arbitrary enough to appeal the decision, and that all but two men received satisfactory treatment on their appeals without delay, indicates that the Seattle system, on the whole, provides adequate protection against being arbitrarily dropped from the list. But the minutes show that the appeal procedure did not afford adequate or speedy relief in two cases—those of Able and King—and that in each of these cases the relationship between the aggrieved man and the union appears to have been the key factor, thus making these two cases particularly important. If more information were available, it might support the union's position in these cases, but even if the full facts showed that the union had used its influence to drive Able and King out of the industry on arbitrary grounds, the system would not stand completely condemned. The Seattle appeal procedures suffer only from the same limitations as those in other industries—if either the employer or the union moves to discharge a man and the other party will not defend him, the existence of a formal, reasonable procedure cannot by itself ensure his reinstatement.* Nevertheless, the cases of Able and King suggest that procedural safeguards against arbitrary deregistration could be considerably strengthened by more clearly specifying the grounds for expulsion from the industry.

It is conceivable, of course, that other men may also have felt they were arbitrarily deregistered, but did not protest the action. Even if this happened, which in view of the success achieved in most appeals seems unlikely, it would not necessarily imply a weakness in the procedures. No grievance system will protect those who fail to use it. On the other hand, if anyone decided not to appeal his case because he was afraid to question either the union's or the committee's action, this *would* reflect a serious weakness in the system. Interviews with employers, union officials, longshoremen, and staff members of the National Labor Relations Board in Seattle, brought forth no hints that intimidation of this sort is a factor on the Seattle waterfront. Able's behavior supports this contention, because he made full use of the appeal procedure even after a majority of the membership of Local 19 had voted to exclude him. It is reasonable to conclude that Seattle longshoremen are at least as adequately protected against losing their jobs as workers in any other unionized

---

* In the 1951 agreement, the grievance procedures were improved, from the point of view of individual workers, by providing that an aggrieved worker can personally appeal the decision of the JLRC to the area committee, and ultimately to the area arbitrator.

industry, and that they are considerably better protected than in most.

Where the union plays such an important role in dispensing jobs, disciplining workers, and processing grievances as it does in West Coast longshoring, the extent to which the men can continue to enjoy a high degree of economic security and control over other conditions of their work environment, depends on the degree to which they participate in running their union. The history of the union reveals a strong tradition in Local 19 that all major and, indeed, most minor issues must be referred to the membership. It is notable that the agreement provides: "The Union shall be entitled to one night per month for membership meeting purposes," and no work is performed on that night except under special circumstances.* Estimates of meeting attendance during the summer of 1951 varied from 600 to 700, and summer meetings were said to be less well attended than winter meetings.

Annual elections by secret ballot are held for the following offices: president, vice-president, recording secretary, financial secretary (treasurer), business agent, executive board (15 members), labor relations committee (3), dispatchers (5), delegates to longshore caucus and international conventions (varied from 7 to 12 in period studied), safety committee (4), shop stewards, trustees, janitors, sergeant-at-arms.

Local 19 rents voting machines from the city hall for use in these elections, and the turnover of major office holders, with defeated incumbents returning to the docks, reflects a healthy democracy in the local. Another advantage to the membership is the accessibility of union officers and committees. The grievance committee meets in the hiring hall each week and the 15-man executive board every two weeks.

Through their union, Seattle longshoremen have achieved substantial control over their work environment. Their freedom to select their jobs from among those available by "pulling their peg," to choose the type of work group they belong to, and, within reasonable limits, even to decide not to work at all without losing their job, all testify to a mastery over their environment which is rare in industry. For men who devote their lives to longshoring, one of the most advantageous features of the hiring system is the way it expands the worker's productive years by consciously reserving the easier jobs for older men and for men who have been injured. This points up an aspect of longshore work which does not appear at first to be related to the hiring system. In ports where the shape-up exists, accident prevention is largely ignored,[17] but since the Seattle system

---

* During the emergency immediately following the outbreak of the Korean War, for example, members of Local 19 temporarily gave up their right to the "stop work meeting night" at the request of the Army and Navy.

prevents discarding men injured on the job, the parties have a strong and continuous incentive to improve safety standards. This is done through a job-level safety committee composed of employer and union representatives, who go over the records of all accidents each month and attempt to determine their causes in an effort to prevent recurrence. Disputes over safety conditions are handled by the Joint Labor Relations Committee in the same manner as other grievances.

All features of the hiring system combine to give the longshoremen a feeling of self-sufficiency, dignity, and self-respect which is envied by many "noncasual" workers in industry. An outsider cannot fail to be impressed with the intense pride Seattle longshoremen take in their hiring hall. When they learned that my purpose in wandering around the building day after day was to study the system, longshoremen frequently took occasion to strike up a conversation in the coffee shop or in the hall, and invariably they asked, "Well, what do you think of our hall? Can you think of any way to improve it?" In sharp contrast with their attitude toward the old hiring system, which they referred to as "working out of the fink hall," ILWU members have repeatedly urged their critics, running from individual citizens to congressional investigating commitccs, to "visit the hiring hall and see for yourself how it operates."[18] A comment by Eric Hoffer is pertinent.* When asked why he works as a registered longshoreman (in San Francisco, where conditions are similar to those in Seattle), he replied that he likes the men he works with, and continued, "It would be hard to find another occupation with so suitable a combination of freedom, exercise, leisure, and income."[19]

Temporary Labor Pool Men

Although the hiring system should be judged primarily in terms of its impact on the regular labor force—the registered men—it is appropriate to consider its impact on new men who are considering longshoring as a permanent occupation. The system offers them as close an approximation to an apprentice status as is possible in an industry where employment is casual, since they have second preference in employment, rotation in hiring, and a chance to accumulate seniority toward full registration. Pool men receive the same wage rate as regular longshoremen and, although their earnings are not as high as those of regular men (since they are not dispatched until the regular men are all working) the earnings data for pool men show (table 6) they can expect to receive "adequate" earnings.

---

* Hoffer is the author of the philosophical treatise, *The True Believer* (New York: Harper and Brothers, 1951).

Since the men represented in the table are dispatched in rotation, it is reasonable to infer that men in the lower earnings range were, for one reason or another, not making themselves regularly available for work. Some men were only trying out longshoring as a possible occupation, and having found it not to their liking, dropped out of the industry during the year. The fact that some casual workers, who are dispatched *after* pool men, earned surprisingly high incomes (as will be shown below) suggests that other pool men could have put themselves in the higher earnings brackets if they had wished to do so.

TABLE 6

ANNUAL EARNINGS OF TEMPORARY LABOR POOL MEN
SEATTLE, 1951

Annual earnings in dollars	Number of men	Per cent of total
5,000 and over	81	11.5
4,000 to 4,999	160	22.8
3,000 to 3,999	123	17.4
2,000 to 2,999	81	11.5
1,000 to 1,999	100	14.1
0 to 999	160	22.7
	705	100.0

Source: Payroll records, Washington Area, Pacific Maritime Association.

When a man considers getting a foothold in a new occupation, he needs to know about any obstacles in his way. Potential longshoremen in Seattle have the advantage of knowing that arbitrary barriers to employment which exist in many industries are absent here. The coast agreement prohibits discrimination "because of union membership or activities, race, creed, color, national origin, or religious or political belief," and this clause is scrupulously observed in the Seattle hiring hall.*

In terms of providing the benefits of an apprenticeship status which gives them adequate earnings and full use of the grievance machinery, the hiring system is highly beneficial to the temporary pool men. It is less satisfactory for them than for the regular men, because pool men have no voice in the union and therefore only limited control over their work environment. Less information about jobs is available to them, and they

---

* This conclusion is based on personal observation and interviews with representatives of the Washington State Board Against Discrimination in Employment and the Seattle Urban League. Both were asked if they knew of any instances of discrimination in the industry. Both agencies stated that longshoring has an excellent record on this score, and that when new men are employed members of minority groups stand an equal chance.

are discouraged from passing up jobs when being dispatched. At the same time, it is difficult to see how the hiring system could be improved for them without losing the essence of decasualization—the limitation on the number of registered men in the port.

Casual Workers

The effect of the hiring hall on the casual workers who work on the waterfront is hard to evaluate, because we know neither who they are nor what they want the hiring system to do for them. In 1951—when shipments to Korea provided unusual activity in the port—more than 3,700 casual workers were dispatched from the hiring hall. The distribution of their earnings may be seen in table 7.

TABLE 7
ANNUAL EARNINGS OF CASUAL WORKERS
SEATTLE, 1951

Annual earnings in dollars	Number of men	Per cent of total
5,000 and over	46	1.2
4,000 to 4,999	33	.9
3,000 to 3,999	48	1.3
2,000 to 2,999	73	1.9
1,000 to 1,999	148	4.0
0 to 999	3,372	90.7
Total	3,720	100.0

Source: Payroll records, Washington Area, Pacific Maritime Association.

The 3,372 men whose earnings were in the $0–$999 bracket were presumably sent to the hall from the State Casual Labor Office and worked for only one day or for a short period at most. The parties have always recognized the need to hire casual workers on this basis and have made provision for them in the system. It is more difficult to speculate about those with higher earnings. It is possible that most of the high-earners came from the fishermen's union, but where the rest of the men came from and what they wanted from the hiring system is as much of a mystery as it was in New York. One would expect that men working regularly enough to earn $4,000 or more a year would prefer to put themselves on the Temporary Pool Board where they would have several advantages they do not enjoy as casual workers. However, the motivations of these men is less important for our present purposes than the fact that 79 casuals worked regularly enough to earn $4,000. This suggests that the dispatching system would be more efficient if more men were added to the Temporary Pool Board—or if the number of registered longshoremen were increased.

From the point of view of these casual workers—whoever they may be —there are advantages and disadvantages in the hiring system. Centralizing information about employment opportunities in the port is a gain to most casuals, because it saves them the need to tour the port in search of work. They pay no fees to support the hiring hall but, on the other hand, they receive only some of the benefits enjoyed by the registered and pool men. Indeed, from the point of view of these casual workers, the market might be more adequate in one sense if it permitted them to "float" in and out at will and take their chances on getting work. This is necessarily a conjecture, because the abandonment of the present hiring hall would almost certainly carry with it the destruction of the satisfactory working conditions which are a result of the hiring system.*

It is manifest that the hiring hall gives longshoremen a high degree of satisfaction in their work. Through the union's prominent role in the hall they have achieved enviable earnings and have reduced to a minimum the uncertainties and discomforts usually associated with casual employment. Paradoxically, the importance of the union in the industry imposes a cost on the longshoremen. If they are to preserve the benefits they have won, it is imperative that they continue to take an active part in the union. Although it is not customary to regard active participation as a "cost" to union members, the extent to which most unionists—indeed, most Americans—prefer to acquiesce in policies formulated and administered by the leaders of their organizations, so long as they are not called upon to take action themselves, makes it apparent that fulfilling the obligations of membership in democratic institutions *is* widely regarded as a sacrifice. To date, the longshoremen have not considered this "cost" too great, and during their tumultuous history they have had innumerable opportunities to face the decision whether they will be active union members. It will be interesting to see whether the cost might not appear increasingly onerous if the "new look" eventually replaces the earlier tradition of having to fight every step of the way.

The Union

In addition to serving as an instrument for the achievement of its members' objectives, any legitimate union has a separate objective of its own— its survival as an institution. The security of a union as an institution is

---

* One morning when I was in the hall, I saw a casual worker who had been sent up from the State Casual Labor Office trying to slip the dispatcher a bill as he reached in
(Note continued on following page.)

directly linked to its ability to control the jobs within its jurisdiction—to require that all the workers who hold these jobs contribute to the support of the union and be subject to its discipline. The test, then, of the hiring hall as far as the ILWU is concerned, is its effect on the union's ability to control the jobs on the waterfront.

It is manifest that Local 19 exerts a substantial degree of such control. Almost all Seattle longshoremen are union members, and the great majority enthusiastically support the union and approve of its right to exercise disciplinary power over them. By helping decide who will be registered, the union is able to protect itself against an influx of antiunion men; and by electing the dispatchers who, in practice, take the place of employers in the hiring process, Local 19 is able to prevent any employer favoritism which might be designed to win the loyalty of workers away from the union.

Since the advent of the "new look," the union has had no reason to fear attempts by the employers to weaken its position, but it has been open to attack from another direction—legal action under the Taft-Hartley Act. Shortly after the 1948 strike, two Seattle longshoremen by-passed the industry's grievance machinery, taking their complaints to the National Labor Relations Board in cases which point up clearly the impact of the law on a union's ability to demand that individual members support majority decisions. In view of the possible significance of these two complaints, a detailed discussion of them follows.[20]

The first was filed by one Clarence Purnell, who had been a registered longshoreman and a member of Local 19 since 1942. Purnell contracted arthritis and, early in 1948, purchased a barber shop, telling a friend that his condition prevented him from working outside in bad weather. When the 1948 strike began in September, Purnell went to Phoenix, Arizona, consequently failing to report for picket duty as is required of each member of Local 19 during a strike.* After the strike ended, he returned to Seattle. In January, 1949, he was brought before the executive board of Local 19 where, after a hearing on his unexcused absence during the strike, he was ordered to pay the customary fine of $25 a day for each day he had failed to report for picket duty. Unfortunately for Purnell's

for his dispatching slip. When the dispatcher handed him the dispatching slip, he also handed back the bill. When I asked the dispatcher about the incident, he explained, "Once in a while a guy who's worked on the East Coast is sent up here . . . If we ever took any of that stuff, the regular guys'd tear us apart."

* The by-laws of Local 19 require that during a strike or lockout "all members shall report daily at the Hall to receive instructions, unless other provisions are made by the membership meeting." Members who are unable to do their share of picketing appear before the local's clearance committee which recommends to the membership whether or not the applicants should be excused from picket duty.

pocket book, the 1948 strike had been one of the longest of the ILWU's many protracted strikes, and the total amount of his fine was $2,400.* The executive board reminded him that he could work for 30 days before paying the fine, but he did not accept work on the waterfront because, according to his subsequent testimony, he was too sick to work "in the cold and wet of that winter." Later in the month, he asked the chief clerk in the hiring hall for a statement of his availability for work which he needed to draw unemployment compensation and which would help him in getting another job. The chief clerk refused to give him the certificate, telling him he could still work for 30 days without having to pay any part of the fine. Purnell replied that he was not physically able to work. He then telephoned the head of the employers' association and asked him for a statement of availability.

Apparently angered when the employers also declined to give him the statement, he went to the National Labor Relations Board and filed unfair labor practice charges against both the union and the employers. In April, 1950, before the case came before the NLRB trial examiner, Purnell sold his barber shop and opened a larger one. During part of this time he also worked at an airport "because the work there was inside work and he was not bothered by the weather."

In his original complaint, Purnell's charges were directed against Local 19, but he later amended them to include the International Union, the Waterfront Employers of Washington, and certain Seattle stevedoring concerns, alleging that the employers and the union had committed unfair labor practices by agreeing to give preference in employment to union members in the 1948 contract, and by the manner in which they actually operated the hiring hall under the agreement.[21]

The trial examiner hearing Purnell's case dismissed the complaint against the International Union under section 10b, on the grounds that Purnell had named the ILWU as a party to the alleged violation of the law more than six months after the practices had occurred. As to the substance of Purnell's accusations, the trial examiner recommended dismissing the charges of discrimination against both the employers and Local 19 because, "In order for there to be a discriminatory refusal to employ, it is axiomatic that the individual must have been an applicant for employment." He concluded:

> In fact Purnell did not want to work. His name is still on the plug board, and the dispatcher testified, at least, that if Purnell

---

* The official records of the 1948 strike indicate that it lasted 95, rather than 96, days so there must have been a meeting at which attendance was compulsory the

(Note continued on following page.)

176

had plugged in in the customary manner, he would have been, and still would be, dispatched. As Purnell has never tested the truth of this testimony, there is no proof to the contrary.[22]

He also dismissed Purnell's further charge that the employers had violated section 8a (2), which makes it an unfair labor practice for an employer to dominate, interfere with, or contribute to the support of a union, by paying 50 per cent of the cost of operating the hiring hall. This payment, the trial examiner concluded, was made, not to the union, but to a separate entity composed of both employer and union representatives:

> For anyone with any reading knowledge of Pacific Coast waterfront history, past or present, to even suggest that . . . the WEW [Waterfront Employers of Washington] is dominating or interfering with the ILWU or Local 19 by these payments . . . is being so completely unrealistic as to be laughable.[23]

However, he agreed with Purnell—and incidentally with the finding in the earlier NLRB case—that the parties had clearly violated the Taft-Hartley Act by including in the 1948 contract a clause giving preference to union members.

The other unfair labor practice charge was brought by Albert G. Crum, who had worked on the waterfront since 1936. Crum had become a registered longshoreman and a member of Local 19 in 1939, and had worked as a member of a regular gang most of the time until 1944, when he became a full-time employee of a stevedoring company in a job over which Local 19 did not have jurisdiction. In 1946, he left this job and bought a 220-acre farm in Idaho where he harvested the hay crop that year. For the next two years, Crum spent most of his time on the farm, but visited Seattle several times when there was no farm work to be done, working occasionally as a longshoreman.

In August, 1948—during the 80-day injunction period preceding the strike—he was in Seattle for a few days and dropped into the hiring hall. The dispatcher urged him to go out on a job, but Crum at first replied that he didn't want to work. Finally, he agreed to take a job supposed to last about four hours, but he actually worked long enough to earn $122. Shortly thereafter, he again left the city, and was absent during the 1948 strike. Like Purnell, Crum failed to ask the clearance committee to excuse him from picket duty, and when he returned to the waterfront several

---

day before the strike began. Although on its face the aggregate size of the fine is startling, neither the trial examiner nor the NLRB commented on it in the subsequent NLRB case, presumably considering that Purnell had no justifiable complaint since he had not exhausted the remedies open to him to avoid the fine.

months later, he was fined $2,400 for having failed to report during the strike, and given 30 days in which to pay. He continued to work as a gang member in the usual fashion for the next 30 days, but when he telephoned the hall on January 27, 1949, to find out whether his gang had been dispatched, he was told, "There's a bug behind your name and you won't be dispatched . . . until the fine is paid."

Like Purnell, he then went to the Waterfront Employers office and to several individual employers, asking them if they would hire him if he were sent out by the hall, and received assurances that they would. In April, 1949, on a motion by the union, the Joint Labor Relations Committee deregistered Crum on the basis of low earnings.* Three months later, Crum filed his unfair labor practice charges against the ILWU and the Waterfront Employers of Washington. A year and a half later, just prior to the hearing before the NLRB trial examiner, he amended his charge to add Local 19 as a respondent.

In January, 1951, a few days after the close of the hearings—but more than two months before the trial examiner announced his decision—Crum appeared before the Joint Labor Relations Committee and asked to be put back on the registered list, promising that he would make himself regularly available for work. The union initially opposed Crum's reinstatement, arguing that such action would tend to substantiate the charge that he had been discriminatorily deregistered, and that it might affect the amount of any back-pay award ordered by the NLRB. Later in the meeting, however, union members of the committee asked Crum if he would drop his case if he were reinstated. Crum replied that he would like to drop the case if it were in his power but that the NLRB would not permit him to do so. The union then asked him to confer with his lawyer about withdrawing the charges, and the matter was held over until the next meeting of the Joint Labor Relations Committee. During the next two months, the employers proposed several times that Crum be reinstated but the union refused, saying they had not yet heard from Crum about withdrawing his charges. Finally, the committee agreed to hold the matter over until the NLRB decided the case. [24]

Later that spring, the trial examiner's report on both Crum's and Purnell's cases was issued. The examiner concluded that Crum had been discriminated against under section 8a (3) since he had been refused em-

---

* Apparently the deregistration procedure is not always invoked as promptly as it might be. The evidence before the NLRB on the employment experience of both Purnell and Crum indicates that if their registrations had been questioned earlier Crum would have been deregistered at the end of 1948 and Purnell might have been deregistered at the same time. Had that been done, the facts upon which their discrimination charges were based would never have arisen.

ployment because his membership had been terminated "for reasons other than the failure to tender the periodic dues and initiation fees uniformly required" of the members of Local 19, and he recommended that the Waterfront Employers be required to reimburse Crum for any loss of pay he had suffered.* However, he concluded that Crum's deregistration in April on the ground of "low earnings" was not a violation of the Taft-Hartley Act and accordingly made no recommendation that Crum's registration be restored. The recommendation for back pay was limited to the period between January 27 (when Crum had been refused work) and April 20 (when he had been deregistered).[25]

The National Labor Relations Board handed down their decision in February, 1952. They sustained all charges against all parties. Giving section 10b a different interpretation than had the trial examiner, the board found that the six-month limitation did not bar Purnell's charges against the ILWU, or Crum's charges against Local 19. They also held the ILWU legally responsible for participation of Local 19 in the hiring hall. Accordingly, their order in both cases held against the Waterfront Employers, the ILWU, and Local 19.

In Purnell's case, the board disagreed with the trial examiner that there had been no discriminatory discharge, taking the view that the manner in which Crum was treated made it apparent that if Purnell had actually made application for work it "would have been a futile gesture" which he need not have made in order to support his charge.[26] In Crum's case, the board concluded that the deregistration in April, coming after the discriminatory discharge in January, "did not reflect a 'good faith' application of the waterfront employment policy."[27] Consequently, the parties were ordered to restore both men to full registration status with all hiring-hall privileges, and to reimburse them for all loss of pay they had suffered as a result of the discriminatory discharges.† The board also pointedly ordered all parties, for the second time, to cease giving effect to the preferential-hiring clause in the 1948 contract (which had been abandoned by the parties the previous year).

---

* The trial examiner's reasoning in holding the Waterfront Employers solely responsible for the back-pay award was that the charge against Local 19 was invalid under section 10b because it had not been filed within six months of the commission of the alleged unfair labor practice. He had exonerated the ILWU on the ground that there was no showing that the international union, as distinguished from Local 19, participated in the dispatching process.

† The award left Crum and Purnell free to collect from any one or more of the respondents. The employers' reaction to paying their share of a two-year back-pay award to men disciplined by the union for failing to stand picket duty was understandably not a happy one. See St. Sure's testimony in U.S. Congress, Senate Committee on Labor . . . , *Taft-Hartley Act Revisions,* for the employers' vigorous protests against the NLRB's policy in other back-pay orders in which the employers have become involved under the act.

The board's decision might be counted a financial and moral victory for Purnell and Crum over the forces of "big unionism,"* but to the ILWU it brought home sharply the pitfalls inherent in the Taft-Hartley Act. These cases clearly limit the union's authority to discipline members, even when disciplinary action is based on clearly specified rules which are uniformly applied and which have the endorsement of the majority of the membership, who recognize that the union must possess such authority if it is to be effective.

Purnell's case has further implications. It indicates a type of harassment to which the union may be vulnerable as long as it plays an integral part in the dispatching system. The parties are now in full compliance with the new labor law, because the agreement no longer provides for preferential treatment to union members and, although the NLRB has not yet passed on the issue specifically, the trial examiners in both ILWU cases have made findings that the present operation of the hall in no way conflicts with the Taft-Hartley Act.[28] But if a case like Purnell's can receive favorable attention from the board, it is conceivable that other equally weak charges against the ILWU might be sustained in such volume as to create considerable confusion in the industry.

Even in the face of the Taft-Hartley Act, it seems safe to conclude that Local 19 will continue to enjoy a highly secure position in the industry. If past behavior of the membership is a reliable clue to the future, the union's diminished ability to discipline "free riders" will have little noticeable effect, and the majority of the members will voluntarily continue to support the union. Being secure, Local 19 will undoubtedly continue to direct its primary attention to serving as an instrument for achieving its members' objectives. Under these circumstances, the goals of the union are closely identified with the goals of the members. Having found that the hiring-hall system satisfies the longshoremen, it can be said with equal validity that it satisfies the union.

The Community

How well does the hiring hall serve the public interest?

To answer this question, we need to look first at the economic impact of the hall, and then at its broader social implications. The economic aspects of any hiring system which have implications for the welfare of

---

* Purnell received a substantially smaller check for his back pay than Crum, since the board ordered that in calculating his compensation his inability to work because of his arthritic condition would have to be taken into account. Presumably Parnell had already obtained the satisfaction he sought—his case looks suspiciously like a "spite suit."

the community at large are two-fold. First, the community has an interest in having a hiring system which produces a balance between the number of workers offering their services and those whose services are needed, so that neither the chronic surpluses nor shortages of workers usually associated with a casual-labor market result in a loss of production. The hiring hall meets this test well. Secondly, the community has an interest in having the hiring system facilitate the process of placing workers in jobs they are best fitted for, because this is essential to maximizing the efficient use of the labor force. It has been suggested that this can best be achieved by permitting complete freedom of choice to both employers and workers, modified only by those limitations society has conceded are necessary if workers are to enjoy economic security, such as the seniority principle. Here the hiring hall measures up better in some respects than in others. On the positive side, it gives the longshoremen wide latitude in choosing jobs, coupled with complete job security. In addition, the employment policy of the hiring hall removes many arbitrary barriers to using every man's skills to the best advantage, because it prohibits discrimination on the basis of race, color, or creed. Furthermore, the willingness of the industry to give older and injured men jobs they can handle, probably enables many men to be productive whose manpower would otherwise be lost to the economy.

On the negative side, the employers contend that while under the Seattle system the men have freedom of choice, employers are far less free to select their workers than they were when they could hire steady employees. Indeed, it may be that any increment to productivity resulting from the increased sense of job security the hiring hall gives longshoremen is more than offset by a drop in efficiency which the employers assert has resulted from the abandonment of steady employees.* Unfortunately, our present knowledge of how to measure productivity in longshoring does not permit any meaningful conclusions about the effect of this union policy, or on the larger question of the over-all effect of unionism on efficiency in the industry. The question of whether or not the public is being forced to subsidize inefficiency on the waterfront through higher handling costs must remain moot. But even if the contention of the employers is eventually supported by refined techniques for correlating productivity with specific industry practices, the community at large (if informed) would

---

* I am assuming here that the employers can exercise sufficient authority to weed out incompetent workers from the labor force and, therefore, that the registered longshoremen are as well qualified to perform the work as any other group of men who could be recruited. In other words, the seniority aspect of registration in the hiring hall does not protect incompetents in this industry to any greater extent than seniority does in industry generally.

undoubtedly share the present employer view that the basic framework of the Seattle system is superior to the much-discussed alternative—a government-operated hiring hall.

The lack of consensus in the community about what constitutes approved social behavior makes it more difficult to assess the impact of the hiring hall on social institutions. On the one hand, some results of the hall clearly reinforce the community's standards of acceptable conduct. In a society committed to the ideals of respect for the individual and to the notion that the democratic process is the best way to reconcile conflicts of interest, the dignity and self-respect enjoyed by Seattle longshoremen and their experience with the effectiveness of democratic coöperation, both of which are closely associated with the hiring hall, are obvious social gains. In addition, the system enables regular longshoremen to live at a level which meets the generally accepted concept of the "American standard of living"—a circumstance which tends to make them a conservative force because it gives them a vested interest in supporting the status quo.

On the other hand, the community is ambivalent about the longshoremen's highly developed appreciation of the strength they derive from coöperation, because the public attributes to this factor their ability to cause the community inconvenience and irritation through strikes. The turbulent history of their union has given the longshoremen a reputation for militancy and aggressiveness which sets them off from most other groups in our society. The "in-group" feeling which has grown up among longshoremen has enabled them to ignore strong community disapproval and even to circumvent the law of the land. As recently as 1948, for example, during the final battle over the hiring hall, Seattle longshoremen deliberately violated the intent of the Taft-Hartley Act by engaging in a slowdown during the 80-day injunction, and by boycotting the vote on the employers' last offer which is specifically required before a strike is legal under the national emergency provisions of the act. In recent years, a growing body of people have come to consider behavior of this sort as far from acceptable—indeed, as lawlessness. But almost as many others see unionism as a desirable, even an essential, social institution, and accept as the *conditio sine qua non* of unionism the power to strike effectively when necessary. This group regards behavior such as the longshoremen's in 1948 as legitimate trade-union methods by which workers defend themselves against the effects of restrictive legislation passed by a hostile Congress, and consequently views as healthy the union's lack of concern over generating vigorous public disapproval.

The many shades of difference of opinion on what are acceptable trade union methods—and thus acceptable social behavior—may never be finally resolved, and public policy will probably continue to reflect the shifting popularity of these opposing views of unionism. But regardless of what balance is struck in our labor laws, the experience in both New York and Seattle indicates that the clue to avoiding public intervention in any industry is the avoidance of work stoppages. If Seattle employers and the ILWU can keep goods flowing through the port in an uninterrupted stream (and continue to steer clear of collusive practices detrimental to consumers), they will avoid overt conflicts of interest with the community as a whole. Under these circumstances, they will be able to keep their hiring hall, and the public will grow less concerned about the independent spirit of the longshoremen—indeed, if harmony becomes the new tradition on the waterfront, the longshoremen may lose much of the militancy which stems from being on the defensive and which has caused distress in many quarters during past strikes. If chronic warfare breaks out again, however, the community will undoubtedly concentrate its wrath on the hiring hall which in the public mind symbolizes the industry, and which has contributed so greatly to the bargaining strength of the longshoremen's union.

Whatever society's ultimate judgment is about strong unions, it will surely continue to favor democratic institutions. Accordingly, it should recognize one undisputed benefit to a democratic society in joint administration of the hiring hall. By imposing on both the employers and rank-and-file longshoremen the necessity of active participation in decision-making in order to ensure that the dispatching system continues to serve their interests, the hiring hall provides them with useful experience for the larger duties of citizenship.

7

Government-Operated Halls
The New York Expedient

*The commission shall . . . establish hiring practices
and conditions which will permit the termination
of governmental regulation and intervention at the
earliest opportunity.*
—Waterfront Commission Act.[1]

With privately run hiring halls working successfully in West Coast ports,
why did legislators in New York and New Jersey deem it necessary to
carry government intervention as far as they did in the Port of New York?
It will be recalled that the Waterfront Commission Act, passed at special sessions in the summer of 1953, set up government-operated hiring
halls and created a bistate agency endowed with extraordinary powers,
including the authority to investigate and ban from the longshore industry
not only men who seek work as longshoremen, foremen, and supervisors,
but also those who wish to operate stevedoring companies.

In view of the respect and prestige our society accords to businessmen,
it is indeed a departure from tradition for two state legislatures to enact
laws permitting a government agency to demand that any stevedoring
concern must submit "a photograph and the authenticated fingerprints"
of anyone holding five per cent or more of the company's stock before a
license will be issued permitting them to do business.[2] The law represents
a fundamental rejection of our traditional philosophy that the proper
scope of social control of industry, in contrast to social control of professional services (such as medicine and the law), is limited to the impersonal
regulation of the business enterprise. Never before has this philosophy
endorsed a requirement that all individuals connected with a regulated
business must meet a "morals test."

The Draconian character of this legislation is partially explained by
the monumental extent of the abuses it was designed to correct. The find-

184

ings of the legislatures which passed the reform bills can serve as a reminder of the magnitude of the task facing the legislators:

> The states of New York and New Jersey hereby find and declare that the conditions under which waterfront labor is employed within the port of New York district are depressing and degrading to such labor, resulting from the lack of any systematic method of hiring . . . , corrupt hiring practices and the fact that persons conducting such hiring are frequently criminals and persons notoriously lacking in moral character and integrity and neither responsive or responsible to the employers nor to the uncoerced will of the majority of the members of the labor organizations of the employees;

> that as a result waterfront laborers suffer from irregularity of employment, fear and insecurity, inadequate earnings, an unduly high accident rate, subjection to borrowing at usurious rates of interest, exploitation and extortion as the price of securing employment and a loss of respect for the law;

> that not only does there result a destruction of the dignity of an important segment of American labor, but a direct encouragement of crime which imposes a levy of greatly increased costs of food, fuel and other necessities handled in and through the port of New York district.

> . . . that many of the evils above described result . . . from the lack of regulation of the occupation of stevedores; that such stevedores have engaged in corrupt practices to induce their hire by carriers of freight by water and to induce officers and representatives of labor organizations to betray their trust to the members of such labor organizations.[3]

When the legislators met in June, almost five months had gone by since the Crime Commission had laid bare the evidence underlying this indictment, yet the shape-up was still in existence. The conclusion was inescapable that the industry was not going to reform itself. There were men in the industry, of course, who honestly wanted to attack basic evils on the waterfront, but they had been unable to rally any effective support for self-reform, because the gamut of malefactors who had a vested interest in the shape-up ran all the way from the lowliest loan sharks to the managers of some of the world's largest stevedoring companies.

But it was not merely the continued existence of the shape-up that aroused the indignation of the legislators. The major irritant was the incapacity of either the employers' association or the union to recognize that, this time, they would have to do more than sit back and wait for the storm of public criticism to subside as it had after the many earlier exposés. Even after the Crime Commission's investigation, the parties might still have been able to head off legislative action if they had been more sensitive to the temper of the community. True, both the employers and the union had belatedly offered reform proposals, but after they announced their plans, neither gave the public any real assurance that they intended to put them into practice. The plans themselves reflected the industry's inability to move with the times—the reforms suggested by the parties were considerably less than frontal attacks on the problems they purported to solve.

The Employers' Plan

Toward the end of the Crime Commission's hearings in January, the New York Shipping Association announced that they were willing to abandon their traditional insistence on retaining the shape-up. The employers proposed to divide the port into an unspecified number of districts and set up hiring halls, which they termed (following the European nomenclature) "information centres," in each district. The suggestion that these centers be operated unilaterally by the employers made their plan bear a superficial resemblance to the hiring system established in 1921 by Seattle employers, but other features of the proposal revealed that New York employers had not yet fully accepted the basic principle of regularizing longshore employment.[4]

The labor force was to be divided into three categories. The first was to be composed of "regular gangs," which, like the "company gangs" in the Seattle employers' system, were to be attached to a particular pier. Each regular gang was to be given a port number and this, together with the name and social security number of the gang foreman, was to be registered in the information center in that district. Significantly, these gangs were not to be permanently employed on their regular pier, but were merely to be given first preference in employment. They were to be informed of jobs for the following day by means of bulletin boards in front of their piers. If a gang were not scheduled to work, the gang foreman was to report its availability to the information center. The centers were to be kept informed of needs for gangs throughout the port, and if a gang were needed in another area it could be sent to the center serving that area. While the exchange of gangs between different employers was to be cleared through the centers, individual employers were to be free to designate the specific gangs they desired.

The next category was designated as "regular extra gangs." These would have been similar to the Seattle "hall gangs" in that they were to be hired after the regular gangs, but—and this would have been an important difference—rather than being hired from the center, each gang was to be attached to a specific pier. If gang members were not needed on their regular pier, they were to follow the same procedure as regular gangs.

In the final category were the men who would be hired as individuals. All these men—dock workers, porters, tractor drivers, and men for extra gangs—were to be hired directly from the centers. Each day employers would call the center and order the men they wanted for the following day. This group would roughly correspond to the longshoremen and truckers on the extra board in the original Seattle system, but the men would have had far less job security than their counterparts had in Foisie's scheme, because New York employers were to select men from the hall by name, rather than accepting men sent to them in rotation.

In two respects, the NYSA proposal fell short of the basic requirements of an effective decasualization scheme. First, the employers said nothing about limiting the size of the regular labor force by registering only the number of men required for normal port activity; and second, since they rejected this principle, it would have been impossible to equalize the earnings of all regular men by rotating them among available jobs. The provision to attach "regular *extra* gangs" to each pier clearly implies that the employers planned to perpetuate the chronic surplus at each pier, while the stipulation that employers would be free to pick their men in the hall was a specific rejection of the rotation principle.

As a means of eliminating criminals from the waterfront, the employers proposed relying on the Coast Guard screening program. Every longshoreman was to be required to carry a Coast Guard identification card, and if a man were convicted of larceny or other crime on the waterfront, his card was to be revoked. Presumably, men would have been required to have a card before they could work on commercial cargo as well as in restricted areas of the port. Parolees were to be prohibited from obtaining waterfront employment, and it was further proposed that

> . . . under no circumstances shall an ex-convict be employed as Head Foreman, Gang Foreman, Clerk, Timekeeper, Checker or in any other supervisory capacity or key position, unless and until he furnished proof that he has received a certificate of good conduct or that he has been pardoned.

To solve the problem of wildcat strikes, the employers offered an interesting proposal. A permanent "working" arbitrator was to be selected jointly by the employers and the union, and empowered to assess damages on any of the parties found by him to have caused an unauthorized work stoppage or to have violated the contract. A fund out of which damages were to be paid was to be established by "contributions based on payroll data to be made in equal amounts by all employers, and all employees." Although not specifically so indicated, this proposal apparently would have involved a deduction from each longshoreman's earnings to cover the contributions of "all employees." If the employers had been able to put this proposal into effect, another precedent in labor-management relations would have been set by the maritime industry. Finally, the employers reiterated their insistence that public loaders be licensed and bonded, and that uniform loading rates be prominently posted on the piers.

Actually, the employers' hiring plan would have provided the longshoremen little more than "a shape-up with a roof over it." Since the surplus was to be retained, it is unlikely that the other proposals of the NYSA would have protected the community from frequent work stoppages or criminal activity on the waterfront.* In any case, reformers were aware that a proposal to establish "information centres" unilaterally operated by employers was most appropriately viewed as being of historical rather than current interest. One of the aims of the reformers was to enable the longshoremen to participate in a responsive union, and it was obvious that employer-operated halls which contemplated preserving the chronic surplus of labor would hardly encourage the emergence of democratic unionism. Thus, the NYSA proposal offered no permanent solution to waterfront problems—even if the employers had shown a real interest in putting it into effect.

The ILA Plan

About a week after the employers announced their hiring scheme, the AFL handed the International Longshoremen's Association the ultimatum requiring abolition of the shape-up as a condition of remaining in the federation. ILA officials appointed a committee to study alternative hiring systems and, in March, the New York District Council adopted a plan embodying many similarities to the NYSA proposal.[5]

Under the ILA plan, the labor force was to be divided into four categories. The first were members of regular gangs—who, like those in the employers' proposal, would be given first preference in employment at

---

* When I asked J. V. Lyon if the NYSA had ever considered adopting Foisie's Seattle plan, he replied that they had studied the system (in 1940) but had rejected it. Lyon added the comment: "The trouble with Foisie was, he didn't know how to handle men."

their regular pier. Next in order were "regular extra men," who presumably were to be replacements for regular gangs, since they were to have priority in employment corresponding to that of the regular extra gangs in the employers' plan. In the third category, which had no precise parallel in the NYSA recommendations, were members of "extra gangs" who were to be taken on after the first two groups had been hired. A fourth group, which corresponded to the third category in the employers' proposal, comprised porters, tractor drivers, and extra men, all of whom would be hired individually. No mention was made of formally registering these gangs or individuals, but presumably they were to be designated according to their classifications in some fashion.

Like the employers, the ILA proposed establishing a series of hiring halls—which the ILA termed "employment centers"—but these were to be operated by the union, although they would be financed by the employers through contributions to a "hiring and employment fund." Another deviation from the employers' plan was a requirement that all men be hired individually, and all gangs—even regular gangs assigned to specific piers—be hired through these centers. Upon completion of any particular job, the men were to report back to the centers. The union proposed setting up a six-man board—composed of three employer members and three from the union—"to handle disputes arising from classifications and identification of gangs or individuals," but did not specify how men were to be hired in the centers—whether employers would be allowed to pick their men, or whether some sort of seniority or rotation plan was to be used.

To deal with wildcat strikes, the ILA, like the employers, proposed arbitration, but the union did not endorse the employers' suggestion that the arbitrator have authority to assess damages for contract violations. On the problem of ridding the waterfront of criminal activity, the ILA recommendations were silent and public loading was not mentioned.

What impact this loosely sketched plan might have had on the waterfront does not merit analysis, because it was obvious to everyone that the ILA hierarchy had no serious intention of putting their scheme into operation. It *was* significant that the vagueness of the plan showed reformers that the union—like the employers—could not be counted upon to suggest a useful formula for combating either the economic or social evils of the waterfront. Responsible public officials consequently reconciled themselves to the necessity of finding some new approach, and of implementing it through legislation.

The revelations of the Crime Commission had caused New Yorkers to tell each other with increasing frequency and mounting fervor, "there ought to be a law." After almost forty years of ignoring conditions on the waterfront, the rapidity with which state officials met this demand takes on special interest. The first step in the evolution of the Waterfront Commission Act came in May, when the Crime Commission issued its report outlining its legislative proposals.

The basic elements of their plan—licensing all personnel and setting up government hiring halls—had been suggested to the Crime Commission by Walter P. Hedden, who had served for ten years as director of port development of the New York Port Authority.[6] Since most of the staff members of the Crime Commission were men who had, at best, only a limited acquaintance with the longshore industry before they began their waterfront investigation, it was perhaps to be expected that commission members would give great weight to the Port Authority's recommendations. Reliance on the Port Authority's views was strengthened when commission members learned that the agency had, for several years, been studying waterfront hiring practices in other ports, "particularly those in England."[7]

A somewhat different approach was suggested to the Crime Commission by a private citizen whose experience with the industry lent weight to his recommendations. This was the "waterfront priest"—Reverend John M. Corridan, associate director of the Xavier Institute of Industrial Relations —who submitted a comprehensive plan when asked by the Crime Commission to testify about waterfront conditions. The important differences between the two proposals revolved around the method by which the surplus of men was to be eliminated and the basis on which men were to be hired in the government halls.[8] The Port Authority proposed removing the surplus by the automatic process of deregistering men if they failed to work or to report for work on at least forty days in any six-month period. Father Corridan proposed first to survey the labor force, then to assign men to the different job classifications on the basis of seniority and, in this way, formally to exclude floaters from the labor force. Secondly, the Port Authority specifically rejected the concept of hiring men in rotation, stipulating that employers should be free to choose the men they wanted. Father Corridan did not explicitly endorse rotation, but his recommendation that the agency operating the hall be given authority to equalize the earnings of "regular gangs" and "traveling gangs," and that extra men be dispatched on the basis of seniority, would have considerably limited the employers'

190

free choice of workers. In fact, Father Corridan's plan came closer to embodying the basic features of Frank Foisie's decasualization scheme than any of the other proposals heard by the Crime Commission.

The commission's decision to reject Father Corridan's plan in favor of the Port Authority's can be explained on several grounds. For one thing, the employers were strongly opposed to any plan which restricted their freedom to select workers, and the commission was interested in finding a workable solution which stood a chance of being accepted with a minimum of opposition. Since Father Corridan had no organized group to fight for his program, it was inevitable that his suggestion would receive less consideration. Moreover, his plan to survey the entire labor force would have been more complicated and expensive than the Port Authority's scheme, which would work automatically to exclude surplus workers. It is also possible that political considerations dictated favoring the automatic plan because it avoided putting the government in the position of culling out the labor force.* And since neither the union nor the employers were willing to undertake the survey suggested by Father Corridan, the agency administering the halls would have been put in the unenviable position of having to decide which men had greater seniority and then having to force the employers to accept these men in key jobs.

But perhaps a more important disqualification of Father Corridan's plan was its resemblance to the West Coast system. Few New Yorkers seemed to know much about the hiring system on the other side of the continent, but most of them equated the idea of seniority or rotation with "Harry Bridges's hiring halls" and, consequently, with radicalism and chronic labor strife—an attitude which for years had been nurtured by the NYSA, the ILA, and the New York press. The Crime Commission was highly sensitive to this public attitude (commission members themselves shared the popular conception of the West Coast) and made every effort to keep their proposals immune from attacks on this score. It will be recalled that the statement made by Harry Bridges to the Crime Commission was not introduced into the public record, and that no effort was made to obtain testimony from West Coast employers.† Indeed, the commission carefully refrained from even using the term "hiring hall," preferring instead the designation "employment information centers."

In view of the aversion to the West Coast system so widely held by

_____

* Except, of course, for men eliminated on the basis of criminal activity, to which commission members had reconciled themselves and which public opinion supported.

† The testimony of J. Paul St. Sure, PMA president, before the Senate Labor Committee, in which he expressed the general satisfaction of West Coast employers with their hiring system was given in April but it received little publicity in the New York area.

191

New Yorkers, it is probable that even if Father Corridan's plan had received broad backing, its very resemblance to the West Coast system would have been enough to preclude its enactment into law. Because hiring practices identified with the ILWU were ruled out, the commission was left with little alternative but to adopt the Port Authority's proposal, which was patterned after systems used in European ports.

The next step in the evolution of the Waterfront Commission Act was taken three days after the Crime Commission's recommendations were made public. On May 23, Governor Dewey announced that public hearings would be held on the commission's report and urged any groups who had alternative proposals to appear and present them:

> I would like to avoid establishing a new state agency to supervise the waterfront and its hiring practices if there is any sound alternative. I believe this is also the view of the members of the Crime Commission. The difficulty is that no one has yet proposed any other sound alternative. If there is a better solution, I most earnestly hope it will be presented at the hearings.[9]

The hearings, which began on June 8, brought out the views of many divergent groups in the community. Recommendations were submitted by chambers of commerce, the Board of Trade, the Commerce and Industry Association, the president of the AFL, the State Federation of Labor, various factions in the ILA, the NYSA and other shipping and trucking associations, district attorneys, a police commissioner, a college professor, a Catholic priest (Father Corridan), and a protestant bishop, spokesmen for the legislative and executive branches of the federal and local government, political action groups such as Americans for Democratic Action, the Association of Catholic Trade Unionists, and civic improvement clubs. The consensus of the testimony was that the Crime Commission's recommendations should be enacted without delay.*

Some differences of opinion emerged on procedural questions, but the commission's basic approach—government-operated halls and licensing of all personnel—was endorsed by all who testified, except the ILA, the State Federation of Labor, the manager of one stevedoring company, and the Association of Catholic Trade Unionists. The only point on which this remarkable unanimity showed any serious signs of strain was the relatively peripheral issue of whether public loading should be brought under control by a system of licensing, as the crime commission proposed,

---

* Testimony was confined almost entirely to the commission's first legislative proposal. Their second proposal—to legislate standards for internal administration of unions—received little attention since that bill was not going to be introduced in the pending special session of the legislature.

or outlawed entirely, as many speakers urged persuasively in the hearings.

The ambivalent attitude toward the Crime Commission's bill held by some of its supporters—especially the business groups—came out in recommendations that, although immediate enactment of this legislation was imperative, it should be regarded as necessary only on a temporary basis. As soon as satisfactory labor relations were established on the waterfront, it was argued, the government should withdraw from the industry. The Crime Commission and Governor Dewey indicated that they shared this view, and those who were uncomfortable at finding themselves supporting such an extreme form of government intervention as the proposed bill were apparently mollified by the assurance that the temporary nature of the legislation would be explicitly spelled out in the law.

The possible effect on bona fide collective bargaining or precipitating the government into the heart of the industry was brought up by the ILA and by a few interested outsiders.* All but the ILA representatives, who seemed to be raising this issue as only part of a general attack on the proposed law, appeared to be satisfied when they were assured that a specific statement would be added to the law setting forth the government's intention to support, rather than discourage, representative trade unionism and free collective bargaining.

Frontal attacks on the idea of government-operated halls came almost exclusively from the ILA. Sometime between January and the governor's hearings in June, ILA officials lost their strongest backer on this issue when the NYSA evidently reconciled themselves to the inevitable—in the hearings, even the employers endorsed the principle of state operation. Much of the testimony offered by ILA spokesmen, who included Waldman, Ryan, and Sampson, was a general protest against the plan in its entirety and a discounting of the seriousness of the waterfront problem. However, two union speakers came forward who fully agreed with the Crime Commission's findings as to the extent of waterfront corruption, and who offered specific remedies which could be instituted through collective bargaining. The first of these speakers was Cleophas Jacobs, secretary-treasurer of Local 968 (the "Jim Crow local"). Jacobs outlined a plan to regularize employment by setting up union "employment offices," from which men would be dispatched according to strict seniority. The other was a spokesman for Anthony Anastasia. Asserting that the Long-

---

* Interestingly enough, AFL president Meany did not discuss this aspect of the law in his testimony. The only remarks Meany addressed to this general subject (aside from his comments on the commission's second bill which was not being considered at that time) were his objections to the proposal to prohibit hiring foremen and port watchmen from belonging to the same international union as the longshoremen.

shoremen's, Checkers' and Clerks' Social Club was already proceeding with plans for a hiring hall of its own, the attorney for the club proposed setting up union hiring halls to be managed by a chairman who would be elected once a year, with employers having "a voice in the control of the hall."

There were only two other objections to government halls. One came from Phineas B. Blanchard, manager of a New York stevedoring company, who insisted that the shape-up no longer worked hardships on the men because the use of regular gangs gave them steady employment and high earnings. The other was voiced by James Conroy of the Association of Catholic Trade Unionists, who generally opposed government intervention and who pointed to genuine reforms accomplished in several sections of the port through trade-union action on a local scale.*

There was surprisingly little debate on the Crime Commission's drastic proposal to license stevedoring companies. The NYSA stood almost alone in outright opposition. The Chamber of Commerce of the State of New York was the only other organization to raise an objection, and their opposition was focused on the proposal that licenses would have to be renewed each year, taking the position that it should be sufficient to require the companies to register, to file statements of ownership, and to maintain adequate books and records, in order to hold their licenses. Both the Commerce and Industry Association and the New York Board of Trade endorsed the licensing requirement in its entirety. Apparently their patience with the NYSA had reached the breaking point.

Almost everyone concurred in the commission's recommendation that longshoremen be registered, but one procedural feature of the proposal received some criticism. The Crime Commission had proposed that "refusal to testify . . . or refusal to answer any question relating to activities on the waterfront should constitute sufficient cause for refusing or cancelling registration" in the hiring halls. Opposition to this proposal brought together some strange bedfellows. In addition to the ILA hierarchy (who opposed registration in general), two district attorneys, the Americans for Democratic Action, the Chamber of Commerce of the State of New York, and AFL President George Meany raised specific objections to this basis for excluding men from the industry. Frank Hogan, district attorney for New York County, gave the most eloquent statement of their position:

---

* Of all the people I interviewed in New York in 1951 and 1952, the only person who recognized that West Coast hiring halls were operating satisfactorily, and who felt that New York could profit from the West Coast experience, was a national officer of the Association of Catholic Trade Unionists.

I think it would be a deviation from something that is ingrained in the American concept of jurisprudence. . . . As much as I sympathize with the desire of the Commission to get the information—you must believe me that I have the same problem every day, and sometimes wish that I could cut corners too—but I think it would be a deprivation of their civil rights and that the Legislature should not sanction it.[10]

The crucial question of whether employers should be free to select their workers received less attention in the hearings than any other procedural questions. The possibility that giving employers complete freedom of choice might perpetuate a surplus and mean low earnings for many registered men was recognized by very few of those who testified in the hearings. Father Corridan, Cleophas Jacobs, and James Conroy all implied that it would be necessary to strengthen the job security of registered longshoremen when they proposed that men be hired on a basis of seniority. The idea of hiring in rotation—the basic ingredient in the success of the West Coast system—met with formidable opposition and had only two supporters.

One of these supporters was the spokesman for Anthony Anastasia whose plan for union-operated halls gave employers the right to hire regular gangs, but required them to accept all other workers in rotation. The only other advocate of this view, the City Club of New York, stated the case for rotation most articulately:

> The essential logic of the plan is that it will encourage employers to try to hire the best men and keep them employed, making whatever arrangements are necessary to build the proper relationship between employer and employee. If an employer does not do this, he must take his chances on the rotation system. If an employee, on the other hand, feels that he is not being adequately employed by a regular employer, he too can quit his regular employer and take his chance on the rotation system.[11]

On the other hand, the NYSA insisted that to operate efficiently employers must be free to select, not only regular gangs, but all other employees as well. This position was supported by Walter Hedden of the Port Authority, who argued that rotation was unnecessary because it was anticipated that the Crime Commission's proposed plan would automatically bring the number of longshoremen eligible for employment down from 36,000 to about 25,000. Both Hedden and the NYSA were convinced that 25,000 men could earn adequate wages and, at the same time, handle all the work of the port.[12]

195

Thus the hearings ended without providing Governor Dewey with an acceptable alternative to the Crime Commission's recommendations, drastic as these were. Immediate action was dictated by the overwhelming support for the commission's bill, and by the end of the month the Waterfront Commission Act was placed on the statute books. In view of the almost complete mandate given legislators to adopt the Crime Commission's plan without amendment, the efforts made by the drafters of the final bill to accommodate the few dissenters who had come forward in the hearings were remarkable. Understandably, no compromise was made in the substantive issues involved—the legislators ignored the ILA's opposition to government halls and the NYSA's opposition to licensing stevedores. The legislators also chose to abolish outright the practice of public loading, rather than to license public loaders as the Crime Commission had urged. But the language of the law reflected a genuine attempt to meet almost all procedural objections raised in the hearings. Those who had urged that the law be considered temporary were reassured by a specific provision that government intervention should be terminated at the earliest possible time. Fears that the legislation might be administered in a way which would adversely affect bona fide trade unionism were given consideration in a provision in the law specifically endorsing collective bargaining, and including the language that "nothing in this compact shall be construed to limit in any way the right of employees to strike."[13] The most objectionable features of the proposed registration and licensing procedure were modified in two ways. The stipulation that longshoremen be deregistered if they refused to testify about waterfront activities was omitted from the law, and the chamber of commerce's reservations about licensing stevedoring companies were met by allowing licenses to run for two years, rather than one.

Even on the question of whether employers should enjoy unrestricted freedom to choose their employees in the hiring halls, the legislatures adopted a far more flexible position than the Crime Commission had recommended. The commission's bill had provided that "employers should be entitled to designate such registered dock workers as they may desire,"[14] but the new law pointedly omitted such a guarantee:

> This compact is not designed and shall not be construed to limit in any way any rights . . . to bargain collectively and agree upon any method of selection of such employees by way of seniority, experience, regular gangs or otherwise."[15]

196

Specific instructions to future administrators of the employment information centers were limited to ordering them to adopt policies "to the end that longshoremen and port watchmen shall have the maximum information as to available employment . . . and to the end that employers shall have an adequate opportunity to fill their requirements,"[16] and to permit the establishment of convenient facilities for cashing longshoremen's paychecks.* Thus the law leaves the union and the employers free to work with the staff of the hiring halls in developing whatever kind of hiring system they desire, limited only by the requirement that men be hired through the halls.

Expenses of operating the centers are to be met by assessing employers' gross payrolls at a rate, not to exceed two per cent, which should yield sufficient revenue (about two million dollars) to finance the Waterfront Commission's annual budget. For several reasons, this arrangement commended itself to the legislators. It gives the employers a direct incentive to help find the most efficient system of operating the centers so as to keep expenses to a minimum, and it prevents the NYSA from developing a vested interest in preserving government operation, which they might if the state were paying the bill. This arrangement also strikes at another waterfront evil. The practice of keeping incomplete financial records had made it easy for many stevedoring concerns to cover up bribery and corruption of union officials and shipping-company representatives (and, one suspects, to evade payment of income taxes). Under its power to levy assessments on employers' payrolls, the Waterfront Commission is now authorized to require that

> every person subject to the payment of assessment hereunder shall keep an accurate record of his employment of longshoremen, pier superintendents, hiring agents, or port watchmen, which shall show the amount of compensation paid and such other information as the commission may require. Such records shall be preserved for a period of three years and be open for inspection at reasonable times.[17]

Controlling the longshore industry by keeping its financial records under close surveillance is, to be sure, a radical departure from past practices on the New York waterfront, but it is not in this arrangement that the significant break with tradition appears. After all, other regulated industries in the United States have to open their books to representatives of administrative agencies. The truly unique features of the law are

---

* The law required that wage payments be made either by check or, if by cash, only when evidenced by a written voucher receipted by the person to whom cash was paid. *N.Y. Laws* (1953), chap. 882, XII 4.

found in its licensing provisions, which add a new dimension to the usual standards of firms operating in publicly regulated industries. Normally, a regulatory agency determines that applicants for licenses "possess good character and integrity" on the basis of standard character references and evidence of financial responsibility. The commission's requirement that persons holding as little as five per cent of a stevedoring company's stock must submit fingerprints and photographs suggests the far-reaching character of this new dimension. If a stevedore has ever been convicted of treason, murder, manslaughter, a felony, or a variety of misdemeanors (such as drug addiction), or if he *attempts* to violate the Waterfront Commission Act, he must submit to the commission evidence of good conduct for the preceding five years before his company can hold a license. In addition, stevedoring companies can be refused permission to operate if they are discovered attempting to bribe either a shipping-company representative or a union official at any time "after July 1, 1953."[18]

The conditions under which pier superintendents and hiring foremen can be barred from the waterfront are even more stringent than those applicable to employers. In general, the Waterfront Commission is empowered to demand from applicants for licenses any facts and evidence "as may be required by the commission to ascertain the character, integrity, and identity of the prospective licensee."[19] Men may be disqualified from holding these jobs for all the reasons which apply to stevedores but, in addition, hiring foremen and superintendents can be barred from the industry if they have received kickbacks, if they have coerced longshoremen to make purchases from or to utilize the services of any person, or if they have loaned money to or borrowed money from a longshoreman where interest was charged.

It is significant that, unlike the protection afforded stevedores, the law includes no statute of limitations for offenses disqualifying hiring foremen and superintendents. The absence of any language clearly prohibiting an *ex post facto* ruling in cases involving these men may permit the Waterfront Commission to exclude them for past actions, and other provisions of the law suggest that the legislators may have intended to enable the commission to do so. The relevant provisions state that "it shall be sufficient to prove only a single act (or a single holding out or attempt) prohibited by law, without having to prove a general course of conduct, in order to prove a violation," and furthermore, that "this compact shall be liberally construed to eliminate the evils described therein."[20]

In addition to the probe revolving around past and present criminal behavior, hiring foremen and superintents must meet two more tests. They are prohibited from belonging to a union which represents longshoremen or port watchmen,* and they are disqualified if it is determined that

> the prospective licensee knowingly or wilfully advocates the desirability of overthrowing or destroying the government of the United States by force or violence or shall be a member of a group which advocates such desirability, knowing the purpose of such group includes such advocacy.[21]

Ironically, the group in whose behalf the Waterfront Commission Act was presumably drafted—the longshoremen—are required to meet more stringent tests than any other group in the industry. The arrangements for screening longshoremen are described in different language—here the references are to "registration" rather than licensing—but the practical effect is identical. The Waterfront Commission can require from longshoremen any "facts and evidence as the commission may prescribe to establish the identity of such persons and his criminal record, if any."[22] Longshoremen may be declared ineligible for registration because of past crimes or misdemeanors on all the same grounds as employers and supervisory employees. They are also subject to the same political test as that applicable to supervisory employees. For longshoremen, however, there are two additional qualifications. A man can be deregistered

> whose presence at the piers or other waterfront terminals . . . is found by the commission on the basis of the facts and evidence before it, to constitute a danger to the public peace or safety.[23]

He may also lose his registration if he is found to be guilty of

> wilful commission of or wilful attempt to commit at or on a waterfront terminal or adjacent highway any act of physical injury to any other person or of wilful damage to or misappropriation of any other person's property, unless justified or excused by law.[24]

It is true that the same article of the law which sets forth these two provisions specifies that none of these licensing requirements are to be construed to limit in any way the right of workers to organize, to bargain collectively, or to strike. It is also true that at the time the law was passed the legislators may well have viewed these two provisions as arming the commission with means to prosecute public loaders and to protect longshoremen from being coerced by other longshoremen or union officials who were antagonistic to the new hiring arrangements. But this screening

---

* The language of the law does not prohibit foremen from joining a separate union, even if it is connected with the same congress or federation as that of the other two groups, but clearly rules out affiliation with the same international. Other licensing requirements for port watchmen are almost identical with those for hiring foremen.

program suffers from the same weaknesses as other screening programs —loosely drawn standards are often subject to widely differing interpretations depending on the circumstances. If the AFL organizing campaign on the waterfront meets with resistance from ILA members and the port is tied up while the two factions battle it out, is it not possible that a leader of an unpopular faction might seem to commission members to constitute "a danger to the public peace and safety"? And drawing a parallel from the West Coast experience, did it not seem to some people that certain Seattle longshoremen were inflicting "wilful damage to . . . other persons' property" during the turbulent period when quickie strikes and job action were almost daily occurrences?

Although this legislation was viewed in 1953 as a temporary expedient, our experience with other "temporary" legislation has shown that laws once enacted tend to endure. This legislation may remain on the books long after the public has forgotten the sympathy it felt for the exploited longshoremen when the law was passed. If prolonged and costly work stoppages occur in the future, members of the Waterfront Commission may be subjected to such strong public pressure that they will be forced to place different interpretations on these registration provisions than the lawmakers intended. It is less likely that the legislative intent will be perverted with respect to stevedores, but again drawing on the West Coast experience, we have seen that bitter quarrels over policy decisions can arise among members of an employers' association. Furthermore, "free riders" are no more popular among organized employers than among organized workers. A strong employers' association could conceivably use the numerous licensing requirements in the law to harass a nonconforming firm in order to "bring it into line." In 1953, several stevedores operating in New York were either outside the New York Shipping Association, or were not subject to its discipline.

Given the range of possible interpretations which might be read into the licensing requirements, the procedures open to persons who want to appeal a decision of the commission take on special significance. It is encouraging that the procedural safeguards outlined in the law appear to afford considerably more protection to appellants than those provided in most screening programs.

The commission is required to give not less than 10 days notice of its intention to revoke a license or registration, and to state the reasons for its action. It is, however, empowered to suspend persons temporarily if the commission believes that retention of the license or registration "would be inimical to the public peace and safety."[25] No one's license or registration is to be revoked, nor is an application to be denied, without a hearing in which the aggrieved person may be represented by counsel. The commission has the power to issue subpoenas and to administer oaths in connection with these hearings, but is also required to issue subpoenas "at the request of and upon behalf of the licensee, registrant or applicant."[26] Furthermore, and this is an exceptional privilege in such proceedings, the person being "tried" is entitled to cross-examine witnesses against him.[27] Hearing officers are not bound by common law or statutory rules of evidence and, as already noted, the legislators instructed the commission that the law is to be interpreted liberally. However, any person against whom an adverse finding is made has the right of judicial review. By establishing these eminently reasonable appeal procedures, the lawmakers made a genuine attempt to protect persons against arbitrary action by the Waterfront Commission, and there is no reason to believe that these procedures will prove inadequate protection under normal conditions.

The New York waterfront, however, appears to be headed for unsettled times. American labor history is replete with examples of industrial disputes engendering such peculiarly violent reactions that it is possible, if not probable, that procedural safeguards—however reasonable—may not always give men who become highly unpopular with the public the protection they would enjoy if the grant of authority to the commission had been more clearly delineated. When emotions are running high, the impact on the ability of the union to use its traditional weapons may be similarly restricted. In labor-management disputes, timing is often of great importance. If, under some unique set of circumstances, a key group of men are found to be "inimical to the public peace and safety," and these men are suddenly told that they no longer have the right to pursue their activities on the waterfront, their right to cross-examine witnesses in hearings 10 days later, and to obtain judicial review of a commission decision months later, may not be fully meaningful. Perhaps such a pessimistic view of the Waterfront Commission's ability to withstand public pressure is unwarranted, but only time will tell.

Having done their best to provide as fair treatment to stevedores, supervisory personnel, and longshoremen as seemed compatible with the reform plan, the legislators evidently were unable to restrain themselves from taking a back-handed swipe at the one remaining waterfront group who was responsible for much of the trouble in the port—the ILA hierarchy. The provisions of the Waterfront Commission Act which deal directly with the union made no apparent attempt to treat this group fairly or, it would appear, even constitutionally. The act declares it to be unlawful for any person to solicit or collect dues from registered longshoremen on behalf of any labor organization

> if any officer or agent of such organization has been convicted
> . . . of a felony unless he has been subsequently pardoned
> . . . or has received a certificate of good conduct from the
> board of parole.[28]

The legislators were undoubtedly aware that this section, if enforced, would more than likely precipitate a substantial amount of litigation without seriously curtailing the activities of the ILA, but perhaps they felt that its mere presence in the statute might have a deterrent effect on the union while New Yorkers waited for the AFL to expel the ILA and establish a new union. The whole section has the appearance of having been tacked on almost as an afterthought—the Waterfront Commission is not charged with enforcing it, and it is quite out of character with the general approach of the other features of the law.

A Shape-up With a Roof Over It?

The licensing provisions of the act seem to be well designed for the job of eliminating from the waterfront many persons who have practiced abuses under the shape-up, but it is difficult to predict how well the law will cure the basic condition which gave rise to these waterfront evils— the insecure employment and low earnings of many longshoremen. That few, if any, New Yorkers were aware of the complexities inherent in the task of putting an effective decasualization scheme into operation was clearly revealed both in the Crime Commission's recommendations and in the testimony given in the Dewey hearings. New York reformers could have profited from the lessons the longshore industry has learned in Seattle. As early as 1921, Seattle employers saw that, if regular longshoremen were to have any real job security, stevedores would have to give up their freedom to select individual workers from the hiring hall, the nucleus of the labor force would have to be carefully limited to a very small part of the total number of men hired in the course of a year, and finally that many casual workers were still going to be needed and would play an important part in the industry.

The reform proposal which won out in New York is predicated on the belief that in the course of operation, the employment centers will automatically produce a registered labor force of about 25,000 men, and on an assumption that this number of men will be able to earn adequate incomes and perform all necessary work of the port. This means reducing the number of men eligible to work as longshoremen to about two-thirds of the number who have worked on the waterfront in any recent year. But, paradoxically, if longshoring in Seattle is comparable to longshoring in New York—and there is no reason to doubt this assumption—25,000 men are almost certainly too large a *regular* labor force to enable all men to earn adequate incomes, and too small a *total* labor force to handle all work of the port in a 12-month period. Years of experience with a hiring hall in a casual-labor market have taught Seattle employers and the union that having a regular labor force of more than about 1,400 men would result in low earnings, "unemployment claims and dissatisfaction." But the 1,400 registered men (70 per cent of whom earned $4,000 or more in 1951) represent only one-fourth of the total number who work in the port during the year. In fact, a comparison of the earnings of all men who worked in each port reveals that, contrary to the notion that a hiring hall eliminates the need for casual workers, Seattle hired a higher percentage of casual workers than New York did under the shape-up (60 per cent as compared with 50 per cent).

TABLE 8

ANNUAL EARNINGS OF LONGSHOREMEN
SEATTLE, 1951, AND NEW YORK, 1950

Annual earnings in dollars	SEATTLE			NEW YORK		
	Number	Per cent of total	Cumulative percentage	Number	Per cent of total	Cumulative percentage
5,000 and over	883	14.9	14.9	692	1.9	1.9
4,000 to 4,999	529	8.9	23.8	2,519	6.9	8.8
3,000 to 3,999	360	6.1	29.9	5,636	15.4	24.2
2,000 to 2,999	249	4.2	34.1	4,958	13.6	37.8
1,000 to 1,999	323	5.5	39.6	4,208	11.5	49.3
0 to 999	3,576	60.4	100.0	18,527	50.7	100.0
Total	5,920	100.0	—	36,540	100.0	—

Source: Payroll records, Washington Area, Pacific Maritime Association; *Board of Inquiry*, p. 54.

The Seattle experience suggests that many more casual workers than was anticipated by the Port Authority will be needed on the New York waterfront from time to time. Fortunately, the law authorizes the commission to give temporary registration to casual workers if additional workers are needed at any time, and, presumably, the rigid licensing requirements will be suspended for workers who are hired on this basis.[29] However, if casual workers are to be hired more or less regularly, the question arises whether 25,000 is actually the optimum number of men to keep permanently registered. It has been demonstrated that the total amount of work in the port in a typical recent year was only enough to provide about 14,000 longshoremen with full-time employment.[30] If 25,000 men are registered and hired at the discretion of hiring foremen, the effect on the earnings and job security of many longshoremen is obvious. The solution to the problem is equally apparent—the regular men must be protected against the competition of casual workers, whether permanently or temporarily registered, through some system of job priority such as seniority or rotation. If hiring foremen who have roughly 14,000 jobs to dispense can choose among 25,000 men or more, it is inevitable that private "arrangements" will continue to be made between foremen and workers, even if the formal hiring takes place in a government-operated hall. A New York employment information center will then be little more than "a shape-up with a roof over it."

Thus the ultimate solution to the basic problem still rests with the employers and the union. The rules they agree on can spell the success or failure of the whole scheme. The technical administration of whatever hiring arrangements are adopted presents no insuperable problems, because the Waterfront Commission staff has the advantage of being able to draw on the West Coast experience and experience gained by the New York State Employment Service in operating hiring halls in three different industries where employment, although not as irregular as in longshoring, is intermittent.[31] The problems confronting the managers of these halls are similar to those facing the Waterfront Commission, and the apparent success of the employment service halls indicates that the dispatching job confronting the Waterfront Commission presents no unique problems.

Several features of the waterfront reform augur well for the ultimate adoption of dispatching rules which will give meaningful job security to the men. For one thing, the law gives the longshoremen a better chance to obtain a bona fide union than they have had for thirty years. Whether this union will be a rejuvenated ILA or a new AFL union is less important than the emergence of a representative union. The screening features of the law should remove from the waterfront many of the strong-arm men who have, in the past, been used by the employers and the ILA hierarchy to keep the longshoremen in line, and the establishment of 13 hiring halls in the port makes it a logical development for the present 31 ILA locals to be consolidated into 13 which will serve the men attached to each hiring hall. Although the men working in regular gangs will not be reporting into the halls regularly, the rest of the men will be brought together in the halls almost daily and will have more communication with each other than they were ever able to achieve under the shape-up and the gerrymandered structure of the old ILA. Since both the men in regular gangs and the men hired in the modified shape-up in the halls will still have only a tenuous claim on jobs, they will have a strong incentive to push for reforms in their union in order to bargain for more satisfactory dispatching rules.

204

Thus it seems likely that the union will ultimately embark on a campaign for rotary hiring similar to the drive the ILWU and other maritime unions launched in the 1930's. The response of the employers will largely determine whether, under the Waterfront Commission Act, the New York waterfront is to be peaceful or turbulent. The past behavior of the employers indicates that they may put up strong resistance, but there appears to be some basis for thinking that their policies may change. The act will presumably relieve the industry of some of the corrupt practices which gave many stevedores a vested interest in opposing reform, and those stevedores who want to conduct their affairs according to accepted standards of legitimate and responsible business practice may in the future be able to exercise greater influence in the employers' association. It seems reasonable to expect this group will have the intelligence to take advantage of the lessons learned on the West Coast, and that they will reach the same conclusion Seattle employers reached thirty years ago—that the unique nature of longshoring makes it impossible for the men to have decent working conditions unless the employers accept some sort of priority system of hiring, whether it be seniority or rotation.

Once a responsible union and a responsible employers' association evolve and reach agreement on this principle, the next step will be to begin retiring the government from the industry. The Seattle experience shows the positive advantages to both parties (and to the community) when the employers and the workers in the industry face up to, and solve, their own problems. When the employers and union in New York reach a level of maturity where they are capable of handling their own affairs, New York stevedores and longshoremen will finally be able to enjoy the self-respect and dignity their counterparts on the West Coast have enjoyed for years.

Recent Developments

As 1955 began, I found that the fifteen months then ended, crowded though they were with dramatic events, had wrought no meaningful changes on either of the two waterfronts. In Seattle, longshoremen were being dispatched to their jobs from the hiring hall and the "new look" phase of labor-management relations was moving quietly into its seventh year. In New York, the hopefully awaited AFL organizers had come and gone and the Waterfront Commission Act had been in effect for a year, but longshoremen were still shaping up for work each morning and still paying their union dues to the ILA. With few exceptions, the same ILA officials and employers whose conduct had aroused the public demand for waterfront reform were doing business as usual, circumventing the law whenever possible.

Incredibly, the AFL managed to throw away one of the most favorable organizing opportunities ever presented to a union. The New York longshore agreement expired on September 30, 1953—a week after the AFL convention expelled the discredited ILA—and Joseph Ryan hurried back from his defeat in St. Louis to try to persuade the employers to sign a new agreement immediately. Under NLRB rules, this would have precluded a representation election between the ILA and the new AFL union for at least a year. The employers seemed willing to acquiesce, especially when they found Ryan proposing an even better bargain than his usual request for "a dime an hour." To forestall this maneuver, the AFL served notice on the employers that they were filing with the NLRB for an election, and Dave Beck, speaking for the new union, publicly urged Governor Dewey to persuade the employers not to sign a "cut-rate" contract with the ILA. Beck's appeal (as quoted in the *New York Times* on September 26, 1953) contained an interesting explanation of why the governor should act:

206

> We see every evidence that the New York employers are bent on signing a contract they think will save them money, even though it means freezing racket control on the piers and making the job of honest unionism much harder. It was exactly that attitude on the part of waterfront employers that gave Harry Bridges his hold on the West Coast.

At this point, even before the new union had time to put its organizers on the docks, the cordial encouragement the AFL could count on from the New York press and from federal and state officials became apparent. The New York Shipping Association was immediately subjected to appeals from Governor Dewey and other public officials, and from private groups like the New York City Anti-Crime Committee, urging the employers not to sign with the ILA. The shipping association reluctantly yielded to this pressure on September 30, but demanded as a *quid pro quo* that President Eisenhower grant the employers the protection of a Taft-Hartley Act injunction against the coast-wide strike which desperate ILA officials had set for the next day. Federal officials apparently did not expect any show of strength from the rapidly disintegrating ILA—they did not set in motion the machinery for obtaining a national emergency injunction until asked to do so by the employers. But the ILA struck the next day, and for a week shipping came to a standstill in all Atlantic Coast ports while a Presidential board of inquiry was hurriedly appointed and held its hearings, after which the attorney general was free to obtain a court order enjoining the work stoppage. The strike proceeded in an atmosphere of suppressed excitement, with the AFL wisely remaining on the sidelines. New York newspapers assured their readers that the work stoppage, which everyone knew would soon be enjoined, was preferable to a settlement with the ILA, and pointed out that when the injunction went into effect, the new AFL union would have almost three months in which to complete its organizing campaign.

But during those three months the AFL campaign never quite got off the ground. Confident of an easy victory, the new union put little of its $1,000,000 campaign fund into the organizational techniques such as mass rallies, questionnaires on grievances, leaflets, and newspaper ads, which had been perfected in the 1930's for appealing to large groups of workers. Instead, the AFL tried to reach longshoremen through organizers assigned to local pier areas. Some of these organizers were highly effective campaigners for the AFL—men who emerged from the rank and file like John Dwyer in Manhattan and Tony Mike De Vincenzo in Hoboken, for example—but no indigenous leader appeared who was capable of rallying followers in all sections of the port. (Gene Sampson, who had been regarded by many New Yorkers as the most influential insurgent leader on the waterfront, joined the AFL forces early in the campaign, but was unable to carry with him more than a handful from the local he had represented for 32 years.) In other sections of the port, the AFL accepted the assistance of several well-known hoodlums whose past records in the ILA made some longshoremen begin to doubt the AFL's assurances that the new union would be free from racketeering. Using these men was a mistake. Racket-free unionism was the only plank in the AFL campaign platform.

The AFL did not attempt to formulate a broader program for several reasons. Men who were active in the campaign were sure that many, perhaps most, longshoremen were disgusted with the ILA, but no one knew what sort of positive program would appeal to the majority. A variety of working practices had long been established in different sections of the port, and a port-wide program offering a new and unfamiliar substitute for practices longshoremen were used to might have frightened off men the AFL was trying to reach. Also, the AFL realized that a strategically situated nucleus of ILA members had a vested interest in the old system; these men could be expected to use their influence to create mistrust and fear of any new plan.

Another obstacle to presenting an integrated program to the longshoremen was that the men conducting the campaign had conflicting plans in mind for the future of the waterfront. (Of the five-man committee appointed at the AFL convention to direct the affairs of the new union, only Dave Beck of the teamsters and Paul Hall of the sailors' union took part in the organizing effort.) Beck's interest in the longshoremen was apparently limited to getting the men who load and unload trucks on the piers out of the longshoremen's union and into his International Brotherhood of Teamsters. He remained in his Washington headquarters except for brief visits to New York, and showed little interest in helping to work out a program which would have broad appeal among the rank and file. Paul Hall's actions during the campaign led many to believe that he envisioned a new longshoremen's union as merely a useful adjunct of his New York sailors' union and saw the waterfront as a handy source of jobs for his sailors when they were out of work. Hall, though more willing than Beck to stage a strong effort, did no more than Beck to develop a program which would offer the longshoremen job security and give them a union free of officials with dubious scruples. When longshoremen who expected the AFL to establish responsible unionism offered their services at campaign headquarters, they soon perceived the narrow objectives of the men in control of the campaign fund. Thus, as the campaign got under way, men from the waterfront were mistrustful of Hall and Beck.

George Meany, president of the AFL, realized that things were not starting off well, and in the third week of the organizing drive, put a new man in charge—Ace Keeney, a trouble shooter for the International Association of Machinists. The task of reconciling the aims of the diverse factions in the organizing committee would have been challenging even to a man intimately familiar with the waterfront. For Keeney, a stranger to the complexities and personalities involved, the hazards of the assignment proved insuperable. Relations between the various factions in the organizing committee ultimately deteriorated to the point where each faction was sending out its own organizers and hiring its own attorneys to speak for the committee in dealings with government agencies and the employers. To the rank and file, Keeney remained a shadowy figure and the longshoremen never knew who was really directing the campaign.

The men were further confused by the behavior of other AFL unions in the New York area. Early in the organizing drive, ten top New York AFL officials petitioned President Meany for permission to bring the ILA "back into the family" and forget about the new union. Meany flatly rejected this suggestion, but the campaign had been under way for six weeks before he succeeded in eliciting pledges from the major AFL councils in New York that they would support the organizing drive. Martin Lacey, president of the teamsters' joint council in New York, was the instigator of the petition to Meany. Lacey not only was friendly with many ILA officials, but he and Dave Beck had long been in opposing factions in the teamsters' union, and Lacey was reluctant to help Beck extend his enclave in New York. The teamsters' joint council was the last group to announce they would go along with Meany and, even after giving this pledge, some teamster officials in New York continued to support the ILA throughout the campaign.

The longshoremen, who might well have been wondering whether the AFL regarded them as anything more than pawns in some larger maneuver, next had to evaluate the unexpected behavior of John L. Lewis, president of the United Mine Workers. Lewis, a bitter enemy of George Meany and the AFL, had been meeting with Beck and David MacDonald, president of the CIO steelworkers' union, to explore the possibility of forming a new labor federation. In the middle of the AFL waterfront campaign, Lewis loaned the nearly bankrupt ILA $200,000.

Terms of the loan were not made public, but it was rumored that Lewis had demanded a clean-up within the union as a condition of the loan. In any case, several ILA officials issued statements in November demanding that Ryan resign from the presidency. Mike Clemente, an ILA official who had fared none too well in the Crime Commission hearings himself, and who later went to jail for extortion, told a *New York Times* reporter that the following conversation ensued when he demanded that Ryan step down for the good of the union:

> Ryan said to me, "But why do you say that to me now when I've got an indictment hanging over my head?" And I said to him, "So what, I've got three indictments hanging over mine."

Either in response to urging from John L. Lewis or to impress the rank and file, the ILA held a special convention on November 18, 1953, at which Ryan was retired and given the title of president emeritus. If the delegates contemplated proving to the longshoremen that the ILA was at last capable of cleaning its own house, that purpose was lost when the convention absolved Ryan of the charges of stealing union funds and awarded him a pension of $10,000 a year. Captain William V. Bradley, who had been president of the New York Tugboat local since 1937, was elected to succeed Ryan. Bradley qualified for the job chiefly because the union wanted a man from New York, and Bradley was a rarity among the union's New York officials—he had not been charged in the Crime Commission hearings with abusing his union office.

A week after Captain Bradley's election, the AFL committed one of the major blunders of the campaign. People in a better position than Dave Beck to know the longshoremen's attitudes had been fearful that if Beck carried out his intention to split off the loaders and absorb them into the teamsters' union, it would turn many longshoremen against the AFL. Father Corridan made a special trip to Washington to try to convince Beck to drop his plan, but on November 24 Beck announced that he had chartered a new teamsters' local to take over the 2,500 loaders. Paul Hall issued a statement applauding Beck's action and promising to help the new local get on its feet. A short time later, any longshoreman who had refused to believe that Beck was determined to see that loading jobs were done by teamsters must have been convinced when he learned that Beck had offered New York trucking firms a $2,000,000 loan to set up an equipment pool which would enable them to take over the functions of the outlawed public loaders.

The AFL's appeal to the longshoremen was further weakened when, despite AFL claims that the ILA remained in power only by using violence and intimidation, AFL sympathizers themselves resorted to strong-arm tactics. In the earliest days of the campaign, AFL supporters equipped to give battle invaded the area controlled by Anthony Anastasia, who was determined to keep the Brooklyn waterfront in the ILA camp. Pitched battles resulted. Who started the fights was not clear, but longshoremen could see that the AFL was no less willing than the ILA to use coercion in order to win. The most flagrant use of force by the AFL occurred late in the campaign when 75 AFL supporters invaded the Newark port area and wrecked the offices of an ILA local.

As the expiration date of the 80-day injunction neared, the Presidential board of inquiry reconvened and reported that the employers had not made a clear and definite last offer to the ILA and that, in any event, rivalry between the competing unions was the paramount issue. Accordingly, the NLRB called off plans for a vote on the last offer and, instead, scheduled a representation election for December 22 and 23. Tension on the waterfront mounted as the days for voting approached, erupting into stonings, fist fights, and several stabbings as the men went to the polling places. Even with the poverty of alternatives offered them, more than 85 per cent of the eligible longshoremen cast ballots. When the votes were counted, 9,060 men had voted for the old union, 7,568 for the AFL, and 95 for no union. The ILA could not claim an immediate victory, however, because the votes of an additional 4,397 men had been challenged.

If the election results came as a surprise to everyone else, they came as a humiliating shock to the AFL. When federation officials recovered from the initial impact of the news, they demanded that the NLRB set aside the election on the grounds that the ILA had used intimidation and gang violence to influence the vote. Governor Dewey supported the AFL petition, citing acts of violence reported to him by police. NLRB officials agreed to investigate the charges, thus giving the AFL another period of grace in which to continue its campaign. Week after week went by without a decision from the NLRB. During this time, the port was the scene of frequent work stoppages as ILA and AFL longshoremen battled about who should control particular dock areas.

In late February, 1954—more than two months after the election— the sporadic skirmishes came to a head in a dispute reminiscent of the jurisdictional tugs of war which kept the West Coast in a turmoil during the 1930's. ILA supporters at a Hudson River pier forced the discharge of an AFL shop steward; immediately, AFL longshoremen picketed the pier. At this point, the split in the New York teamsters' organization came into the picture. The head of Local 807 of the teamsters' union was a strong supporter of the AFL longshoremen's union, and members of his local refused to cross the AFL picket line. The dispute spread as ILA members on other piers refused to load or unload trucks driven by members of Local 807, but continued to serve trucks driven by members of other teamster locals which supported the ILA. Local 807 retaliated by picketing piers where this was happening.

In an attempt to end these tie-ups, the NLRB charged the ILA with engaging in a secondary boycott and, on March 4, obtained a restraining order requiring ILA members to go back to work. Curiously, the court order did not enjoin the AFL or Local 807 from picketing. Instead of ending the localized work stoppages, the board's action brought to a head the growing irritation ILA supporters felt toward the NLRB for delaying a decision on the December election. The day after the court order was issued, ILA men struck in most sections of the port. President Bradley toured the docks trying to persuade the men to obey the order, but his efforts were totally ineffective. Four days later, with the strike spreading to more and more piers, the NLRB asked the court to fine the ILA $100,000 and to imprison three key local officials for violating the restraining order. While the judge was signing the papers directing the union to show cause why the NLRB petition should not be granted, 500 ILA longshoremen defiantly picketed the courthouse.

The mayor of New York attempted to mediate the dispute. When he failed, the AFL began laying plans to open the port. Members of the organizing committee who had worked as longshoremen and had participated in earlier waterfront strikes tried to persuade the top AFL strategists that this plan could be disastrous to the organizing drive, just as they had advised Beck against chartering his loaders' local, but on the sixteenth day of the walk-out, Paul Hall began trying to run men through the ILA picket lines. He had powerful support—the mayor, other city officials, and the personnel of the Waterfront Commission all worked closely with the AFL in the effort, as they saw it, to break the strangle hold of ILA gangsters who were tying up the port. Irate business men and public officials were convinced that if adequate protection could be provided against ILA goon squads, the 7,500 men who had voted for the AFL would go back on the job, and at least some of the men who had supported the ILA would be persuaded to abandon their discredited officials. After the AFL had been trying this new approach for four days, however, only 1,200 of the usual 15,000 longshoremen were on the job.

What was wrong? Inadequate police protection seemed to be the answer; Mayor Wagner accordingly increased the number of policemen assigned to the piers, and the Waterfront Commission announced that it could guarantee to men who were willing to work a police guard from the information center to the job. Even with these assurances, the trickle of men to the piers increased only slightly. With public irritation over the tie-up mounting each day, AFL strategists become increasingly embar-

rassed by their inability to produce more followers among the longshoremen. They finally decided to save the situation by augmenting their numbers with unemployed sailors. The men were loaded into completely covered vans which rumbled to the piers while detachments of mounted police
held back the surging ILA pickets. Even this maneuver failed to produce
enough men to open the port.

Why longshoremen did not respond in greater numbers to this opportunity to break the hold of the ILA is an intriguing question. Some longshoremen were prevented from working, according to the Waterfront
Commission, because employers were collaborating with the ILA to keep
the AFL off the waterfront. Almost daily during the strike, the commission
complained that men had to be turned away from the information centers
for lack of job assignments, even though the harbor was filled with ships
waiting to be worked. The commission named some employers who
refused to send in any orders for men at all, and others who refused
to hire any but ILA men. Instances were reported where employers
professed they were willing to hire men but the hiring foremen who
worked for them refused to blow their whistles for a shape-up. The employers answered the commission's charges by saying that the commission was
trying to force them to hire men who were not qualified longshoremen and
who would have endangered life and property had they been put to work.

Fear must have kept many longshoremen from going to work. The
ILA hierarchy's past record of using violence to keep dissidents in line
would have been enough to intimidate most men, and daily reports of men
who crossed the picket lines being beaten, stoned, and knifed made others
skeptical of official assurances that men who worked would be protected.
Some men who were willing to face the personal risk of running the
gantlet of ILA pickets did go to work but left the docks when their families received threatening phone calls at home.

Some people who participated in the strike, including some AFL supporters, believed that the main reason longshoremen failed to respond
to the AFL's call to open the port was because the men felt it was a legitimate strike. Longshoremen who would have ignored the pickets if they
had represented only the mobsters felt a sense of identity with men who
insisted they were striking—in March—to force the NLRB to decide
who had won the December election, so that whichever union won could
get on with the job of negotiating a new contract to replace the one which
had expired six months earlier. Men who viewed the strike in this light
could not be persuaded to go through the picket lines merely to accommodate the NLRB, Mayor Wagner, the New York business community,
and Governor Dewey and his Waterfront Commission.

When the strike was in its twentieth day, Captain Bradley and his ILA advisers finally took courage from the failure of the AFL to open the port and gave the strike official sanction. Captain Bradley's announcement brought a new flood of demands from the business community that public officials do something about the strike which, it was feared, would now spread to the tugboats in New York harbor as well as to other Atlantic Coast ports. When Governor Dewey was asked if he planned to take any action, he replied obliquely, reminding reporters that as governor he had the power to remove the mayor and police commissioner of New York City "if there is a breakdown of law enforcement." Stung by this threat, Mayor Wagner appealed to President Eisenhower to take whatever federal action was necessary to end the shutdown. In his message to the President, the mayor accused the NLRB of prolonging the strike by the board's "interminable delay" in reaching a decision on the representation election. President Eisenhower did not reply to Mayor Wagner directly, but the next day a spokesman for the NLRB said that procedures for reaching a decision in the election had been streamlined.

A few days later, 1,000 ILA supporters caravaned to Washington and picketed the White House, urging the President to intercede in their behalf with the NLRB, which was then holding hearings on the representation election. While longshoremen were picketing in Washington, a group of government officials including Governor Dewey, the secretary of labor, and representatives of the federal attorney general's office, were meeting in New York to plan a "legal crackdown" against the strike, which they described as a criminal conspiracy. The officials made it clear that while the crackdown would be directed primarily against the ILA, it would also be applied to any employers who obstructed the opening of the port.

Whatever action the government officials may have had in mind, the crackdown never materialized. Three days after the threat was made, the NLRB announced its decision to set aside the first election and hold a new vote. At the same time, the board told the ILA that if the union did not end the strike "forthwith," the ILA would be left off the ballot. Either the board's ultimatum or the announcement of a decision on the election brought the work stoppage to an end on April 2—the twenty-ninth day of the strike.

Too exhausted and impoverished by the hectic events of the past month to resume civil war, ILA and AFL longshoremen worked side by side with few skirmishes while they awaited the second election, scheduled for May 26. The ILA was under continuous attack right up to the day of the election. With the vote only two weeks away, the almost bankrupt union was found guilty of violating the injunction issued during the strike and fined $50,000. Eight of its locals were fined an additional $42,000, and three local officials were sentenced to jail. Five days before the election, the union's funds were impounded by the court, and on the day longshoremen went to the polls they read that the ILA had been placed in receivership by a federal judge.

The ILA was dealt a heavy blow from still another government source three days before the vote when an official of the Waterfront Commission announced that he had forwarded to a federal district attorney documentary proof that two of Anthony Anastasia's lieutenants had gone to the West Coast to meet with Harry Bridges and that the ILWU had given them more than $3,000. The commission spokesman acknowledged to newsmen that there was nothing illegal in one union soliciting financial assistance from another, but explained that he wanted to call the attention of the federal government to the presence of possible subversion on the piers so that the government could take any action it might deem appropriate. Captain Bradley heatedly denied that the ILA had either sought or accepted help "from Harry Bridges or from any other Communist element," and he accused the Waterfront Commission of seeking to influence the coming election in favor of the AFL. Then, on the eve of the election, New York newspapers carried the story that the federal district attorney had asked the FBI "to check into possible hook-ups between Communist forces on the West Coast and followers of Anthony Anastasia." As the incident was presented to the public, ILWU contributions to the ILA sounded sinister indeed, and AFL organizers tried to turn the sensational disclosures to their advantage.

Although any example of coöperation between the ILA and the ILWU was newsworthy (the two unions had not been on speaking terms since 1937), the incident was hardly sinister. During the strike in March, 42 Brooklyn longshoremen had been charged with acts of violence and suspended from their jobs by the Waterfront Commission. Anthony Impliazzo, president of Local 327-1, and Thomas Di Bella, a Brooklyn longshoreman, had gone to the West Coast to raise money to help the suspended men. The ILWU had been following developments in New York with great interest because of the implications for the West Coast if the New York waterfront fell under the control of Dave Beck and Paul Hall—the eastern lieutenant of Harry Lundeberg. The ILWU gave Impliazzo and Di Bella a cordial reception, and locals up and down the coast extended invitations to the Brooklyn men to address their meetings. After Impliazzo summarized the March strike and explained to West Coast longshoremen that he and Di Bella were there on behalf of men who had been screened off the waterfront by a government hiring hall,

ILWU members in most locals voted to contribute to the defense fund. All told, they gave more than $13,000—an average of one dollar a member. Reports of meetings at which Impliazzo and Di Bella appeared were written up in issues of the ILWU newspaper, the first report appearing a week before the Waterfront Commission presented its "documentary evidence" to the federal district attorney.

With all these last-minute developments to consider, longshoremen went to the polls on May 26, 1954. New Yorkers eagerly awaited the results, confident that the elaborate precautions being taken to prevent the ILA from intimidating voters would ensure a hands-down victory for the AFL. The six polling places were guarded by 2,500 policemen, and the balloting was described by the regional director of the NLRB as the most orderly he had ever seen. When the results were announced, the vote was close but the ILA was in the lead—the old union had 9,110 votes and the AFL had 8,791. The only consolation was that, again, there were enough challenged ballots—1,797 of them—to leave the issue in doubt. Three months went by while the NLRB studied the challenges, during which the waterfront remained relatively quiet. Finally, on August 27, the board announced that the ILA had won by 263 votes (the final tally was 9,407 for the ILA and 9,144 for the AFL). The board reluctantly certified the old union as the exclusive bargaining agent for the longshoremen, which foreclosed another representation election for at least a year. The AFL decided to give up the fight and departed, as A. H. Raskin of the *New York Times* put it, "with indecent haste," leaving their 9,000 followers in New York to make their own peace with the men who had been running the waterfront for years.

What influenced the longshoremen to vote as they did remains a mystery. Many voters must have been negatively rather than positively motivated, because both unions deserved to lose; the ILA for its historic betrayal of its members, the AFL for its egregious campaign. One guess is as good as another as to what tipped the scales in favor of the ILA, but my guess is that the overzealous support given the organizing drive by all branches of government put the kiss of death on the AFL.

Even as the ILA survived the AFL organizing drive, waterfront exploiters and their shape-up survived the Waterfront Commission Act. The commission labored mightily to carry out its mandate to screen undesirables off the waterfront; at the end of the commission's first year of operation, some fifty hiring foremen and pier superintendents had been forced to give up their jobs, and almost three times as many longshoremen had been denied registration. The removal of these men had an imperceptible effect on the waterfront spoils system. In fact, not all of them were removed—some of the most notorious hoodlums who were screened off blandly went back to their old piers by taking jobs as maintenance men or carpenters' helpers, jobs over which the Waterfront Commission had no jurisdiction. The licensing requirements for stevedoring companies had only a minor effect on the composition of the New York Shipping Association; one firm sold out and left the port, withdrawing its application for a license when it became apparent that the application would be rejected. Even public loaders, outlawed a year earlier, were, according to the Waterfront Commission, still doing business, though in altered form—sharing fees with stevedoring companies and renting equipment at suspicious rates. Reformers who had thought that licensing would be an effective weapon with which to clean up the waterfront had, at the end of a year, little evidence to support their belief.

The commission labored with equal vigor to find an alternative to the shape-up. The bistate agency's hands were tied, however, because the law under which commission officials operated expressly prohibited them from imposing any system of dispatching men which limited the freedom of employers to choose their workers. People with a vested interest in the shape-up were still in power, and every proposal offered by the commission to modify the hiring system was rejected by the NYSA and ILA with such comments as "unsound," "fraught with dangers," "asinine," "an economic burden."

As a result, a Waterfront Commission information center, in which hiring was conducted under the watchful eyes of commission officials, was, in January, 1955, a shape-up with a roof over it. In the old days, a hiring foreman conducting a shape-up at the pier would first call for regular gangs and then pick extra men from the shape-up in the street; under the commission's rules, regular gangs reported directly to the pier and the hiring foreman went to the information center to pick extra men. In some centers, each hiring foreman was allotted a space in the hall with a white semicircle painted on the floor. When he was ready to begin hiring, he stepped inside the semicircle, the men shaped up behind the line, and he picked the men he wanted. Hiring foremen who normally picked large numbers of men were provided with a platform so that they would be high enough to see over the crowd. In other centers, instead of the hiring foreman having a fixed place, sections of the hall were designated according to job classifications, such as hold men, deck men, dock men. The hiring foreman made up a gang or picked replacements by going from one shape-up to the next.

It is not surprising that shape-ups were frequently conducted in union offices or on the street and then reënacted in the information centers by means of the "toothpick gimmick," described earlier, or some variant of it. As a commission official complained late in 1954, "it seems as though the process is done outside the centers and then recorded there." Nor is it surprising that after a year of trying to clean up the waterfront, commission investigators were still spending much of their time running down reports of kickbacks and other abuses traditionally associated with the shape-up. If the purpose of the waterfront reform law was to improve the lot of the rank-and-file longshoreman, at the end of its first year the law was still on trial. As the Waterfront Commission put it in the agency's first annual report:

> Longshoremen have expressed disappointment that the [act] does not eliminate the element of favoritism by hiring agents. This can only be accomplished by the adoption of some objective method of hiring such as seniority or rotation. This, however, is beyond the powers of the commission.

As the commission began its second year, the agency launched an attack on the underlying cause of the longshoremen's disappointment, using the only weapon available under the law. The commission had learned from a year's experience that on an average day there were no more than 15,000 jobs available on the docks and that no more than 20,000 men were employed at peak periods, yet 40,000 men were registered. "Such an imbalance," a commission official said, "breeds crime, kickbacks, and corruption, and leaves many honest men with empty pockets." He pointed out that some men on the registration list actually had full-time jobs in other industries but when they came down to the waterfront for overtime work, they were favored by hiring foremen and ILA officials. In order to protect the regular men, the commission announced plans to cut 15,000 "part-timers, favorites, and poachers" from the list.

Even as logical a plan as this met with violent opposition from the parties. Employers denounced the plan as "ill-advised" and "repugnant to the process of collective bargaining." The ILA threatened a court test to review the commission's right "to impose its will on the intelligence of labor and management," and union officials immediately began spreading rumors among the rank and file in an attempt to discredit the commission's motives. Implying that this was a move to get rid of ILA men, the general organizer of the union suggested that the commission should, instead, drop every man who had not worked on the waterfront before the agency was created.

Ironically, union officials and employers had good reason to believe

218

they could enlist the support of some longshoremen in their efforts to frustrate the commission, even though the plan was in the men's own interest. From the first, some longshoremen had viewed the agency with apprehension, as they would any agency carrying out a screening program, especially when screening involved fingerprinting and subjecting the men to a security check. Other longshoremen were distrustful of the agency because of the behavior of commission officials during the March strike. Then, under heavy public pressure and exasperated by the obstructionist attitudes of the NYSA and ILA, the commission had proved incapable of maintaining the impartial attitude toward the strikers which was presumably contemplated by the legislators of New York and New Jersey when they included in the reform law language safeguarding "the right of employees to strike." Longshoremen who felt the strikers had a legitimate complaint naturally objected to the commission's active coöperation with the AFL and police in trying to break the strike. Even those longshoremen who supported the AFL must have been worried by the implications of the commission's threat to bar 143 men from the industry for their actions in the strike. While AFL longshoremen might have approved of the commission's suspending 52 men who were charged with specific acts of violence, most union workers would have been worried by the fact that 91 of the suspended men were charged with engaging in a traditional union tactic—mass picketing. Thus the Waterfront Commission could look forward to the prospect of having to overcome hostility among the longshoremen, as well as outright obstruction from the NYSA and ILA officials, in any attempt to put into effect even the limited reforms which the commission was empowered to establish.

The first contract negotiated after the Waterfront Commission Act went into effect reflected the determination of the ILA to circumvent the commission and the willingness of the shipping association to coöperate in the effort. As soon as the union was certified by the NLRB, the parties reopened negotiations and, except for a two-day strike in October which was settled by a 10-cent wage increase retroactive to the previous October, negotiations followed the traditional pattern laid down in the quarter-century when Ryan was spokesman for the ILA. At Thanksgiving, the parties announced a new two-year agreement which they proudly recommended to their members. The contract gave the longshoremen a 17-cent wage increase. It gave employers a no-strike clause and provision for appointment of an arbitrator who was to have power to levy fines and suspend workers for violations of the contract. It gave the ILA a two-year reprieve from another NLRB election and also a union shop, which meant that the 9,000 men who had voted for the AFL would have to pay dues to the ILA. The shipping association agreed to recognize as part of the contract the diverse working practices prevailing in various sections of the port, thus freezing in place an obstacle to development of a port-wide reform program. But the most significant provision had to do with new hiring arrangements—employers agreed to notify union locals each day of the number of men they would need the following day. This meant that despite efforts of the Waterfront Commission to the contrary, ILA officials would be more firmly in control of the spoils system than ever —they would know exactly how many of their designees to send to the information centers the next morning to be picked in the shape-up. As one ILA official jubilantly said to me of the new arrangement, "Now we'll ignore the commission's centers—hiring is going to be done right here in my local."

Following a tradition laid down by President Emeritus Ryan, Captain Bradley tried to sell the contract to his members by promising a clean-up within the union as soon as the agreement went into effect: "We are now in a position to do some screening and investigating of rumors of corruption in the ILA. We do not intend in any way, shape or form to tolerate this sort of thing." In a vote supervised by the Honest Ballot Association, the rank and file turned the contract down by a vote of 6,199 against acceptance to 4,590 in favor.

ILA negotiators, having learned to respect the amount of trouble the rank and file could stir up, resumed negotiations with the shipping association and when the agreement was resubmitted to the membership in January, 1955, the no-strike clause had been rendered meaningless and the arbitrator stripped of power. This time, the vote was unsupervised: Captain Bradley explained that the services of the Honest Ballot Association cost $6,000, which he said the ILA could ill afford. He warned members that if they rejected the contract, they would be voting to strike, which, after the hectic year they had just gone through, the members could ill afford. In this vote the contract won overwhelming acceptance— the ILA reported that 11,266 votes had been cast in favor of the agreement to 4,206 against it.

New Yorkers settled back with relief to enjoy the fruits of two years of peace and quiet on the waterfront, but it is possible that with a weaker hand than Ryan's at the helm of the international union, struggles for power among second-level ILA officials might keep the port in a turmoil. Ryan, after escaping a conviction on charges of stealing union funds by virtue of a mistrial (perhaps jury members were impressed by one of Ryan's defense witnesses — Harvey Matusow), was sentenced to six months in prison and fined $2,500 for accepting gratuities from employers in the form of contributions to his "anti-Communist fund."* Except for his absence, the cast of characters in the ILA is virtually unchanged. Trouble is brewing between local war lords in more than one section of the port, and Captain Bradley has neither the valuable connections in New York labor circles nor the political influence which Ryan was always able to call on when he needed help in keeping his subordinates in line.

Among the second-level officials in the ILA who are working to broaden their spheres of influence, the man who seems most able to rise to a dominant position in the port is Anthony Anastasia. He is now securely entrenched in the ILA officialdom as an international vice-president and as head of Local 1814—the product of amalgamating the six Camarda locals—the 5,000 members of which come to his Longshoremen's, Checkers' and Clerks' Social Club in Brooklyn to make the necessary arrangements for work on the waterfront. Furthermore, Anastasia is extending his influence into other areas of the port by welcoming into his club longshoremen who supported the AFL and, as a result, are having a difficult time reëstablishing cordial relations with ILA officials in other locals. Anastasia is picking up additional supporters by advocating rotation in hiring. Ever since a decent hiring system was set up on the West Coast, some longshoremen in New York have wanted to adopt the system, and as soon as Anastasia became a union official he became a champion of this cause. In January, 1955, he told me that he had lost none of his determination to have a hiring hall for his members. When I asked him if men would be hired in rotation as they are on the West Coast, he responded, "I'm working toward that, but Rome wasn't built in a day."

The peace and quiet New Yorkers hope to get from the new two-year contract will be shattered if Anastasia tries to put rotary hiring into practice. Employers with whom he has built up a cordial relationship will turn against him; ILA officials, already unfriendly to him, will fight him with all the weapons at their command. When work stoppages inevitably result, New Yorkers, who think of him as "Tough Tony, brother of the notorious Albert Anastasia of Murder, Inc.," will demand that the government do something. Government officials have already demonstrated their readiness to try to curb his influence by suggesting, as they did on the eve of the second NLRB election, the possibility of "hook-ups between Communist forces on the West Coast and followers of Anthony Anas-

---

* Technically, Ryan was found guilty of violating Section 302(b) of the Taft-Hartley Act, which makes it a crime for a representative of employees to accept money from an employer. Ryan's conviction was reversed in July, 1955, however, by a Federal Court of Appeals which held, interestingly enough, that the term "representative" meant the bargaining agent—the union itself—and therefore that Ryan was guilty of no crime since he was not a "representative" under the law.

tasia." Anastasia resents the way he has been characterized in the public mind and he wants public approval. Knowing what will be involved if he tries to emulate the West Coast hiring system, he may lose enthusiasm for the project.

Anastasia may not be the man to lead the fight for rotary hiring but he has shown more willingness to do so than anyone else. Perhaps the battle will never take place—the old system demonstrates remarkable staying power. Perhaps New York longshoremen will be shaping up in information centers—or, more accurately, in hiring clubs or saloons around the corner from the information centers—as long as ships come and go in New York harbor.

Seattle longshoremen look forward in 1955 to a promising future. Because recent months have reinforced the rational collective-bargaining relationship which the "new look" brought to the West Coast, longshoremen are getting increased benefits from the rational operation of the industry. Their most recent gain will come in February, when the industry's welfare fund begins paying the bills for dental work needed by longshoremen's children. The record of the "new look" in preventing work stoppages continues to be impressive, marred only by occasional tie-ups of steam schooners caused by the traditional conflict between West Coast sailors and longshoremen over who will work steam-schooner hatches. It is regrettable that this dispute has not yet been resolved (it was especially troublesome in Los Angeles in 1954), but it should not seriously affect the industry's growing reputation for providing reliable service because steam schooners—plying coastal waters—represent only a small part of Pacific Coast shipping.

In Seattle, substantial progress is being made toward eliminating an adjunct of this jurisdictional tug of war as longshoremen in the "exception ports" (Tacoma, Anacortes, and Port Angeles) move toward affiliation with the ILWU. Men in these ports left the ILA when it was expelled from the AFL and affiliated with the AFL longshoremen's union which lost out in New York. They will undoubtedly see the wisdom of affiliating with the ILWU as they work side by side with ILWU men under a new arrangement in which dispatchers in ILWU and AFL hiring halls in all Puget Sound ports call on each other for longshore gangs whenever they are short of experienced men.

Stable relations between the ILWU and the Pacific Maritime Association doubtless will be unshaken even if the government carries out Congressman Velde's proposal to use the Communist Control Act to deprive the ILWU of its legal rights and privileges before the National Labor

Relations Board. Even if the government succeeds in proving that the ILWU is guilty of "Communist infiltration," an unlikely prospect, the union's position will then be no different than that of the United Mine Workers. The UMW has had no legal standing before the NLRB for more than seven years because of John L. Lewis' refusal to sign the non-Communist affidavit in the Taft-Hartley Act, but this has had no significant effect on the bargaining power of the miners. For a union as securely established in the industry as the ILWU, prosecution under the Communist Control Act would be more of a harassment than a serious threat to the union's bargaining power. West Coast longshoremen are also prepared for the possibility that the government may succeed in its current (this will be the fifth) attempt to deport Harry Bridges. If the government deprives the ILWU of Bridges's services, a stand-by president who was elected at the last convention is prepared to take over the presidency.*

Perhaps, instead of listening to the counsel of Congressman Velde and Harry Lundeberg—who in 1953 suggested that such a law as the Communist Control Act be passed and used against his old adversary, the ILWU—government officials would do better to read the *New York Times,* which said editorially two months after the bill became law:

> Following the breaking of ground recently for a new million-dollar headquarters of the International Longshoremen's and Warehousemen's Union in San Francisco, members of the union and shipowners also broke bread, and partook of other viands, at a dinner to take account of their labor-relations stock. Apparently twenty years of collective bargaining on the Pacific Coast has paid dividends for both labor and the employers.
>
> Both sides agree that the San Francisco waterfront is free of the gangsterism and racketeering that have plagued the Port of New York. It seems too bad that the leaders of the International Longshoremen's Association and of the shipping interests of the Port of New York were not present at this most extraordinary gathering. They might have learned a lot.

---

* On July 29, 1955, Bridges was acquitted in a San Francisco Federal District Court which held that the government had failed to prove its case "by clear and convincing evidence."

Source Notes

Note: For full bibliographic information, see pp. 236 ff.

Chapter 1. The New York Waterfront

Mary Heaton Vorse used the apt characterization "pirates' nest" in the title of an article "The Pirates' Nest of New York," published in *Harper's Magazine.*

[1] New York Governor, *Record of the Public Hearings Held by Governor Thomas E. Dewey . . .* , p. 7; hereafter cited as *Dewey Hearings.*

[2] Interview with J. V. Lyon, chairman, New York Shipping Association, February 26, 1952. Lyon declined to make a list of the association's membership available, but a state board of inquiry's report showed its composition as follows: 66 steamship lines and agents; 58 contracting stevedores; 1 contracting cargo repairman; 15 contracting checkers and clerks; 2 contracting maintenance agencies; 19 contracting marine carpenters.

[3] See New York (State), Board of Inquiry on the Longshore Industry Work Stoppage, October–November, 1951, Port of New York, *Final Report,* p. 40; hereafter cited as *Board of Inquiry.*

[4] The Atlantic Coast District of the ILA covers locals from Cape Hatteras to Canada and Newfoundland, but the Canadian locals were not included in negotiations with the NYSA.

[5] Carpenter, *Employers' Associations and Collective Bargaining in New York City,* p. 255.

[6] The specific employment figures submitted for 1950 were: 36,540 longshoremen; 2,572 checkers; 140 dock bosses; 229 assistant clerks; 320 temporary assistant clerks; 307 head clerks; 932 carpenters; 51 carpenter snappers; 28 carpenter temporary foremen; 876 miscellaneous; 41,995 total. *Board of Inquiry,* p. 51. Lyon later stated that employment in 1951 was 48,858 but did not indicate the number of longshoremen included in this figure. *New York Times,* Feb. 21, 1952. Since the most recent hours and earnings data available are those for 1950, the employment figures for that year are used.

[7] *Board of Inquiry,* p. 43.

[8] Barnes, *The Longshoremen,* p. 93.

[9] *Ibid.,* p. 256.

[10] This unusual development was the outgrowth of the formation by European waterfront unions of the International Federation of Ship, Dock and River Workers, with Tom Mann, an English unionist, as its president, and longshore officials from Belgium, Holland, and France on its executive board. Tom Mann, *The Position of Dockers and Sailors in 1897* (London: The Clarion Newspaper Company Ltd., 1897).

[11] The ILA had been organized in 1892 in Detroit as the International Association of Lumber Handlers. The name was later changed to ILA, and in 1902 to the Inter-

national Longshoremen, Marine and Transport Workers' Association, when the union expanded its membership to include not only longshoremen, but also marine firemen, oilers, and watertenders. Andrew Furuseth, president of the International Seamen's Union, protested this raid, and in 1907 Samuel Gompers ordered the longshoremen to restrict themselves to shoreside workers under the former name.

[12] See copy of agreement in New York (City) Mayor's Committee . . . , *Report on Dock Employment* . . . , p. 73.

[13] Barnes, *op. cit.*, p. 127.

[14] This was substantially the proposal the McHugh organization had made eighteen years earlier. Charles B. Barnes, investigator for the commission, offered a similar suggestion, based on Williams' *The First Year's Working of the Liverpool Docks Scheme*. It was later discovered in Liverpool that the mere establishment of regular shaping times was a wholly inadequate solution.

[15] U.S. Congress, Senate Commission on Industrial Relations, *Industrial Relations,* p. 2191.

[16] *Ibid.,* pp. 2194-2195.

[17] Monthly Labor Review, IX (Dec., 1919), 95–115.

[18] This was a board set up in World War I for "the adjustment and control of wages, hours, and conditions of labor in the loading and unloading of vessels." It was created in August, 1918, by an agreement between the U. S. Shipping Board, the secretary of war, the secretary of labor, the AFL, the ILA, and the principal shipping operators on the Atlantic and Gulf coasts. The parties agreed to accept as binding the decisions of the commission. (The source of this information, and of further notes in this chapter not otherwise attributed, is the *New York Times.)*

[19] U.S. National Adjustment Commission, *Chairman's Report for the Period Ending December 31, 1918.*

[20] No termination date for the original commission had been set, but some of its members had represented wartime agencies. When the war ended they had withdrawn and the commission had gone out of existence. Soon after, the U. S. Shipping board proposed its reëstablishment, and the ILA and employers concurred.

[21] The following studies appeared in the 1930's: Swanstrom, *The Waterfront Labor Problem;* Chambers, *Labor Unions and the Public;* Ogg, *Longshoremen and Their Homes.* During the 1920's, the ILA published a semiannual magazine, *The Longshoremen's Journal,* which was apparently discontinued in 1932. Issues of this journal are collectors' items today. The New York City Public Library, for example, has been able to obtain only two issues, one published in 1931 and one in 1932.

[22] See O'Brien, "Longshoremen Stabilize Their Jobs," *American Federationist,* pp. 573–574. O'Brien was a vice-president of the ILA.

[23] U.S. Congress, Senate Committee on Commerce, *Amending the Merchant Marine Act of 1936,* pp. 1192–1204.

[24] See *Longshoremen's Journal,* 1931, and Velie, "Big Boss of the Big Port," *Collier's,* p. 38.

[25] U.S. Congress, Senate Committee on Commerce . . . , *op. cit.,* pp. 1201 ff. For an interesting commentary on Ryan's relations with Tammany Hall, see Velie, *op. cit.,* p. 38.

[26] Swanstrom, *op. cit.,* p. 38.

[27] Barnes, *op. cit.,* p. 100.

[28] *New York Times,* Feb. 17, 1953.

[29] See testimony of James C. Kennedy, president of Daniels and Kennedy; and of Joseph P. Ryan, before the New York Crime Commission, *New York Times,* Dec. 4, 1952, and Jan. 31, 1953.

[30] *New York Times,* Jan. 9, 1953.

[31] New York Crime Commission, Fourth Report . . . to the Governor . . . , pp. 12–16; hereafter cited as *Fourth Report of Crime Commission.*

[32] *New York Times,* Dec. 4, 1952.

[33] Bell, "Last of the Business Rackets," *Fortune,* p. 196.

[34] Carter, "Behind the Waterfront Rackets," *Compass,* Dec. 3 and 9, 1951.

[35] See George Cable Wright in the Sunday "News of the World," *New York Times,* Jan. 4, 1953.

[36] Vorse, "The Pirate's Nest of New York," *Harper's Magazine,* p. 53. Ryan's comment reflected the metamorphosis in the character of the union. In 1914, Walter B. Holt, an ILA organizer, had stated the strong objections of the ILA to efforts of social workers to get the union and the stevedores to help rehabilitate former convicts. U.S. Congress, Senate Commission on Industrial Relations, *Industrial Relations,* p. 2191.

[37] Joseph P. Ryan's testimony, *New York Times,* Jan. 31, 1953.

[38] Alex Di Brizzi's testimony before the New York State Crime Commission, *New York Times,* Jan. 20, 1953.

[39] *Fourth Report of Crime Commission,* p. 22. Florio had perjured himself when he denied before a New Jersey grand jury that he had extorted $2,000 from a stevedoring company to supply longshoremen to unload sugar. When he pleaded guilty and was sentenced, Florio was discharged from his job as international organizer. *New York Times,* Dec. 20, 1952.

[40] Bell describes the process in the article cited above, and longshoremen described it to me in 1952.

[41] This and other cases are discussed in Malcolm Johnson's Pulitzer-Prize-winning series of articles in the *New York Sun,* which ran during November and December, 1948. The quotation in the text appeared on November 9, 1948. See also the testimony of Dominick Genova before the Crime Commission, *New York Times,* Jan. 22, 1953; and *Fourth Report of Crime Commission,* p. 24.

[42] Principal stockholders and officers in Allied Stevedores were Mickey Bowers (a convicted bank robber); John Keefe (vice-president and business agent of Local 824); John Potter (a veteran public loader); and Patrick Connolly (executive vice-president of the ILA). *Fourth Report of Crime Commission,* p. 53, and *New York Times,* Jan. 23, 1953.

[43] *Board of Inquiry,* p. 28.

[44] Josephson, "Red Skies Over the Waterfront," *Collier's;* Bell, *op. cit.,* Vorse, *op. cit.;* U.S. Congress, Senate Special Committee . . . , *Third Interim Report,* hereafter cited as *Kefauver Committee Report;* and *New York Times,* Dec. 19, 1952.

[45] *New York Times,* Jan. 31, 1953.

[46] *New York Sun,* Nov. 8, 1948.

[47] *New York Sun,* Nov. 23, 1948. The letter was reproduced in the article.

[48] New York (County), District Attorney, *Report* . . . , p. 46.

[49] Ryan and Joseph Adelizzi, then managing director of the Motor Carriers' Association, were cochairmen, and Hugh E. Sheridan, impartial chairman of the New York City trucking industry, was appointed arbitrator.

[50] New York (City), Mayor's Joint Committee . . ., *Labor Conditions* . . ., pp. 24–30; and *New York Sun,* Nov. 16, 1948.

[51] U.S. Congress, Senate Subcommittee on War Mobilization . . ., *Mobilization of Shipping Resources,* p. 13.

[52] Quoted in New York (City), Mayor's Joint Committee . . ., *op. cit.*, p. 6.

[53] *Fourth Report of Crime Commission*, p. 28.

[54] Technically speaking, the contract did not provide for a closed or union shop. The language of the relevant clause merely gave preference to "men who regularly worked on a pier." This provision had not been effective in ensuring priority to union members and the men were unwilling to sacrifice other demands for what they considered a meaningless provision.

[55] *Monthly Labor Review*, LXVII (Sept., 1948), 289. Members of the board were Saul Wallen, labor attorney, Boston; Julius Cass, attorney, New York; and Joseph Miller, labor consultant, Washington, D. C.

[56] The Supreme Court had held on June 17, 1948, that premium payments to longshoremen, at time-and-a-half for night, weekend, holiday, and mealtime work, constituted part of the regular rate of pay, and hence could not be considered as overtime compensation due under the Fair Labor Standards Act. The court decided that the regular rate of pay should be computed by adding the premiums for work at irregular hours to straight-time pay received during the week. These premiums were held to be in the nature of a shift differential for work at undesirable hours, since they were not paid because regular hours had previously been worked. Therefore, the computation of time-and-a-half pay could loosely be termed "overtime on overtime." See *Bay Ridge Operating Company v. Aaron, et al.* (1948), 334 U.S. 446; 68 Sup. Ct. 1186; 92 L.Ed. 1502.

[57] Under the Taft-Hartley Act, after the expiration of an 80-day injunction, the NLRB conducts a secret ballot among the employees on the question of accepting or rejecting the final offer made by the employers. If the majority vote to reject it, the union is free to proceed with the strike.

[58] The eligible voters (that is, the ILA members in the port) totaled 14,938. This number included the 12,664 longshoremen; 1,660 checkers and dock foremen; 484 clerks; and 130 cargo repairmen. Interview with Aaron Weissman, field examiner, NLRB, 2d Region, New York City, January, 1952.

[59] *Last Offers of Settlement*, submitted to the Presidential board of inquiry, October 21, 1948. Ryan had testified in court against ILA members who were claimants in the overtime cases, explaining that payment of these claims would force employers to reduce the wage rate.

[60] *Statement of Maritime Policy*. This was a news release, issued on July 24, 1950, by the U.S. Department of Labor. The federal agencies involved were the Department of Labor, the Department of Commerce, the Coast Guard, the Federal Bureau of Investigation, and the Office of Naval Intelligence.

[61] Familiarly known as the "Magnuson Act," after its sponsor—Senator Warren G. Magnuson of Washington—it was passed by the 81st Congress on August 9, 1950. It amends Section 1, Title II, of the act of June 15, 1917 (40 U.S. Stat. 220). See *Security of Vessels and Waterfront Facilities*, U.S. Coast Guard.

[62] Interviews with Captain F. G. Eastman, U.S.C.G., chief, Intelligence Division, and Captain H. T. Jewell, U.S.C.G., chief, Merchant Vessel Personnel Division, in Washington, D.C., February 6, 1952.

[63] *New York Times*, Dec. 28, 1952.

[64] *Board of Inquiry*, pp. 37–39.

[65] The Anti-Crime Committee is a private organization, composed of prominent New Yorkers. Its purpose is to act as a watchdog to prevent the recurrence of laxity in law enforcement which has long plagued New York City. Contrary to public opinion, the committee does not duplicate the work of the police, but works through the press to give publicity to problem areas condoned or ignored by the city officials.

[66] Members of the board were Martin P. Catherwood, dean of the New York State School of Industrial and Labor Relations, Cornell University; Rt. Rev. John P.

Boland, member of New York State Board of Mediation; and Dean Alfange, a a New York City attorney.

[67] *Board of Inquiry*, p. 8.

[68] *Ibid.*, pp. ii–iii.

[69] *New York Times*, March 3, 1952.

[70] *Ibid.*, April 30, 1952.

[71] *Ibid.*, May 10, 1952.

[72] *Ibid.*, July 23, 1953.

[73] *Ibid.*, July 25, 1953.

[74] Among those who retained their own attorneys were Ed Florio; Michael Clemente; Harold and Mickey Bowers; Chris Porto, delegate of Local 1142; Captain William V. Bradley, president of the ILA United Marine Division (the tug and barge workers); and Anthony Marchitto, delegate of Local 1247, New Jersey. Other than Ryan, the only major official who agreed to be represented by Louis Waldman was Alex Di Brizzi. *New York Times*, Dec. 1, 1952.

[75] *Dewey Hearings*, p. 229.

[76] *Ibid.*, pp. 233 and 247.

Chapter 2. The Shape-Up

[1] New York (City), Mayor's Joint Committee . . ., *Labor Conditions* . . ., p. 6.

[2] *Board of Inquiry*, p. 56.

[3] For an extended discussion of this process, see Beveridge, *Unemployment, A Problem of Industry*, p. 98 ff.

[4] Where not otherwise specified, the material in this chapter is based on interviews with representatives of the parties, public officials, and other informed persons. Interviews and observations were made in 1951 and 1952.

[5] New York (City), Mayor's Joint Committee . . ., *op. cit.*, p. 7; *Dewey Hearings*, p. 46; and *Fourth Report of Crime Commission*, pp. 37–38.

[6] Lyon, *Report* . . ., p. 4. Although not so labeled, this was, in essence, a minority report submitted by Lyon as the NYSA member of the Subcommittee on Labor Conditions of the Mayor's Joint Committee on Port Industry. The majority report is cited above as New York (City), Mayor's Joint Committee . . . , *Labor Conditions* . . .

[7] *Board of Inquiry*, p. 73.

[8] Quoted in an article by Stephen Fischer in the *Compass*, Aug. 12, 1949. See also, testimony before the Crime Commission, *New York Times*, Jan. 20, 1953.

[9] Testimony of "John Doe" before the Crime Commission, *New York Times*, Jan. 20, 1953. See also, the report of the Hudson County (New Jersey) Grand Jury which investigated "criminal conditions existing on the waterfront" quoted in the *New York Times*, Sept. 28, 1951.

[10] *Compass*, Aug. 12, 1949.

[11] *Jersey Observer*, June 8, 1951.

[12] *New York Times*, Feb. 14, 1953.

[13] U.S. Congress, Senate Committee on Commerce . . . , *Amending the Merchant Marine Act*, p. 1204; and *New York Sun*, Dec. 8, 1948.

[14] See Carter's series in the *Compass*, especially Dec. 4, 1951. I corroborated the information in interviews in Hoboken and with the New York City Anti-Crime Committee.

[15] U.S. Congress, Senate Subcommittee on Preparedness . . . , *Investigation of the Preparedness Program,* p. 16.

[16] See affidavit of New York County District Attorney Frank Hogan before the New York County Grand Jury, reproduced verbatim in the *New York Herald Tribune,* April 19, 1952. See also, *New York Times,* March 29, 1953.

[17] Lyon, *op. cit.,* p. 7.

[18] *Jersey Journal,* June 1, 1951; and *New York Times,* Feb. 11, 1949.

[19] Testimony of Jones F. Devlin, *New York Times,* Dec. 5, 1952.

Chapter 3.   Who Wanted the Shape-up?

[1] Title of an 1874 pamphlet about the New York waterfront by Joseph Jennings.

[2] Lyon, *Report* . . . , p. 2.

[3] *Ibid.,* p. 3.

[4] Citizens Waterfront Committee, *The New York Waterfront,* p. 13.

[5] U.S. Congress, House Subcommittee . . . , *Safety in Longshore . . . Work,* p. 33 and pp. 125–126.

[6] *Board of Inquiry,* p. 77.

[7] *Ibid.,* p. 9.

[8] Swanstrom and Ogg examined the employment records of a small number of longshoremen and found that underemployment was a problem for the men studied, but the samples were statistically insignificant and the studies are twenty years old.

[9] U.S. Department of Labor, Bureau of Labor Statistics, *Handbook of Labor Statistics,* p. 121.

[10] J. V. Lyon, quoted in *New York Times,* Feb. 21, 1952.

[11] See data on total labor force in *Board of Inquiry,* Table II, p. 51.

[12] *Board of Inquiry,* p. 20.

[13] *Ibid.,* p. 21.

[14] John J. Gannon's testimony, *New York Times,* Jan. 21, 1953.

[15] Stephen Fisher's series in the *Compass,* Aug. 11–14, 1949.

[16] *New York Sun,* March 15, 1949.

[17] Barnes, *The Longshoremen,* p. 93.

[18] *New York Times,* Jan. 21, 1953.

[19] *Fourth Report of Crime Commission,* p. 33.

[20] Waldman, *Final Report* . . . , p. 7.

[21] Testimony of Alex Di Brizzi and Joseph B. Franklin, *New York Times,* Jan. 20, 1953.

[22] *New York Times,* Feb. 1, 1953.

[23] George Horne, the *New York Times* shipping specialist, Nov. 4, 1951.

[24] Lyon, *Report* . . . , p. 2.

Chapter 4.   The Seattle Waterfront

[1] From "Union Maid," words by Woody Guthrie.

[2] Washington (State), Bureau of Labor, *Third Biennial Report, 1901–1902,* p. 94; *Fourth Biennial Report, 1903–1904,* p. 146.

[3] U.S. National Labor Relations Board, *Decisions and Orders,* vol. 7, p. 1007; hereafter cited as 7 NLRB 1007.

[4] Gramm, "Employers Association Development in Seattle and Vicinity."

[5] Washington (State), Bureau of Labor, *Tenth Biennial Report, 1915–1916,* pp. 245–246.

[6] *Ibid.,* p. 213.

[7] Kerr, "Collective Bargaining on the Pacific Coast," *Monthly Labor Review,* p. 652.

[8] Members of the Puget Sound Commission were Henry M. White, a special agent of the national commission; K. J. Middleton of the Waterfront Employers Union; and J. C. Bjorklund, a Tacoma ILA official. The union had been so completely defeated in California that no similar panels were created there.

[9] U.S. National Adjustment Commission, *Chairman's Report . . . ,* pp. 164–165.

[10] A copy of the agreement is on file in the Tacoma Public Library. See also, 32 NLRB 673–674.

[11] Seattle General Strike Committee, *Seattle General Strike,* p. 13.

[12] From an historical note in the *Dispatcher,* ILWU biweekly newspaper published in San Francisco, May 31, 1946. The SS *Delight* was a vessel operated by the U.S. Shipping Board. This board had been instrumental in setting up the Shipbuilding Adjustment Commission, the agency which had played such an unpopular role in the Seattle general strike.

[13] Foisie, *Decasualizing Longshore Labor and the Seattle Experience.* This publication is not widely available but the system is summarized in the *Monthly Labor Review,* XV (Dec., 1922), 121 ff.; and in the *Survey,* XLIX (Oct. 15, 1922), 96–97.

[14] One wage negotiation was carried to arbitration in 1924 and resulted in a 10-cent increase. *Monthly Labor Review,* XVIII (March, 1924) 579.

[15] The system then in use in Bristol, Liverpool, and London—probably the ports in question—is described in Whyte, *Decasualization of Dock Labour.*

[16] *Monthly Labor Review,* XXXVII (Dec., 1933), 1303.

[17] *Ibid.,* p. 1306. See also, U.S. Congress, Senate Joint Committee, *Labor-Management Relations,* p. 6.

[18] Foisie, *op. cit.,* p. 21.

[19] U.S. National Recovery Administration, *Proposed Code of Fair Competition for the Shipping Industry.* The reasons for the rejection are obscure. According to T. G. Plant, it was because of the international character of the industry. "Vessels of all nations call at American ports, all of which vessels will be subject to the provisions of the Code . . . " Waterfront Employers Union of San Francisco, *Statement of Thomas G. Plant . . . ,* p. 7.

[20] Eliel, *The Waterfront and General Strikes, San Francisco, 1934,* p. 7.

[21] From the "Proposed Agreement Submitted by the President's Mediation Board," quoted in full in Eliel, *op. cit.,* pp. 189–192. Members of the board were Charles A. Reynolds, Henry F. Grady, and J. L. Leonard—the heads of the regional labor boards of Seattle, San Francisco, and Los Angeles. These regional labor boards were set up under the National Industrial Recovery Act.

[22] For insights into the San Francisco general strike, see Taylor and Gold, "San Francisco and the General Strike"; Cross, *A History of the Labor Movement in California,* pp. 258–261; Eliel, *op. cit.;* and Mike Quin, *The Big Strike.*

[23] The source of subsequent material in this chapter, unless otherwise specified, is the *Seattle Times.*

[24] These unions were the Sailors Union of the Pacific (SUP); the Pacific Coast

Marine Firemen, Oilers, Watertenders and Wipers' Association; the Marine Engineers' Beneficial Association; the Masters, Mates and Pilots' Association (MMP); and the Marine Cooks and Stewards' Association (MC&S).

[25] Eliel, *op. cit.,* pp. 28–29.

[26] *Ibid.,* pp. 206–207.

[27] Quin, *op. cit.,* p. 61.

[28] *San Francisco News,* May 29, 1934.

[29] Eliel, *op. cit.,* p. 37.

[30] The other striking unions were the SUP; Marine Engineers; Marine Firemen; MMP; MC&S; Radio Operators; Ship Wrights and Boat Builders; Machinists; and Boilermakers.

[31] Members of the board were Archbishop Hanna of San Francisco, chairman; O. K. Cushing, a San Francisco attorney; and Assistant Secretary of Labor Edward F. McGrady. They were authorized to hire investigators, subpoena records and witnesses, and to make findings of fact. *Monthly Labor Review,* XXXIX (Aug., 1934), 317.

[32] In only one port—the small lumber port of Raymond, Washington—did a majority vote against accepting the board's offer to arbitrate. In Raymond, the vote was 61 "no" and 37 "yes."

[33] The award is quoted in full in *Decasualization of Longshore Work in San Francisco,* WPA Research Project No. L-8, pp. 122–127.

[34] The unions involved were the SUP, MMP; MC&S; Marine Firemen; Marine Engineers; and the Radio Operators. The Boilermakers, Machinists, and Teamsters participated in the meeting but did not remain active in the organization.

[35] See U.S. Congress, Senate Subcommittee of the Committee on Education . . . , *Violations of Free Speech* . . . , pp. 117–125; Brooks, *Unions of Their Own Choosing,* pp. 18–25; and Eliel, "Labor Peace in Pacific Coast Ports," p. 429.

[36] See Eliel, "Labor Peace . . . ," *Harvard Business Review,* p. 429.

[37] Coast Committee of Shipowners, *ABC's of the Maritime Strike,* pp. 7 and 13.

[38] ILA, Local 38-79, *The Maritime Crisis, What It Is and What It Isn't,* p. 10.

[39] *Seattle Times,* Nov. 1, 1936.

[40] Interview with Bill Gettings, Northwest Regional Director, ILWU, in Seattle in 1951. See also Selig Perlman's article in Marquand, *Organized Labor in Four Continents.*

[41] *Monthly Labor Review,* XLIV (April, 1937), 817–827; and Quin, *op. cit.,* p. 232.

[42] 7 NLRB 1016. See also, *Maritime Report,* 1 (March 6, 1947). This publication was one of a series of news releases published in San Francisco by the Waterfront Employers Association of the Pacific Coast.

[43] Roth, "Objectives of the San Francisco Employers Council," p. 8.

[44] *Seattle Times,* April 30, 1937.

[45] 7 NLRB 1054, and Committee for Industrial Organization, Western Regional Office, *What the CIO Means to the Maritime Industry.* The coast-wide vote was 11,441 in favor of affiliation to 3,349 against. In Seattle, the vote was 1,130 to 329.

[46] International Longshoremen's and Warehousemen's Union, *Proceedings of the First Annual Convention* . . . , 1938, pp. 76–77.

[47] See 32 NLRB 676–680.

[48] *Seattle Times,* Dec. 1, 1936.

[49] Perlman, in Marquand, *op. cit.,* p. 374.

[50] American Federation of Labor, *Proceedings of the 57th Annual Convention* . . . , p. 519. See also Chaplin, *Wobbly,* chapters 32, 33.

[51] American Federation of Labor, *Proceedings of the 57th Annual Convention* . . . , pp. 520–521.

[52] Wayne Morse, *Arbitrator's Award* . . . , Sept. 5, 1940.

[53] Tacoma voted 523 in favor of the ILA to 55 for the ILWU; Anacortes, 33 to 0; and Port Angeles 78 to 5. 33 NLRB 846.

[54] Eliel, "Labor Peace . . . ," *Harvard Business Review,* p. 347.

[55] Seattle Joint Labor Relations Committee, *Minutes* . . . , June 2, 1944; hereafter cited as *JLRC Minutes.*

[56] *Ibid.,* Feb. 9, 1954.

[57] See U.S. Department of Labor, National War Labor Board, *Termination Report* . . . , vol. 26, pp. 514–566; hereafter cited as 26 WLR 514–566.

[58] The employers considered the walking bosses, or foremen, as first-line supervision and refused to bargain with them. They had no objection to bargaining with checkers (who are actually clerical workers) but opposed their being in the same union as the longshoremen. For the walking boss dispute, see 19 NLRB p. 140 ff.; 71 NLRB 82–117; 72 NLRB 366; Kerr and Fisher, "Conflict on the Waterfront," *Atlantic Monthly;* U.S. Congress, Senate Joint Committee, *Labor-Management Relations,* pp. 51–52; *Seattle Times,* Feb. 26 and April 17, 1946; and the 1951 issues of the *Dispatcher.* For the checkers' dispute, see 71 NLRB 129; 90 NLRB No. 166, p. 15. Mimeographed.

[59] *Seattle Times,* April 4, 1946. Members of the board were Fowler Harper, Indiana Law School professor; Federal District Judge Lloyd Black of Seattle; and James L. Fly, Federal Communications Commission member.

[60] The first serious attempt to improve safety in Pacific Coast longshoring was made in Seattle in 1924, when the employers hired a safety engineer to study the problem. A voluntary safety code existed on the Coast from 1929 to 1946. See Joseph H. Travers, *Accident Prevention in the Pacific Coast Maritime Industry.* The ILWU had unsuccessfully attempted to obtain a safety code as part of the collective bargaining contract in 1944. See 26 WLR 532–533. The code negotiated in 1946 was incorporated in the contract in November. See *Pacific Coast Marine Safety Code, 1949 Revision,* a handbook published jointly by the ILWU and PMA. In 1947, with the assistance of the WEA, ILWU, and ILA, the Washington State Department of Labor and Industries adopted a set of safety standards for longshoring, published in *Safety Standards for Longshore, Stevedore and Waterfront Warehouse Operations.*

[61] An employer who discriminates against an employee in violation of section 8a (3) also violates section 8a (1) which makes it an unfair labor practice to "interfere with, restrain, or coerce employees in the exercise of their rights guaranteed in Section 7." Section 7 guarantees, among other things, the right to join, or refrain from joining, a union. It is also an unfair labor practice under section 8b (1) for a union to "restrain or coerce . . . employees in the exercise of the rights guaranteed in section 7" and, under section 8b (2), for a union to "cause or attempt to cause an employer to discriminate against an employee in violation of" section 8a (3).

[62] Congress amended the act in 1951, eliminating the requirement of the union-shop election, after it became abundantly clear that holding the elections involved a substantial and needless expense. Union-shop elections were authorized in 44,795 of the 46,119 polls. Of the 6,542,564 workers eligible to vote, 5,547,478 exercised their franchise. Of these, 5,071,988 (91 per cent) voted for the union shop. *Sixteenth Annual Report of the National Labor Relations Board, 1951* (1952), p. 10.

[63] Senate Committee on Labor . . . , *Maritime Hiring Halls,* p. 7.

[64] *Shoreside Report,* subtitled "A Report to Waterfront Personnel on Facts of Common Interest," was published in San Francisco by the Waterfront Employers Association of the Pacific Coast. The quotation is from the first issue (April, 1948).

[65] 90 NLRB No. 166, pp. 27–28. Mimeographed.

[66] Harry Shulman, Yale law professor, was appointed chairman of the board. Board of Inquiry, *Report to the President on Labor Disputes in the West Coast Maritime Industry* (June 11, 1948), pp. 54–60.

[67] *Shoreside Report,* 1 (June 21, 1948). See also 90 NLRB No. 166. Mimeographed.

[68] WEA news releases during the month of July, 1948.

[69] 90 NLRB No. 166, p. 32. Mimeographed.

[70] The description of the interchanges between the negotiators is drawn from the report of the trial examiner in a subsequent NLRB case. 90 NLRB No. 166, p. 37. Mimeographed.

[71] WEA news releases and *Shoreside Report,* Sept. and Oct., 1948; also Pacific American Shipowners Association, *White Paper, Pacific Coast Maritime Strike.*

[72] WEA news release, Oct. 18, 1948.

[73] *Shoreside Report,* 1 (Dec. 7, 1948).

[74] WEA news release, Dec. 7, 1948.

[75] *Marine Digest,* 28 (Dec. 11, 1948), 3.

[76] Kerr and Fisher, "Conflict on the Waterfront," *Atlantic Monthly,* p. 20.

[77] *Ibid.,* p. 18.

[78] *Shoreside Report,* 1 (April 26, 1948). See also, California Legislature, *Report of the Senate Fact-Finding Committee . . . ,* Part Two, pp. 105–153.

[79] *Seattle Times,* Aug. 6, 1949.

[80] 90 NLRB No. 166, p. 60. Mimeographed.

[81] *Ibid.,* p. 4.

[82] U.S. Congress, Senate Committee on Labor and Public Welfare, *Communist Domination of Certain Unions,* p. 79.

[83] ILWU, *Union Busting: New Model,* p. 21.

[84] Interviews with Lt. Commander M. C. McGuire, U.S.C.G., chief of Seattle port security unit; and Captain E. G. Eastman (who was then in charge of screening long-shoremen at the national level); in Seattle and Washington, D. C., in July, 1951, and February, 1952.

[85] See arbitration award of David M. Roderick, Washington Area arbitrator, decided March 20, 1950.

[86] *JLRC Minutes,* June 20 and July 3, 1951.

[87] ILWU, *Union Busting . . . ,* p. 2.

[88] On this point, see National Planning Association, *Causes of Industrial Peace Under Collective Bargaining.*

Chapter 5. The Hiring Hall

[1] ILWU, *Union Busting . . . ,* p. 6.

[2] The material in this chapter is based on interviews and personal observations made in August, 1951, and May, 1954, and correspondence with the parties.

Chapter 6.   Who Wants the Hiring Hall?

[1] The minutes of the committee's hearings were examined from 1944 through August, 1951.

[2] Letter from D. W. Cornell, Washington Area manager, PMA, to me, April 18, 1952.

[3] *JLRC Minutes,* July 21, 1950.

[4] *JLRC Minutes,* July 21, 1944, through May 4, 1945, and Sept. 27, 1950.

[5] See 26 WLR 538. During World War II, there were 67 "preferred men" working steadily for certain companies in Seattle, but after the war the practice of steady employees was abandoned at the insistence of the union.

[6] 26 WLR 538.

[7] *Loc. cit.*

[8] U.S. Department of Labor, Bureau of Labor Statistics, *Cargo Handling . . . ;* and Foisie, *Decasualizing . . .*

[9] The minutes of the JLRC meeting of July 28, 1948, contain a quotation from a decision of Arthur C. Miller, the coast arbitrator in 1947, which refers to adverse decisions on the employers' charges by Wayne Morse when he was the coast arbitrator in 1942, by the NLRB in 1945, by the Presidential fact-finding board of 1946, and by Coast Arbitrator Clark Kerr in 1947.

[10] Slichter, *Union Policies and Industrial Management,* p. 174. Total tons of cargo were taken from the ships' manifests, and the total man hours worked from stevedoring company payrolls.

[11] International Longshoremen's and Warehousemen's Union, "Report of Local 1–19," *Proceedings of the Second Annual Convention . . . 1939,* pp. 200–201.

[12] U.S. Congress, Senate Committee on Labor . . . , *Taft-Hartley Act Revisions,* p. 1317.

[13] *Ibid.,* p. 1322.

[14] *Ibid.,* pp. 1324–1325.

[15] *Ibid.,* p. 1318.

[16] *JLRC Minutes,* Nov. 3, 1947.

[17] U.S. Congress, Senate Subcommittee of the Committee on Education . . . , *Safety in Longshore and Harbor Work.*

[18] See, for example, U.S. Congress, Senate Committee on Labor . . . , *Hiring Halls in the Maritime Industry,* p. 431.

[19] *The New Yorker,* 27 (April 28, 1951).

[20] 98 NLRB No. 44, mimeographed; decided Feb. 6, 1952.

[21] The employers were charged under section 8a (1) and 8a(3); the union under Section 8b (1) (A) and 8b (2).

[22] U.S. National Labor Relations Board, Division of Trial Examiners, *Intermediate Report . . . ,* p. 18, mimeographed; hereafter cited as *Intermediate Report.*

[23] *Ibid.,* p. 13.

[24] *JLRC Minutes,* Jan. 31 and Feb. 14 and 28, 1951.

[25] *Intermediate Report,* pp. 20 and 22.

[26] 98 NLRB No. 44, p. 12. Mimeographed.

[27] *Ibid.,* p. 19.

[28] 90 NLRB No. 166, p. 49. Mimeographed. Also *Intermediate Report,* p. 14.

[1] *N.Y. Laws* (1953), Chap. 882, Part I, ix 3(e), hereafter cited as *Waterfront Commission Act.*

[2] Waterfront Commission of New York Harbor, *Regulations,* section 3.4; hereafter cited as *Regulations.*

[3] *Waterfront Commission Act,* Part I, i.

[4] New York Shipping Association, *Recommendations Relating to Waterfront Labor Employed on Piers and Wharves.*

[5] *New York Times,* March 11, 1953.

[6] *Statutory Plan Recommended by the Port of New York Authority to Improve Waterfront Labor Conditions* (New York: Jan., 1953). The Port of New York Authority is a bistate agency established in 1921 by agreement between New York and New Jersey to develop and regulate transportation facilities in the harbor area.

[7] *Dewey Hearings,* p. 6.

[8] Corridan, *Recommendations on Labor Conditions* . . .

[9] *Dewey Hearings,* p. ix.

[10] *Ibid.,* p. 71.

[11] *Ibid.,* p. 173.

[12] *Ibid.,* p. 23.

[13] *Waterfront Commission Act,* Part I, xv.

[14] *Fourth Report of Crime Commission,* p. 69.

[15] *Waterfront Commission Act,* Part I, xv 2.

[16] *Ibid.,* Part I, xii 2.

[17] *Ibid.,* Part II, sec. 2A 2.

[18] *Ibid.,* Part I, vi 3(b)(f)(g).

[19] *Ibid.,* Part I, v 2(d).

[20] *Ibid.,* Part I, xiv 6 and xvi 3.

[21] *Ibid.,* Part I, v 3(c).

[22] *Ibid.,* Part I, viii 2.

[23] *Ibid.,* Part I, viii 3.

[24] *Ibid.,* Part I, viii 5(3).

[25] *Ibid.,* Part I, xi 3.

[26] *Ibid.,* Part I, xi 5.

[27] *Regulations,* Section 9.9.

[28] *Waterfront Commission Act,* Part II, 8.

[29] *Ibid.,* Part I, ix 5.

[30] See page 70.

[31] Since 1941, the employment service has administered the Manhattan Needle Trades Office for the International Ladies Garment Workers Union, AFL, and in 1951 dispatched workers to 800,000 jobs a year. Since 1949, the service industry office, operating under an agreement with Local 32B, Building Service Employees' International Union, AFL, and the Building Owners and Managers Association has placed from 400–500 workers a month. The hotel placement office, set up in 1951 under an agreement with the Hotel Association of New York City and the Hotel Trades Council, AFL, serves as the hiring exchange for about 40,000 workers.

Bibliography

Books

Barnes, Charles B. *The Longshoremen*. New York: Russell Sage Foundation, 1915.

Beveridge, William H. *Unemployment, A Problem of Industry*. New York: Longmans, Green, 1930.

Brooks, Robert R. R. *Unions if Their Own Choosing*. New Haven: Yale University Press, 1939.

Butler, Richard J. *Dock Walloper*. New York: G. P. Putnam's Sons, 1933.

Carpenter, Jesse Thomas. *Employers' Associations and Collective Bargaining in New York City*. Ithaca: Cornell University Press, 1950.

Chambers, Walter. *Labor Unions and the Public*. New York: Coward-McCann, 1936.

Chaplin, Ralph. *Wobbly*. Chicago: University of Chicago Press, 1948.

Chegwidden, T. S., and G. Myrridin-Evans. *The Employment Exchange Service of Great Britain*. New York: Industrial Relations Counselors, 1934.

Cross, Ira B. *A History of the Labor Movement in California*. Berkeley: University of California Press, 1935.

Eliel, Paul. *The Waterfront and General Strikes, San Francisco, 1934*. San Francisco: Hooper Printing Company, 1934.

Francis, Robert C. "A History of Labor on the San Francisco Waterfront." Unpublished Ph.D. dissertation. University of California, 1934.

Fulton, Reed. *Stevedore*. New York: Doubleday and Company, 1948. (A novel.)

Gramm, Warren S. "Employer Association Development in Seattle and Vicinity." Unpublished M.A. thesis. University of Washington, 1948.

Gubin, Sidney N. "Technological Changes and Trade Union Policy." Unpublished Ph.D. dissertation. University of California, 1938.

Hardt, John P. "Port Charges in Pacific Coast Ports." Unpublished M.A. thesis. University of Washington, 1948.

Johnson, Malcolm. *Crime on the Labor Front*. New York: McGraw-Hill, 1950.

Lampman, Robert J. "Collective Bargaining of West Coast Sailors, 1885–1947; A Study in Unionism." Unpublished Ph.D. dissertation. University of Wisconsin, 1950.

Liebes, Richard A. "Longshore Labor Relations on the Pacific Coast, 1934–1942." Unpublished Ph.D. dissertation. University of California, 1942.

Marquand, H. Adair, and others. *Organized Labor in Four Continents*. New York: Longmans, Green, 1939.

237

Morgan, Murray. *Skid Road: An Informal Portrait of Seattle.* New York: Viking Press, 1951.

Myers, Charles A., and W. Rupert MacLaurin. *The Movement of Factory Labor.* New York: John Wiley and Sons, 1943.

Noland, E. William, and E. Wight Bakke. *Workers Wanted.* New York: Harper and Brothers, 1949.

Palmer, Dwight L. "Pacific Coast Maritime Labor." Unpublished Ph.D. dissertation. Stanford University, 1935.

Parker, Carleton H. *The Casual Laborer and Other Essays.* New York: Harcourt, Brace and Howe, 1920.

Poole, Ernest. *The Harbor.* New York: The Macmillan Company, 1915. (A novel.)

Quin, Mike. *The Big Strike.* Olema (Calif.): Olema Publishing Company, 1949.

Raymond, Allen. *Waterfront Priest.* New York: Henry Holt, 1955.

Reynolds, Lloyd G. *The Structure of Labor Markets.* New York: Harper and Brothers, 1951.

Reynolds, Lloyd G., and Joseph Shister. *Job Horizons.* New York: Harper and Brothers, 1949.

Robinson, Robert McL. "Maritime Labor in San Francisco, 1933-1937." Unpublished Ph.D. dissertation. University of California, 1937.

Slichter, Sumner H. *Union Policies and Industrial Management.* Washington: Brookings Institution, 1941.

Swanstrom, Edward E. *The Waterfront Labor Problem.* New York. Fordham University Press, 1938.

Travers, Robert. *A Funeral for Sabella.* New York: Harcourt, Brace and Company, 1952. (A novel based on the Panto murder.)

Whyte, W. Hamilton. *Decasualization of Dock Labour.* Bristol: Arrowsmith, Ltd., 1934.

Williams, R. *The First Year's Working of the Liverpool Docks Scheme.* London: King, 1914.

Articles and Pamphlets

American Civil Liberties Union. *Security and Freedom, The Great Challenge.* 13th Annual Report. New York: 1951.

———, Northern California Branch. *Fear and Suspicion.* 1951 Annual Report. San Francisco: 1952.

Bell, Daniel. "Last of the Business Rackets," *Fortune,* 43 (June, 1951).

Carter, Richard. "Behind the Waterfront Rackets," a series of articles which appeared in the *Compass* (New York) in December, 1951.

Citizens Waterfront Committee. *The New York Waterfront.* A Report to the Public of New York City by the Citizens Waterfront Committee Setting Forth Our Oldest and Most Urgent Civic Problem—the Condition of the Waterfront. New York: 1946.

Dawson, A. A. P. "The Stabilization of Dockworkers' Earnings," *International Labour Review,* LXIII (March and April, 1951).

"Decasualizing the Beach in Seattle," the *Survey,* 49 (Oct., 15, 1922).

Eliel, Paul. "Labor Peace in Pacific Coast Ports," *Harvard Business Review,* XIX (Summer, 1941).

Harris, Robin. "Who Is This Mr. Big?" *Sunday News* (New York), Jan. 20, 1952.

Hildebrand, George, and Wytze Gorter. *Maritime Industry of the Pacific Coast, 1930–1948*. Reprint no. 13. San Francisco: Institute of Industrial Relations, University of California at Los Angeles, 1950.

Hopkins, William S. "Employment Exchanges for Seamen," *American Economic Review,* XXV (June, 1935).

———. *Seasonal Unemployment in the State of Washington.* Seattle: University of Washington Press, 1936.

Hutchinson, Keith. "Facts About the Shipping Disputes," *Nation,* 162 (June 15, 1946).

Jennings, Joseph. *The Frauds of New York and the Aristocrats Who Sustain Them.* New York: George W. Van Vorst, Printer, 1874.

Johnson, Malcolm. A series of articles on the New York waterfront, which appeared in the *New York Sun* in November and December, 1948.

Josephson, Mathew. "Red Skies Over the Waterfront," *Collier's,* 118 (Oct. 5, 1946).

Kerr, Clark. "Collective Bargaining on the Pacific Coast," *Monthly Labor Review,* LXIV (April, 1947).

———. "Labor Markets: Their Characteristics and Consequences," *American Economic Review,* XL (May, 1950).

———. *Migration to the Seattle Labor Market Area, 1940–1942.* University of Washington Publications in the Social Sciences, Vol. II, no. 3. Seattle: University of Washington Press, 1942.

Kerr, Clark, and Lloyd Fisher. "Conflict on the Waterfront," *Atlantic Monthly,* 184 (Sept., 1949).

Malm, F. T. "Wage Differentials in Pacific Coast Longshoring," *Industrial and Labor Relations Review,* V (Oct., 1951).

Mezy, Phiz. "West Coast Waterfront Showdown," *Nation,* 167 (Nov. 6, 1948).

National Planning Association. *The Causes of Industrial Peace Under Collective Bargaining.* Washington: 1948–1953. (A series of case studies.)

O'Brien, Simon P. "Longshoremen Stabilize Their Jobs," *American Federationist,* 34 (May, 1927).

Ogg, Elizabeth. *Longshoremen and Their Homes.* New York: Greenwich House, 1939.

Roth, Almon E. "Objectives of the San Francisco Employers Council," in *Addresses given before the Industrial Relations Council of the American Management Association.* New York: AMA, 1939.

Schneiderman, William. *The Pacific Coast Maritime Strike.* San Francisco: Western Worker Publisher, 1937.

Seattle General Strike Committee. *Seattle General Strike.* Seattle: Union Record, 1919.

Taft, Philip. "The Unlicensed Seafaring Unions," *Industrial and Labor Relations Review,* III (Jan., 1950).

Taylor, Paul S., and Normal Leon Gold. "San Francisco and the General Strike," *Survey Graphic,* 23 (Sept., 1934).

Trimble, Peter. "Thought Control on the Waterfront," *Nation,* 173 (July 14, 1951).

Velie, Lester. "Big Boss of the Big Port," *Collier's,* 129 (Feb. 9, 1952).

Vorse, Mary Heaton. "The Pirates' Nest of New York," *Harper's Magazine,* 204 (April, 1952).

239

Public Documents

Board of Inquiry. See New York (State). Board of Inquiry ... *Final Report* ...

California. Legislature. *Report of the Senate Fact-Finding Committee on San Francisco Bay Ports.* 1951 Session. Parts I and II. Sacramento: 1951.

Dewey Hearings. See New York Governor.

Fourth Report of Crime Commission. See New York Crime Commission.

Intermediate Report. See U.S. National Labor Relations Board. Division of Trial Examiners.

Kefauver Committee Report. See U.S. Congress, Senate Special Committee . . .

New York (City). Mayor's Committee on Unemployment. *How to Meet Hard Times, A Program for the Prevention and Relief of Abnormal Unemployment.* New York: 1917.

————. Mayor's Committee . . . *Report on Dock Employment in New York City and Recommendations for Its Regularization.* New York: 1916.

————. Mayor's Joint Committee on Port Industry. *Labor Conditions Affecting Waterfront Commerce.* Report of Subcommittee No. 5. New York: 1951.

New York (County). District Attorney. *Report of the District Attorney . . . 1946–1948.* New York: 1948.

New York (State). Board of Inquiry on Longshore Industry Work Stoppage. *Final Report to the Industrial Commissioner . . . October–November, 1951, Port of New York.* New York: 1952.

————. Board of Inquiry . . . *Transcript of Hearings* . . . New York, 1951.

New York Crime Commission. *Fourth Report of the New York State Crime Commission (Port of New York Waterfront) to the Governor, the Attorney General and the Legislature of the State of New York.* Albany: 1953.

New York Governor. *Record of the Public Hearings Held by Governor Thomas E. Dewey on the Recommendations of the New York State Crime Commission for Remedying Conditions on the Waterfront of the Port of New York.* New York: 1953.

New York Laws. Chapter 882. Albany: 1953.

New York Legislature. Committee on Industrial and Labor Conditions. *Longshore Operations in San Francisco and Portland—A Case Study in Labor Market Organization.* Report No. 39. Albany: 1943.

————. Joint Legislative Committee on Unemployment. Report . . . Albany: 1933.

NLRB. See U.S. National Labor Relations Board.

Regulations. See Waterfront Commission of New York Harbor.

U.S. Congress. House. Subcommittee of the Committee on Education and Labor. *Hiring Practices, Maritime Industry.* Hearings, 81st Cong., 1st sess. Washington, 1949.

————. *Safety in Longshore and Harbor Work.* Hearings, 82nd Cong., 1st sess. Washington: 1951.

U.S. Congress. Senate. Commission on Industrial Relations. *Industrial Relations.* 64th Cong., 1st sess., S. Doc. 415. Washington: 1916.

————. Committee on Commerce and Committee on Education and Labor. *Amending the Merchant Marine Act of 1936.* Hearings, 75th Cong., 3d sess. Washington: 1938.

U.S. Congress (Continued)

———. Committee on Labor and Public Welfare. *Maritime Hiring Halls.* 81st Cong., 2d sess., S. Rept. 1827. Washington: 1950.

———. Committee on Labor . . . *Taft-Hartley Act Revisions.* Hearings, 83d Cong., 1st sess. Washington: 1953.

———. Joint Committee on Labor-Management Relations. *Labor-Management Relations, West Coast Maritime Industry.* 80th Cong., 2d sess. Washington: 1948.

———. Special Committee to Investigate Organized Crime in Interstate Commerce. *Third Interim Report* . . . 82d Cong., 1st sess., Rept. No. 307, pursuant to S. Res. 202. Washington: 1951.

———. Subcommittee of the Committee on Education and Labor. *Safety in Longshore and Harbor Work.* Hearings, 82d Cong., 1st sess. Washington: 1951.

———. Subcommittee of the Committee on Education . . . *Violations of Free Speech and the Rights of Labor.* 77th Cong., 2d sess., S. Rept. 1150. Part 1. Washington: 1942.

———. Subcommittee on Labor and Labor-Management Relations of the Committee on Labor and Public Welfare. *A Bill to Amend the NLRA, as Amended, with Reference to the Building and Construction Industry, and for Other Purposes.* Hearings, 82d Cong., 1st sess., on S. 1973. Washington: 1951.

———. Subcommittee on Labor . . . *Communist Domination of Certain Unions.* 82d Cong., 1st sess., S. Doc. 89. Washington: 1951.

———. Subcommittee on Labor . . . *Hiring Halls in the Maritime Industry.* Hearings, 81st Cong., 2d sess. Washington: 1950.

———. Subcommittee on Labor . . . *To Legalize Maritime Hiring Halls.* Hearings, 82d Cong., 1st sess., pursuant to S. Res. 71 on S. 1044. Washington: 1951.

———. Subcommittee on Preparedness of the Committee on the Armed Services. *Investigation of the Preparedness Program,* 83rd Cong., 1st sess., Comm. Rept. 44. Washington: 1953.

———. Subcommittee on War Mobilization of the Committee on Military Affairs. *Mobilization of Shipping Resources.* 78th Cong., 1st sess., Rept. No. 3. Washington: 1943.

U.S. Department of Labor. *In the Matter of Harry Bridges,* by James M. Landis. Washington: 1939.

———. *Statement on Maritime Policy.* Mimeographed news release. Washington: July 24, 1950.

———. Bureau of Labor Statistics. *Cargo Handling and Longshore Labor Conditions,* by Boris Stern. Bulletin, no. 550. Washington: 1932.

———. Bureau of Labor Statistics. *Handbook of Labor Statistics, 1950 Edition.* Bulletin, no. 1016. Washington: 1951.

———. Bureau of Labor Statistics. *Injuries and Accident Causes in the Longshore Industry.* Bulletin no. 764. Washington: 1944.

———. National War Labor Board. *Termination Report* . . . , Historical Reports on War Administration, 3 vols. Washington: 1948.

U.S. Federal Coördinator of Transportation. *Comparative Labor Standards in Transportation.* Washington: 1937.

———. *Hours, Wages and Working Conditions in Domestic Water Transportation.* Vol. I. Washington: 1936.

U.S. Federal Coördinator of Transportation (Continued)

———. *Unemployment Compensation for Transportation Employees.* Washington: 1936.

U.S. Maritime Labor Board. *Report to the President and to the Congress, March 1, 1940.* Washington: 1940.

U.S. National Adjustment Commission. *Chairman's Report for the Period Ending December 31, 1918.* Washington: 1919.

———. *Labor Costs and Output in the Longshore Industry at the Port of New York.* Washington: 1920.

U.S. National Labor Relations Board. *Decisions and Orders . . .* Washington: (Various years.)

———. Division of Trial Examiners. *Intermediate Report of the Trial Examiner in the Matter of ILWU Local 19, ILWU, Waterfront Employers of Washington and Its Employer-Members; and Clarence Purnell and Albert G. Crum.* Washington: 1951.

U.S. National Recovery Administration. *Code Hearings for the Shipping Industry.* Vol. 1417. Washington: 1934.

———. *Proposed Code of Fair Competition for the Shipping Industry.* Registry no. 1417–1423. Washington: 1934.

U.S. Board of Inquiry in re: New York Shipping Association and International Longshoremen's Association. *Last Offer of Settlement.* Washington: October 21, 1948.

———. *Report to the President on the Labor Dispute in the West Coast Maritime Industry.* Washington: June 11, 1948.

———. *Final Report . . .* Washington: August 13, 1948.

U.S. Shipping Board. Marine and Dock Industrial Division. *Marine and Dock Labor, Work, Wages and Industrial Relations During the Period of the War.* Washington: 1919.

U.S. Treasury Department. U.S. Coast Guard. *Security of Vessels and Waterfront Facilities.* Washington: 1951. (For amendments of Sept. 1951, see *Federal Register,* Sept. 14, 1951, pp. 9312–9313.)

U.S. War Department. U.S. Army. Corps of Engineers. *Port and Terminal Facilities at the Port of New York.* Washington: 1942.

———. U.S. Army. Corps of Engineers. *Port and Terminal Facilities at the Port of Seattle.* Washington: 1941.

U.S. Works Progress Administration. *Decasualization of Longshore Work in San Francisco.* National Research Project no. L-8. Philadelphia: 1939.

Washington (State). Bureau of Labor. *Biennial Report* covering 1897–1931. Variously published in Olympia and Seattle.

———. Department of Labor and Industries. *Safety Standards for Longshoremen, Stevedore and Waterfront Warehouse Operations.* Olympia: 1947.

———. Office of Unemployment Compensation and Placement. *Sixth Annual Report, 1942.* Olympia: 1943.

Waterfront Commission Act. See *New York Laws.*

Waterfront Commission of New York Harbor. *Interim Report on Current Work Stoppage.* New York: 1954. Mimeographed.

———. *Regulations.* New York: 1954. Mimeographed.

242

WLR. See U.S. Department of Labor, National War Labor Board. *Termination Report.*

Employer Publications

Coast Committee of the Shipowners. *ABC's of the Maritime Strike.* San Francisco: 1936.

Foisie, Frank P. *Decasualizing Longshore Labor and the Seattle Experience.* Seattle: Seattle Waterfront Employers Union, 1934.

Lyon, J. V. *Report of Mr. J. V. Lyon.* New York: New York Shipping Association, 1951. Mimeographed.

New York Shipping Association. *Recommendations [to the New York State Crime Commission] Relating to Waterfront Labor Employed on Piers and Wharves.* New York: Jan. 27, 1953. Mimeographed.

Pacific American Shipowners Association and Waterfront Employers' Association of Oregon. *White Paper, Pacific Coast Maritime Strike.* Portland: 1948.

Pacific Maritime Association. New releases during 1949–1951. San Francisco. Mimeographed.

————. *Shippers' Newsletter.* San Francisco: June 20, 1949. Mimeographed.

————. *Strikes and Work Stoppages in the West Coast Maritime Industry.* San Francisco: 1951. Mimeographed.

Travers, Joseph H. *Accident Prevention in the Pacific Coast Maritime Industry.* San Francisco: Waterfront Employers Association of the Pacific Coast, 1948. Mimeographed.

Waterfront Employers Association of the Pacific Coast. *Maritime Reports.* San Francisco: 1947 and 1948. Mimeographed.

————. *Shoreside Report, A Report to Waterfront Personnel on Facts of Common Interest.* San Francisco: April to Dec., 1948. Mimeographed.

Waterfront Employers Union of San Francisco. *Full and By, A Message from the Waterfront Employers Union.* San Francisco: 1921.

————. *Oral Argument of Herman Phleger, Esq., in Behalf of Waterfront Employers, Before the National Longshoremen's Board.* San Francisco: 1934.

————. *Statement of Thomas G. Plant, President, . . . to the National Longshoremen's Board.* San Francisco: 1934.

Waterfront Employers Union of Seattle. *History of Labor Relations.* Seattle: 1921.

Union Publications

American Federation of Labor. *Proceedings of the Annual Convention.* Washington: 1937 (57th) and 1939 (59th).

————. *Report of a Committee Appointed to Evaluate the Report of the Board of Inquiry in the 1951 Strike.* New York: 1952. Mimeographed.

Committee for Industrial Organization, Western Regional Office. *What the CIO Means to the Maritime Industry.* San Francisco: 1937.

Huberman, Leo. *Storm Over Bridges.* San Francisco: Harry Bridges Defense Committee, 1941.

International Longshoremen's Association. *Report of International President Joseph P. Ryan to the Thirty-fifth Convention.* New York: 1951.

International Longshoremen's Association (Continued)

————. *Statement by the Executive Council.* New York: Jan. 7, 1953. Mimeographed.

————. *Statement . . . on the Subject of Christmas Gifts and Gratuities From Employers to Officers of the ILA and Its Locals.* New York: Jan. 8, 1953. Mimeographed.

————. *Statement . . . Concerning Crime on the Waterfront.* New York: Jan. 9, 1953. Mimeographed.

————. *Fourth and Final Policy Statement of the Executive Council of the ILA.* New York: Jan. 11, 1953. Mimeographed.

————. *The ILA Program to Improve and Further Stabilize Labor and Industrial Conditions in the Port of New York.* Submitted to the Board of Inquiry in the 1951 strike. New York: Dec. 6, 1951. Mimeographed.

————. *The Longshoremen's Journal.* Buffalo: Issues for 1931 and 1932.

————. Local 38-79. *The Maritime Crisis, What It Is and What It Isn't.* San Francisco: 1936.

International Longshoremen's and Warehousemen's Union. *Convention Proceedings.* San Francisco: 1938–1953.

————. *Longshoremen, Pacific and Atlantic.* Seattle: 1940.

————. *Statement by Harry Bridges, President, on behalf of . . . before New York State Crime Commission.* San Francisco: 1953. Mimeographed.

————. The *Dispatcher.* San Francisco: 1942–1954.

————. *Union Busting: New Model.* San Francisco: 1951.

Maritime Federation of the Pacific. *Maritime Strike Pictorial.* San Francisco: 1937.

Waldman, Louis. *Final Report on Survey of ILA Locals.* New York: July 28, 1952. Mimeographed.

Miscellaneous

Corridan, Rev. John M., S.J. *Recommendations on Labor Conditions Affecting Waterfront Commerce in the Port of New York, Submitted to the New York State Crime Commission.* New York: Jan. 12, 1951.

JLRC Minutes. See Seattle Joint Labor Relations Committee, below.

Morse, Wayne. *Arbitrator's Award in the Matter of a Controversy between the Waterfront Employers Association of the Pacific Coast, Complainant, and International Longshoremen's and Warehousemen's Union, District 1, ILWU, Local 1–19, and the International Longshoremen's Association, Locals in Tacoma, Port Angeles and Anacortes, Respondents.* San Francisco: September 5, 1940. Mimeographed.

Port of New York Authority. *Statutory Plan Recommended by the . . . to Improve Waterfront Labor Conditions.* New York: Jan., 1953.

Seattle Joint Labor Relations Committee. *Minutes of Committee Meetings.* Seattle: 1944–1951. Mimeographed.

Index

Pacific Maritime Association, 84, 129, 131 n., 132, 162–165, 191, 223; Washington area, 135, 152–156 *passim. See also* Cornell, Darrell W.; Employers; St. Sure, J. Paul

Pacific Maritime Industry Board, 116, 155

Panto, Pete, 22, 37 n.

Papa, Joseph, 40 n., 48 n.

Parsons, Theodore D., 36 n.

Pearson, O. W., 129

Perlman, Selig, 113 n.

Phantom employees, 57

Pineapple-barge incident, 132

Plant, Thomas G., 99, 100 n., 107, 109–110

Police action on the waterfront, 7, 99, 100–102, 213

Politics on the waterfront, 16–17, 58–59, 79–80

Port of New York: described, 1–3; map of, 5

Port of New York Authority: report on public loading, 25 n.; reform proposal, 190–192

Port of Seattle: described, 85; map of, 147

Prisoners of war, 116

Public loaders: function described, 21; reform attempt, 24–25; prohibited under Waterfront Commission Act, 196; staying power, 217

Purnell, Clarence, unfair labor practice charge, 175–180. *See also* Crum, Albert G.

Rackets on the waterfront, 18, 21–22, 30, 44, 48 n., 54–60, 68 n., 75–77, 185

Raskin, A. H., 216

Rathbun, Harry, 131 n.

Riley, John F., 9, 12–13

Ripley, William Z., 12

Ritchie, J. E., 135 n.

Roche, David B., 36

Roderick, David M., 131 n.

Roosevelt, Franklin D., 95, 98, 102, 108, 116 n.

Rossi, Angelo, 99 n.

Roth, Almon E., 110, 128

Rustling cards, 89–90

Ryan, Joseph P.: actions in 1919 strike, 11–14; political acumen, 16–17, 59; and West Coast, 18, 97–100, 102 n., 110, 111–112; and "anti-Communist fund," 18–19, 75; and strong-arm system, 20; and Camarda locals, 23; reform attempts, 23, 29, 76; and public loaders, 24–25; elected for life, 26; actions in 1945 strike, 26–29; actions in later strikes, 30–38 *passim;* clash with Anastasia, 41–43; troubles with Crime Commission, 44; troubles with AFL, 46–48; relations with Governor Dewey, 80 n.; sets up Maritime Trades Department, 118 n.; attempts to forestall AFL organizing drive, 206; retired as president emeritus, 210; conviction reversed, 221 n.

Safety procedures: New York, 64; Seattle, 119, 170–171

Sailors' Union of the Pacific, 19 n., 94 n., 105–106, 112, 114, 119, 138. *See also* Steam schooner issue

St. Sure, J. Paul, 191; West Coast employers' position on hiring halls, 162–165

Sampson, Gene, 27 n., 28, 31, 34 n., 38, 56, 193; "pretender to the throne," 33; bolts ILA for AFL, 207–208

Screening programs: Coast Guard, 35–37, 80, 135–137; U. S. Navy, 36, 136; Waterfront Commission Act, 184, 197–201, 215–216

Seafarers' International Union, 19 n., 35, 42, 48

Seattle Joint Labor Relations Committee, 85, 116, 136, 154, 155, 156, 167–169, 178

Seattle Port Commission, 126

Seattle Port of Embarkation, 126

Senate Committee on Preparedness, 59

Shape-up: on New York waterfront, described briefly, 2; condemned, 4, 25–26, 46, 185; contributes to corruption of union, 6; reforms proposed, 7, 8, 9–10, 26, 47, 80, 186–195; defended by ILA and NYSA, 29; abolished by law, 45, 184 ff.; ILA referendum on, 47; described in detail, 49 ff.; value to employers, 61–69; value to ILA hierarchy, 74–77; community interest in, 77–81; in Waterfront Commission employment centers, 201–204, 216–218; in Seattle, 89, 90, 92; in San Francisco, 94 n.

Sheridan, Hugh E., 40 n.

Ship and Dock Foremen's Union of Washington, 138

Shoreside Reports, 121, 124, 129

Sling loads, 27

Sloss, Judge M. C., 131 n.

Smith, Edwin S., 114 n.

Smith, Mayor Charles, 99, 102

Spencer, Charles, 29

Squires, B. M., 15 n.

Standard Fruit and Steamship Co., 19

250